SACRED

GEOGRAPHY

SACRED
GEOGRAPHY

A Tale of Murder and Archeology
in the Holy Land

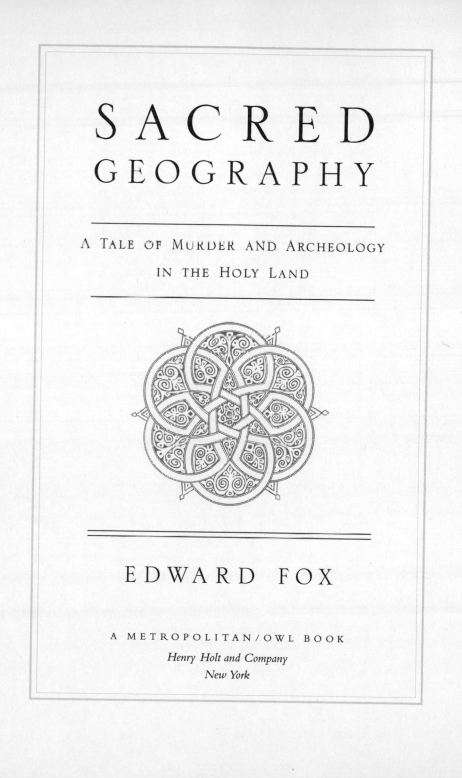

EDWARD FOX

A METROPOLITAN/OWL BOOK
Henry Holt and Company
New York

Henry Holt and Company, LLC
Publishers since 1866
115 West 18th Street
New York, New York 10011

Henry Holt® is a registered trademark of
Henry Holt and Company, LLC.

Library of Congress Cataloging-in-Publication Data
Fox, Edward, date.
    Sacred geography : a tale of murder and archeology in the Holy Land / Edward Fox.
    p. cm.
Includes bibliographical references and index.
ISBN 0-8050-7188-1 (pbk.)
    1. Palestine—Antiquities.   2. Bible—Antiquities.   3. Excavations
(Archaeology)—Palestine.   4. Glock, Albert E.—Assassination.
5. Archaeologists—Palestine—Biography.   I. Title.
DS108.9 .F65 2001
933—dc21   2001030320

First published in hardcover in 2001 by Metropolitan Books

First Owl Books Edition 2002

A Metropolitan / Owl Book

DESIGNED BY FRITZ METSCH

Printed in the United States of America

1   3   5   7   9   10   8   6   4   2

To Emma,
with love

ALBERT GLOCK

SACRED
GEOGRAPHY

PART
I

CHAPTER ONE

O N THE MORNING of Sunday, January 19, 1992, Dr. Albert Glock went to church with his wife, Lois, in the Old City of Jerusalem. The church they attended, the Church of the Redeemer, is a somber nineteenth-century Crusader pastiche, one of several religious institutions clustered tightly around the Holy Sepulchre, the lugubrious and claustrophobic Christian shrine that is traditionally believed to contain the tomb of Jesus Christ and the site of his Crucifixion.

Albert left the service after the Eucharist; Lois stayed to the end. Glock, an archeologist at Birzeit University, the main Palestinian university in the Israeli-occupied West Bank, wanted to get back to his office to work on pottery. He walked through Damascus Gate, the monumental, grimy Ottoman construction at the corner of the Old City where the world of Palestinian Jerusalem rubs uncomfortably against the world of Israeli Jerusalem. Under the wary eyes of Israeli soldiers, Palestinian women in embroidered dresses sell fruit and vegetables on the busy sidewalks, and minibuses and shared taxis depart for the towns and villages and refugee camps of the West Bank. Gray winter clouds clogged the sky, but despite the weather Glock was wearing only his well-worn black leather jacket. At about 10:30, he climbed into his blue Volkswagen van and drove northward out of Jerusalem in the direction of Ramallah. He passed first through Beit Hanina, where he and Lois lived, a Palestinian village that had been absorbed into the northern suburbs of Jerusalem. There he bought an Arabic newspaper, and then stopped at a local bakery and bought a *ka'ak simsim*, a ring of pastry filled with dates and sprinkled with sesame seeds.

The checkpoint separating Jerusalem from the West Bank—a

roadblock of slabs of painted concrete, with a small cabin beside it occupied by Israeli soldiers—was open, so Glock was able to cover the distance from Jerusalem to Ramallah in about half an hour. He drove northward through the city, past the British-built prison inherited by the Israelis, along the road called Radio Boulevard, named after the array of three radio transmission masts built alongside it, also relics of the period of British rule that ended in 1948.

Glock stopped at a house on the outskirts of Ramallah, near the radio transmitters, where the road was muddy and gouged with ice-filled potholes. This was the house of Dr. Gabi Baramki, the acting president of Birzeit, and his wife, Dr. Haifa Baramki, the university's registrar. Nearly thirty years after first coming to Palestine, Glock still thought that it was an Arab custom not to make appointments, and Palestinian courtesy had restrained anyone from telling him this was not the case. On the other hand, Glock may have followed this habit after long experience of the unreliability of local telephone lines, or out of his own abrupt impatience with formality. When Haifa Baramki answered the doorbell and saw Glock in the doorway, she was not expecting to see him, but she was not surprised either.

Haifa told him that Gabi was not at home but invited him in for coffee. Albert declined, but said he would return after he had finished working at the institute. He would come back at about four, he said.

Before he left, Haifa Baramki asked him if he planned to stop at the house of the el-Farabi family in Bir Zeit. If he did, she asked, he might remind Maya el-Farabi,* who was Glock's teaching assistant at the Institute of Palestinian Archeology, where Glock was director, to attend a meeting the next day. The el-Farabis did not have a telephone, and Haifa knew that Albert was a regular visitor to the house. This was an errand that he would have been happy to undertake. Indeed, he was probably intending to stop there anyway. Maya el-Farabi was Glock's closest colleague at the Institute of Palestinian Archeology. He had guided and nurtured her academic career every step of the way, from undergraduate to

*I have used pseudonyms for Maya el-Farabi and her family.

PhD, and had done the same for her younger sister, Huda. If Glock trusted anyone to take over his position as director of the institute, it was Maya el-Farabi. On working days, Glock would often have lunch at the el-Farabi house. As a sign of affectionate familiarity, the el-Farabis gave him a traditional Arabic nickname, Abu Abed, which meant "father of Albert," the name of Glock's eldest son.

Sometime between eleven o'clock and noon, Glock drove out of Ramallah and into a valley where the road to Bir Zeit crossed a bypass road to an Israeli settlement. There was usually an Israeli checkpoint here, with a jeep, a strip of spiked chain across the road, and some surly young soldiers with machine guns slung over their shoulders stopping vehicles and checking identity cards. Glock was slyly proud of his skill at talking his way past these obstacles. Palestinian friends would marvel at how he would appear at their door on days when the Israeli army had imposed one of its frequent closures of the West Bank, which meant that no one was able to travel. He took full advantage of his appearance as a serious-looking, elderly foreigner. He was even careful to establish discreet but cordial relations with a few Israeli soldiers, the ones he saw more than once at the checkpoints, chatting with them, aware of their boredom. If this made it easier to go about his business, he was willing to do it, though he was careful not to seem too friendly with the soldiers when he had a Palestinian passenger sitting beside him.

Covering the distance from Ramallah to Bir Zeit took about fifteen minutes. The road winds around the rocky, rubbly hills and through several villages. Just outside Bir Zeit, he drove past the new campus, built in 1980, which was closed by military order. Farther along stood a limestone quarry at the side of the road, and a scattering of houses, including the el-Farabi house, which he planned to visit later. He knew that Maya had a dentist's appointment in Ramallah that day, and he probably assumed that she would be back home by the time he finished work at the institute. He drove through the compact town, whose position on a ridge gave it a grand view of the valley below, with tiers of crumbling olive terraces—some in use, some not—descending to a narrow plain. It was on this plain where, according to local legend, the

Roman general Titus encamped with his army in 70 C.E. before marching on Jerusalem to besiege it. From this road one can look down into the valley and across toward Ramallah, at the blinking lights of the radio masts, and beyond, to the top of a distant ridge, where the Israeli settlement of Beit El stands on the traditional site of the biblical Bethel. On the slope below Beit El, which housed the military headquarters of the region, sprawled the Palestinian refugee camp of Jalazun. At night, these two enemy settlements, irreconcilable worlds of victor and vanquished, were visible only as streaks of light, the upper one brilliant white, the lower one yellow. When a power cut cast Bir Zeit and the surrounding area into darkness, Jalazun would seem to disappear, while Beit El, with its own source of power, blazed on.

This winter had been the coldest anyone could remember. In Bir Zeit, the worst of winter was usually a few cold, rainy weeks at around the turn of the year. This year there had been heavy snow, which stayed frozen on the ground for days. The snow brought down telephone lines and power cables, cutting off electricity and telephones, and the ice caused water pipes to burst. People in the town had to endure long, bleak spells without electricity, telephone, and water. In the narrow, layered terraces of rocky soil sculpted into the slopes, the cold froze and killed thousands of olive trees.

The olive tree is the emblem of Birzeit University, the main university in the Occupied Territories. It is a good symbol for an institution that prides itself on being the hearth of Palestinian nationalism. The olive tree embodies the virtues the Palestinians like to see in themselves: it is ancient, tough, native, and it has deep roots. The name Birzeit means "reservoir of oil." In the academic calendar of Birzeit University, a day is added to a weekend in the middle of October, and this three-day break is observed as Olive Picking Holiday. The idea is that on this weekend, students return to their homes to help with the olive harvest. In reality, the Olive Picking Holiday is more of a political and nostalgic gesture than a matter of agricultural necessity. Few people any more have olive groves big enough to produce an economically viable crop.

In January 1992, Albert Glock was sixty-seven years old, and in his slow, perfectionist way was getting ready for retirement. He and Lois had been expatriates for so long, and were so deeply immersed in life among the Palestinians, that Glock felt he could never live in the United States again. For many years they had rented a large, comfortable house in Beit Hanina on the main Jerusalem road, with big airy rooms and a large study full of the books and artifacts that Albert Glock had accumulated over the years. Their children—three sons and a daughter—were grown and living their own lives in America. Everything the Glocks had was here, materially and spiritually. Now, on the verge of retirement, they were preparing to move to a smaller house in the same neighborhood. The American way of life—which Glock saw as a condition of comfortable ignorance of the rest of the world—had become foreign to him. He called it "living in the bubble." He had been visiting Cyprus on the periodic trips out of the country he was compelled to make to renew his Israeli visa, and favored settling there. But he had done nothing about it. This academic year he had relinquished most of his teaching responsibilities so that he could concentrate on completing the long-delayed publication of his life's work, the excavation of an archeologically complex site in the northern West Bank called Ti'innik.

The Institute of Archeology was accommodated in an old-fashioned family house with two stories built around a central courtyard that was entered by an ornamental iron gate. It stood on the edge of Bir Zeit's old town, a tight maze of dilapidated Ottoman buildings. Nearby, a car mechanic worked out of a dark cave of a workshop that had formerly been a blacksmith's shop. Down a narrow lane, among the tiny houses, stood a bakery where traditional flat bread was baked in a dome-shaped oven, and beyond it a small Greek Orthodox church in a poor state of repair.

Glock worked alone that day. The shelves in his workroom were filled from floor to ceiling with the cardboard boxes, neatly marked, that contained the excavation material from his digs. The worktables in the room were covered with hundreds of blackened shards of burnt pottery, arranged in a state somewhere between order and chaos. The fragments were from Ti'innik, and Albert was working with Maya and a staff technician on the painstaking business of putting as many of the fragments as possible back together into their original forms as domestic pottery vessels. The pots bore a mysterious pattern of ridges they could not identify. Several vessels had already been reassembled, among them a big two-handled water jar that dominated the room.

Ti'innik is a hamlet in the northernmost part of the West Bank, a few kilometers north of the town of Jenin in the flat, green Jezreel Valley. Nearby is the biblical site of Megiddo, better known as Armageddon, where the Book of Revelation prophesies that the battle to end all earthly battles will be fought. The village stands at the foot of an ancient man-made mound called Tell Ti'innik, which is almost certainly the site mentioned in the Bible as the Canaanite stronghold of Taanach. In 1987, Glock and Maya el-Farabi took the radical step of excavating, not the parts of the site that related to biblical history, which had been the dominant interest of archeologists in the Holy Land since the middle of the nineteenth century, but the more recent Ottoman remains, which had been largely ignored by archeologists.

Some time before three o'clock, he closed up the office and turned the key in the VW. It was his plan to stop off briefly at the el-Farabi house to leave the message for Maya about the meeting. He would not stay long: his appointment with Gabi Baramki was more important. Before he left, he scribbled a note to el-Farabi on the copy of the Arabic newspaper he had bought in Beit Hanina, that day's edition of *al-Ittihad*. He wrote across the top in block capitals, "I may be late tomorrow. Al," and left it where she would see it.

Many of Glock's friends were impressed by the fearlessness with which he drove around the West Bank during the *intifada*, the Palestinian uprising against Israeli rule that had erupted four years earlier. He traveled without hesitation into areas where a vehicle with Israeli license plates, like his, was almost certain to have stones thrown at it by children and teenagers. Glock had endured his share of stones, but he still went where he wanted to go. But lately he had begun to take precautions when he drove the van, aware that it was well known and that he was conspicuous driving it. He would vary his usual routes and check underneath the van before he got into it. He was afraid of something, it seemed, but whether it was a general fear for his safety at a dangerous time or if he was afraid of something or someone in particular is unknowable.

That day, a funeral was taking place at the Greek Orthodox church. The town of Bir Zeit is unusual among West Bank towns in that its population is mostly Christian. Unlike better-known Palestinian towns that have traditionally had Christian majorities, like Bethlehem, the proportion of its population that is Christian has increased rather than shrunk in recent years. The thresholds of the doorways of houses tend to be decorated with a carved relief of St. George slaying the dragon (a motif thought to originate with the Crusades), indicating a Christian household, rather than a Quranic inscription. Most of the Christians in Bir Zeit, in common with most Palestinian Christians, belonged to the Greek Orthodox church. As Glock was leaving the institute, the funeral procession, with its train of cars, came along the narrow road in the opposite direction toward the church. People in Bir Zeit remember that as the funeral procession approached, Glock patiently pulled over to the side of the road to let it pass. His VW van was a familiar sight in the area, and everyone knew it belonged to the American archeologist. They remember that moment as a characteristically modest, thoughtful act of courtesy. They also remember it as the last time they saw him alive.

After the procession had passed, Glock drove out of the town and along the road to the new campus. The el-Farabi house was on this road, about a kilometer outside the town. It was built on a steep slope, below the level of the road, so a person standing on the road looks down on the roof of the house, with its solar panels, hot water tank, and television antenna. Glock parked the van on the gravel shoulder at the side of the road, under a fig tree. It was a dark day, so he left the van's headlights on, not meaning to stay long. The time was just after three o'clock.

Albert Glock walked around to the gate at the top of the driveway, pushed it open, and walked down the concrete ramp. He probably did not hear the sound of a man jumping down into the el-Farabis' garden from the stone wall that ran along the side of the road. The assailant, later described by witnesses as a young man dressed in a dark jacket, jeans, sneakers, and a *kaffiyeh*—the black-and-white cotton scarf favored by many Palestinians—landed softly on a strip of plowed earth planted with olive trees. As Glock strode toward the front door of the house, the man crept up behind him, leveled his gun, and fired three times.

CHAPTER TWO

LBERT GLOCK'S FATHER, Ernest, was born in Nevada in
1891 in a log cabin. Ernest's parents were German-speaking
Catholics; his father came from the Franco-German
province of Alsace-Lorraine, his mother from Switzerland. The
couple had immigrated separately to America, where they met in
Carson City, Nevada, and married in 1892. Seven children were
born before their father disappeared, plunging the family into
penury. The youngest children were sent to an orphanage.

As a teenager, Ernest worked as a farmhand for room and
board. In an autobiographical essay he records the hardships he
endured as a youth, sleeping in a freezing barn, milking cows, feed-
ing hogs, and later herding sheep, which required camping alone
for a week at a time. He would cook his supper on a sagebrush
fire, sleeping with one ear cocked for the sound of a predatory
bobcat or wolf. After a few years of herding sheep he got a job
hauling cordwood. In this job Ernest had to rise at 4:00 A.M. to
drive a team of horses and mules.

Later he was taken in by an aunt and her husband. She was
a convert to the Lutheran Church—Missouri Synod, a St.
Louis–based organization that had been established to care for the
millions of Germans migrating to the United States in the nineteenth century. When Ernest Glock expressed a need to improve
himself by getting an education, his aunt suggested a Lutheran
seminary in California. Before his graduation from the seminary
Ernest was sent as a Missouri Synod vicar and schoolmaster to
Lebeau, Texas, a small town so steeped in German culture that
even the local blacks spoke German.

After graduating, Ernest Glock married a grocer's daughter,

Meta Matulle. He and his wife were sent to Gifford, Idaho: a rural, roadless place, surrounded by forest, where the congregation was again entirely German-speaking, and which is now within the borders of an Indian reservation (the Nez Percé tribe). "During my four and one half years as pastor I did not preach one English sermon," he wrote. Their house in Gifford had no indoor plumbing; their water supply was rainwater and snowmelt from the roof, which drained into a brick cistern; and in the winter the thermometer sometimes touched forty below. This is the house in which, in 1925, Albert Ernest Glock was born. A few months later, the family moved to Grangeville, a larger town not far away. They spent another three years in Idaho before Ernest accepted a "call" to a church in Washburn, Illinois, a small dot on the map northeast of Peoria with a population of nine hundred, where Albert and his two brothers grew up.

It was a claustrophobic, confining upbringing for the three boys, who were each a little more than a year apart in age. As the preacher's children, they were always on show, expected to be models of good behavior. Their father maintained discipline with a paddle. Like most clerical families, the Glocks' social status was higher than their income, and the rigor of their upbringing was mirrored in the plainness of their material circumstances. The house was heated with wood in the winter, and the Glocks bought their groceries on credit. Every day, Meta served supper at five o'clock. The meal was preceded and concluded with prayers. Until they went to grade school at the age of six or seven, the children spoke only High German at home. It was an airless world, conservative and austere. Their mother effaced herself in the duties of a minister's wife, and said little. "But she was the really intelligent one," Albert's younger brother Delmer remembered.

There was little in this upbringing to stimulate the minds of the three intelligent boys. The town of Washburn—inhabited mostly by retired farmers, and surrounded by expanses of flat farmland—offered few distractions. Their father, Ernest, was a practical man with limited intellectual interests, and he disapproved of popular amusements like movies and dancing. His library was dominated by dry volumes of Lutheran theology.

Temperamentally, the boys were not rebellious. They dared not challenge their father's firm belief that the Pope was the Antichrist, as Missouri Synod doctrine held. So when Albert sought a means of escape from this restricted world, he quietly found one for himself in the voracious reading of books.

Delmer Glock was convinced that his brother's interest in the archeology of Palestine originated not in the text of the Bible but in the swashbuckling children's adventure stories of Richard Halliburton, which were published in America in the 1920s and 1930s. In one of these books, *Richard Halliburton's Second Book of Marvels: The Orient,* first published when Albert was thirteen, one finds, after descriptions of the Seven Wonders of the Ancient World, chapters recounting the exploration of "Timbuctoo," the discovery of Victoria Falls by Livingstone, a meeting with "Ibn Saud" (the King of Saudi Arabia) in a tent outside Mecca, and visits to Petra and the Dead Sea. In addition, there is a swaggering account of an attempt to explore a "secret tunnel" in the Temple Mount in Jerusalem. This may have been the spark that ignited Albert's curiosity, kindled on the dry wood of an already abundant knowledge of the Bible. Exploration of the Temple Mount, the seat of the biblical Temple, was and remains the holy grail of biblical archeology, its central mystery, its ultimate prize, and a subject so thickly encrusted with myth and legend that the facts about it are easily forgotten. The cult of exploration of the Temple Mount, of which Halliburton gave a simplified children's version, may have turned the homely familiarity with the Bible that Albert Glock already possessed into a genuine adventure.

Halliburton wrote:

The more I heard about the caverns and tunnels and shaft, the more curious I became about them. How exciting it would be if someone *could* explore the entire passage, the passage lost all these centuries. If someone found the tunnel, it would lead—if the legend turned out to be true—right into the treasure-caverns from underneath. The reward of such an adventure might be the long-lost Ark of the Covenant, or the mummy of Israel's greatest king.

I resolved to be that someone myself. . . . Was I about to make one of the greatest discoveries in Bible history?

Albert Glock no doubt drew inspiration for his career as an archeologist from many sources, not just the accounts of a famous American adventure writer. But when he was still a teenager, he traveled on a freighter to Europe, just as Halliburton did, and years later he was excavating an ancient mound in Palestine, seeking to make discoveries in Bible history himself.

Albert showed a determined independence of mind that was unusual in a place where few aspired to individualism. "He was always off doing *something*," his brother Richard recalled, "and we were never sure what it was." Richard remembers being mystified by the sight of his older brother writing Sanskrit and cuneiform characters on a piece of paper. "I don't know *where* he got it from," he said.

At the age of thirteen, Albert told his father that he wanted to enroll at a residential preseminary high school for boys in Milwaukee, two hundred miles away. The school was a German-style *Gymnasium* where students learned Latin, Greek, and Hebrew. Its purpose was to prepare boys for the Lutheran ministry. Albert's parents could afford the fees, which were $200 per year, but not the cost of transportation. So from the age of thirteen, and for the next five years, Albert would hitchhike the two hundred miles between Washburn and Milwaukee. Later, he announced that he wanted to specialize in the Old Testament, source of the legends of Solomon and the Temple and the ancient civilizations of the Near East.

Albert Glock's motive in going to school in Milwaukee was a desire to get out of Washburn, to see the world, as much as a dedication to the Lutheran ministry. Seeing the way out that their older brother had found, Albert's younger brothers, Delmer and Richard, followed his path to the Missouri Synod ministry via the *Gymnasium* in Milwaukee. The boys took full advantage of their newly won freedom. By the time they had reached their late teens, they had hitchhiked to all forty-eight states in the Union.

Once they were in their mid-twenties, they were all Lutheran ministers.

Lutherans of the Missouri Synod subscribed unconditionally to the version of Christianity embodied in the classic works of Martin Luther and were unimpressed with anything written later. Drinking from this pristine well of pure doctrine, based on a belief in the Bible as "the inspired, inerrant and infallible word of God," Missourians saw themselves as forming "the only true visible church on earth." Although it was the plan of the Missouri Synod leadership gradually to adopt English in church rites as soon as most of its members had acquired the language, and once the work of translating the Lutheran classics was completed, the cultural and doctrinal conservatism of most members of the church were inseparable. To Missourians, their native German tongue was the divine language of the Bible, as translated by the blessed Luther himself, and they only reluctantly gave it up completely in church services as late as World War II, spurred on by popular anti-German feeling in the United States.

The Missourians remained apart and solitary in their righteousness: it was not until the 1960s that they would agree to join Christian organizations that included other denominations. This attitude was reinforced by their social and cultural homogeneity: they were almost all German Americans (there was also a Scandinavian element), and they were in and of the agricultural Midwest. As late as the mid-1960s two-thirds of them lived within a three-hundred-mile radius of Chicago.

Their separateness and common identity were not just ethnic. Members of the church did not need to look outside for education. LCMS pastors were trained at an LCMS seminary—Concordia Theological Seminary, St. Louis—and the children of LCMS members attended LCMS elementary schools, whose teachers were trained at an LCMS teachers college. As late as the 1930s, lectures in theology at Concordia Seminary were in Latin.

In 1932, the church published a synopsis of its beliefs, bearing the plain title *A Brief Statement of the Doctrinal Position of the Missouri Synod*. The document proposes a universe that came into being in exactly six twenty-four-hour days. "Since no man was present when it pleased God to create the world," it argues, "we must look for a reliable account of creation to God's own record, found in God's own book, the Bible." Missourians reject any scientific explanation of the origins of man and the universe that contradicts the biblical account, whatever the intellectual difficulties this may cause.

The *Statement* also sets out that salvation is achieved exclusively by divine grace. The Gospels and the Sacraments are the tools given man to promote receptiveness to this divine grace. Good works alone are insufficient for salvation: the idea is anathema to the Missourians. They also believe that the Pope is the fulfillment of biblical prophecies of the Antichrist. Catholics, Anabaptists, Unitarians, Masons, "crypto-Calvinists," and "synergists" are all held to be in dangerous error. Missourians repudiate "unionism," "that is, church-fellowship with the adherents of false doctrine."

These tenets were the result of decades of collegial deliberation by pious, solitary, scholarly Lutherans, conducted in earnest conferences in small towns on the midwestern plains, based on a prior faith in the Bible as the infallible word of God. It is a Protestantism of the windswept American plains: pure, primitive, austere, unworldly. This is the doctrine—transmitted via the golden chain of Christ, the Bible, Luther, and the Missouri divines—that Ernest Glock taught his sons at their family devotions. Albert later admitted that he had privately scorned his father's worldview, seeing it as narrow and exclusive of all but the concerns of his Missouri Synod flock.

Ernest was ambivalent about his son's scholarship: he thought basic seminary training was enough. But Albert, young and intellectually hungry, continued to enlarge his field of study. In 1949 he spent a year in Europe studying theology, and took classes in biblical criticism at the University of Heidelberg; he then returned to America to study Near Eastern Languages at the University of Chicago.

His study of biblical Hebrew would set Glock in opposition to one of the most intellectually constraining articles of the *Brief*

Statement: "Since the Holy Scriptures are the Word of God, it goes without saying that they contain no errors or contradictions, but that they are in all their parts and words the infallible truth, *also in those parts which treat of historical, geographical, and other secular matters*." Historical and geographical matters were precisely what interested Albert Glock. His scholarly intellect was too keen, and his nature too individualistic, to accept this traditional dogma unquestioningly. Nevertheless, he graduated from Concordia Theological Seminary in St. Louis in 1950.

The following year, he married Lois Sohn, also a German American, the daughter of a professor of Lutheran theology, and he seemed set for the quiet and stable life of a Lutheran clergyman. He spent the next seven years as a pastor in Normal, Illinois, not far from where he had grown up, apparently happy in his vocation: in the earnest, collegial spirit of Lutheran pastors, he closed his letters "yours in Christ," *"agape,"* and "peace."

But his studies in ancient Hebrew continued. While still serving as a pastor in Normal, he enrolled at the University of Michigan, where his thesis adviser was George Mendenhall, a biblical scholar who introduced to biblical studies the Marxist-oriented "peasants' revolt" model of the origin of ancient Israel. His theory was opposed to the orthodox view, which held that Israelite tribes invaded Canaan and defeated the indigenous Canaanites. Mendenhall believed that a kind of theocratic liberation movement emerged within Canaanite society, gradually transforming it into what would ultimately be called "Israel." His theory, revolutionary in its day, was an early instance of a history of ancient Israel that was distinct from the biblical account. Mendenhall's approach was an important formative influence on Albert Glock, who received his doctorate in 1968.

Glock was coming to realize that scholarship suited his temperament far better than the chores of a clergyman. Many years after completing his doctoral thesis, Albert wrote in his diary that he "had wasted seven years in Normal, Illinois." He didn't have the patient personality of a clergyman, who, as part of his daily business, must suffer gladly the lonely, the pedantic, and the boring. In

1956, he was offered a job—or "answered a call," to use the Missouri idiom—to teach Old Testament history and literature at Concordia Teachers College, River Forest, Illinois, the teachers college for the Missouri Synod elementary school system.

The Missouri Synod's insistence that the Bible is the inerrant and infallible word of God created among its scholars a tension that developed in the late 1950s and early 1960s into a controversy that finally caused the church to split. A liberal wing believed their faith in scripture was not undermined by analyzing the Old Testament historically. The liberals argued that the Old Testament was not the work of Moses but of later authors, writing from the eighth century B.C.E. and afterward. The official line of the Missouri Synod was that the books traditionally attributed to Moses were written by Moses, and likewise that all the other books of the Bible were written by their traditional authors.

The leadership of the Missouri Synod, representing the conservative mainstream, sought to stamp out this heresy, which was threatening to engulf the entire church. To put reason before faith in studying the Bible was the beginning of the end of religion, they argued. Worst of all, this heretical fire had broken out in the church's theological engine room, the Concordia Theological Seminary. One of the means the leadership used to extinguish it was to demand allegiance to the *Brief Statement* by the forty or so dissident professors at Concordia. The professors were unwilling to do this, arguing it infringed their right to academic freedom.

Although Glock was teaching elsewhere, at Concordia Teachers College, he took the side of the dissidents, since this was the direction he, too, was following in his biblical studies. In 1960, at age thirty-five, he wrote an article in defense of the dissidents entitled "A Critical Evaluation of the Article on Scripture in 'A Brief Statement' of the Lutheran Church–Missouri Synod." The tone of the article was conventionally and respectfully pious, but the criticism it contained attacked the Missouri Synod's uncompromising doctrine at its heart. The church's theology is locked in the seventeenth century, he wrote, resulting in "a serious breakdown of communication when speaking to our age." He then went on to propose a historic shift in the church's doctrine, away from its most distinctive feature, its stubborn belief in the literalism of the Bible, toward an emphasis on its meaning and spirit.

After Glock read the article at a meeting of his department at Concordia Teachers College, they insisted that it be locked in a safe and not allowed to circulate. For Albert, the episode was his first public act of opposition. He saw it as the symbolic sealing of his fate. Henceforth, he would always be a dissident.

Ultimately, the rebels of Concordia Theological Seminary accepted defeat. They left the church and founded Seminex, a "seminary in exile." Their departure strengthened the conservatives' grip on Missouri Synod doctrine. Seminex survived in the wilderness, training Lutheran pastors who were not recognized by the Missouri Synod, until 1988, when it voted itself out of existence and joined the more liberal Evangelical Lutheran Church of America.

In one of his unpublished essays, written when he was at Birzeit, Albert Glock described himself as "a skeptical white American tending to minority views." Taking the side of the liberals in the Missouri Synod split was like rebelling against his father. Taking the minority view was an instinct that he was to follow at every crossroads in his life.

CHAPTER THREE

IBLICAL ARCHEOLOGY BEGAN in about the year 325 of the common era. Shortly after acquiring the eastern provinces that included Palestine, Emperor Constantine—the first Christian emperor and the founder of Byzantine civilization—sent his mother, Flavia Julia Helena Augusta, the Empress Dowager, to lead a mission to Palestine. The immediate political purpose of the journey was to assert Constantine's authority in the province and to promote Christians and Christianity in the imperial state among a mostly non-Christian population. As physical signs of this new dispensation, a number of churches and basilicas were commissioned in the course of the Empress Dowager's visit, including a church over the Holy Sepulchre, the presumed tomb of Christ. A local cult of the relic of the cross on which Christ was crucified had already come into existence at some point in the intervening three centuries, though how and when remains obscure.

The Empress Helena died in about 328, in her eighties. Some fifty years after her death, a legend began to circulate about her and her visit to Palestine. Here is the legend, from the *Church History* of Tyrannius Rufinus, written about 400 C.E.

Helena, the mother of Constantine, a woman of outstanding faith and deep piety, and also of exceptional munificence . . . was advised by divinely sent visions to go to Jerusalem. There she was to make an enquiry among the inhabitants to find out the place where the sacred body of Christ had hung on the Cross. This spot was difficult to find, because the persecutors of old had set up a statue of Venus over it, so that if any Christian wanted to worship Christ in that place, he seemed to be worshipping Venus. For this reason, the place was not much frequented and had all but been forgotten. But when . . . the pious lady hastened to the spot pointed out to her by a heavenly sign, she tore down all that was profane and polluted there. Deep beneath the rubble she found three Crosses lying in disorder. But the joy of finding this treasure was marred by the difficulty of distinguishing to whom each Cross belonged. The board was there, it is true, on which Pilate had placed an inscription written in Greek, Latin and Hebrew characters.

Helena was unsure whether what she had found was the true cross. To allay her doubts, the bishop of Jerusalem, Macarius, determined that divine proof was needed. He led Helena and her entourage to the house of a woman who was mortally ill with a serious disease. One by one the crosses Helena had found were shown to the sick woman. When the third cross was brought to her, the woman leapt out of bed, cured. This miracle identified the third cross as the true cross.

When the queen saw that her wish had been answered by such a clear sign, she built a marvellous church of royal magnificence over the place where she had discovered the Cross. The nails which had attached the Lord's body to the Cross, she sent to her son. From some of these he had a horse's bridle made, for use in battle, while he used others to add strength to a helmet, equally with a view to using it in battle. Part of the redeeming wood she sent to her son, but she also left part of it there preserved in silver chests. This part is commemorated by regular veneration to this very day. . . .

This legend has been woven into later historical narratives as if it were fact, but it is a pious fiction, emanating from the imperially supported church in Jerusalem. (In his account of the life of Constantine, written in about 338, the time of Helena's death, the bishop Eusebius, chronicler of the early church in Palestine, mentions her piety and her commissioning of churches, but says nothing about finding the true cross.) The purpose of the legend is to burnish Constantine's reputation as a Christian emperor. The symbolism in what happened to the nails is obvious: incorporated into the emperor's helmet (other versions of the legend say diadem or crown) and his horse's bridle. The sacred power of Christ is incorporated into Constantine's imperial implements of war and governance, giving supernatural legitimacy to his military and civil authority.

The legend also enhances the reputation of Jerusalem as the home of sacred relics, and reflects the inauguration at that time of a tradition that persists to this day of the search for the physical remains of biblical history as a dimension of Christian spirituality. It establishes the idea of the Holy Land as one of the universal features of the Christian faith: a transcendental geography imposed on the mundane geography of southern Syria. In subsequent centuries, Jerusalem and surrounding sacred sites were the prized destinations of Christian pilgrims, and splinters of Helena's true cross and other relics were sold as sacred souvenirs for the pilgrims to take home with them. Thus Helena's account was an advertisement, intended to promote the pilgrimage industry, not a report.

Helena's excavation techniques have been improved upon, but her archeological assumptions have proven remarkably durable, persisting well into an age of scientific rationalism. She knew what she was looking for, and—with divine inspiration—she found it.

———

BEFORE HELENA'S VISIT, Christian pilgrimages to Palestine originating from outside the country were unknown. Visiting sacred sites was a local cult, preceding Judaism, Christianity, and Islam. The Church's earliest authorities considered it theologically unnecessary for Christians to tread the land that Jesus' feet had trodden. Besides, the anti-Christian policy of the Roman authorities that governed Palestine discouraged Christian visitors. After Constantine's institutionalization of Christianity in the Roman empire, pilgrimage was encouraged as a natural expression of piety. Monasteries and hostels were built to accommodate pilgrims. In the first centuries after Constantine, the numbers of pilgrims making the journey rose and fell in response to changing political conditions in the Mediterranean and the countries through which they were obliged to pass.

These early pilgrims were either very rich or very determined, as the journey was long, arduous, and expensive. Pilgrimages would often take several years to complete. One of the earliest pilgrims to leave a written account was a nun named Egeria, probably from Spain, who visited Palestine in the years 381 to 384. Her narrative, of which only a fragment survives, shows her conducting her pilgrimage as a kind of liturgical ritual. Accompanied by monks, at every point of interest she and her party would offer prayers. She ascended Mount Sinai, where Moses received from God the stone tablets inscribed with the Ten Commandments, as if she were performing the ceremony of the stations of the cross.

Throughout her narrative she describes little that was not related to the network of hundreds of minor and major Christian shrines that by the time of her visit had been established in the region. Where a sacred site had previously been pagan, a Christian legend would be created to absorb it into the new landscape of religious meaning. From her point of view the whole country existed as an enormous church. It was a land whose holiness, combined with its unfamiliarity to a European, rendered it unreal: pilgrims depended on local guides and storytellers who wove inspiring tales of miracles and marvels about the sites on the pilgrim circuit, more or less based on familiar stories in the Old and New Testaments, sometimes wholly original. In the Holy Land, the hands and feet of Jesus would press into stone as if it were Plasticine, leaving a permanent and easily identifiable imprint. (This folkloric impulse is one that all faiths followed to create religious marvels: the rock inside the Dome of the Rock in Jerusalem bears a mark that is interpreted as both the footprint of Christ and the handprint of the Prophet Muhammad.)

A pilgrimage was not a fact-finding mission. The point was to be amazed. The pilgrim beheld a holy site to enhance the faith that had brought him there, not to allay doubt through the acquisition of data. This corpus of religious folklore grew prolifically in the centuries after Constantine and became part of what it meant to be a Christian. In the case of Jerusalem, the Holy Land's focal point, the physical city came to be totally overshadowed by an idealized version that bore little resemblance to the original. In maps,

Jerusalem was often depicted as a circle, with a round wall enclosing the sacred sites, as if it were one of the spheres of the cosmos. Besides the tomb of Christ and the site of his Crucifixion, the Church of the Holy Sepulchre came to include the tomb of Adam (directly underneath the cross), and the center of the world itself: the shrine became a model in miniature of the Christian cosmos.

To increase the pilgrim's sense of awe, the interior of the Church of the Holy Sepulchre was improved and augmented, with spiritual power conveyed by ritual, by art, and above all by the hallowed objects that had come into contact with the body of Christ in the course of his Passion and Crucifixion. A seventh-century account by a monk of the Scottish monastery on the island of Iona (basing his account on what a fellow monk told him) records that the Church of the Holy Sepulchre contained the cup that Jesus used at the Last Supper (made of silver, with two handles, and large enough to hold "a French quart"), the vinegar-soaked sponge that was thrust into Jesus' mouth by a soldier, the spear that was used to stab him, and the cloth that was placed over his body.

The power of the cult of the Holy Land was such that reverence for the Holy Sepulchre was not extinguished after the church and its contents were systematically demolished in the year 1009. The demolition was carried out by soldiers based in nearby Ramla, the local administrative center, acting on the order of the mad Fatimid Caliph Abu Ali al-Mansur al-Hakim bi-Amrih Allah, who was waging a particularly eccentric campaign of persecution of Christians and Jews in his dominions, which included Palestine. (At one point al-Hakim required the Christians of Cairo to identify themselves in public by carrying large wooden crosses; Jews were compelled to carry wooden posts. He also banned the sale of *mulukhiyya*, a spinach-like vegetable, as well as fish without scales, wine, beer, grapes, and honey. He forbade women from going out of doors or even looking out of the window, and eventually he came to believe himself to be God incarnate.) The destruction was thorough: according to an Arab historian, al-Hakim's governor "did all he could to uproot the Sepulchre and to remove all trace of it, and to this effect he dug away most of it and broke it up." The destruction of the shrine stopped the pilgrim trade abruptly for a time, but once the church was rebuilt (1042–1048) by the Byzantine emperor Constantine Monomachus, with the destroyed tomb of Christ replaced by a replica, the number of pilgrims became greater than ever.

Al-Hakim's demolition of the Holy Sepulchre spurred the launch of the first Crusade, a military campaign decreed by Pope Urban II to seize the Holy Land from Muslim rule. The Pope's call ignited the popular imagination in western Europe, and the capture of Jerusalem in 1099 inspired a new burst of growth in the Christian cult of the Holy Land. The Dome of the Rock, the Islamic shrine built on the site of the Israelite Temple, was now seen as the Temple of Solomon itself, and the place where, in the Gospel narrative, Jesus was presented to the priests. The "Temple" was absorbed into the "way of the cross," the pilgrims' tour of the sites associated with the life and death of Jesus. In the Jerusalem of the Crusaders, a new cult of the Temple came into being, established by the Templars—the Poor Knights of Christ and of the Temple of Solomon—a religious military order that made its headquarters inside the Dome of the Rock. They developed a system of gnostic mysticism—secret religious knowledge—based on a sacred geometry of the octagon (after the octagonal shape of the Dome of the Rock) and on a concept of God as the architect of the world, as Solomon had been the architect of the Temple.

The Christianization of the Holy Land was accomplished through the "discovery" of countless new sacred relics, most of which were carried back to Europe. Besides further fragments of the true cross, Christians "found" the nails of the true cross (again), Jesus' crown of thorns, the lance used to pierce Jesus' side (which became the Crusaders' battle standard), as well as the bones of the Old Testament patriarchs (at Hebron) and those of numerous saints. The typical method for finding relics was for a monk to find an object and then "discover" its sacred identity in a dream. The proliferation of fragments of the true cross famously prompted the Protestant reformer John Calvin to scoff, at the close of the Middle Ages, that if all these fragments were collected, they would be "comparable in bulk to a battleship" (an assertion that is carefully refuted in the 1913 *Catholic Encyclopedia*, which argues that they would all add up to no more than about a third of a whole cross weighing seventy-five kilograms).

This corpus of legend was always changing and growing. It survived the Reformation and a powerful Protestant critique. The Crusader way of the cross evolved, by the fourteenth century, into the tradition of the Via Dolorosa: the route through the streets of the Old City of Jerusalem that Christ took on his final procession to his public execution. The discovery of such sites as the spot where Jesus fell for the third time was ascribed to Empress Helena, although the configuration of the sites (conforming to the traditional narrative of the stations of the cross) changed over the centuries, and the sites the modern tourist sees were fixed only as recently as the nineteenth century.

Layer upon layer of popular myth, legend, tradition, pious fantasy and delusion, and endlessly repeated secondhand scholarship have accumulated in the sacred geography of the Holy Land over the centuries, like artifacts in an archeologist's mound. The facts were lost in the obscurity.

THE BIBLICAL ARCHEOLOGY that began in the nineteenth century, of which Albert Glock was an inheritor, was a Protestant critique of the traditions and legends that had accreted in the course of centuries of pilgrimage by European Christians. The medieval tradition that began with Helena seemed primitive and pagan to the Protestant sensibility: nineteenth-century biblical archeology was an attempt to impose the Reformation on how Christians saw the Holy Land. The first notable expedition in this reforming spirit was made by the American biblical scholar Edward Robinson and his colleague Eli Smith, an Arabic-speaking missionary, in two journeys to Palestine, the first and most substantial one in 1838, the second in 1852. Robinson is important because he introduced Protestant rationalism and Protestant piety into the western encounter with Palestine. That is, he was determined to avoid the Helenic tradition as much as possible, and to try to see things in a new way. "We early adopted two general principles, by which to govern ourselves in our examination of the Holy Land," he wrote. "The *first* was, to avoid as far as possible all contact with the convents and the authority of the monks; to examine everywhere for ourselves with the Scriptures in our hands; and to apply for information solely to the native Arab population. The *second* was, to leave as much as possible the beaten track."

Emphatic typography expresses the principle Robinson followed in his three-month journey through the biblical landscape: *"All ecclesiastical tradition respecting the ancient places in and around Jerusalem and throughout Palestine, IS OF NO VALUE, except so far as it is supported by circumstances known to us from the Scriptures, or from other contemporary testimony."* This was a radically new approach. For the first time, a respected scholar was able to say and to demonstrate what an uncountable number among the generations of travelers had noticed but not dared to say: that a good many of these traditions didn't make sense historically or rationally. Most conspicuously, the complex of shrines inside the Church of the Holy Sepulchre, which supposedly contains both the site of the Crucifixion and the tomb of Christ (not to mention the stone on which the body of Christ was anointed for burial and related sacred attractions), are manifestly unrealistic and convincing only when seen through the lens of faith. "I am led irresistibly to the conclusion," he wrote, "that the Golgotha and the tomb now shown in the Church of the Holy Sepulchre, are not upon the real places of the crucifixion and resurrection of our Lord. The alleged discovery of them by the aged and credulous Helena, like her discovery of the cross, may not improbably have been the work of pious fraud."

This conclusion was the most publicly sensational of Robinson's observations, and it was hotly debated for decades afterward with the arguments for and against the historicity of the site falling along sectarian lines: the Catholics (who had maintained a stake in the Holy Sepulchre since the Crusades, and therefore had a vested interest) arguing for it, and the Protestants arguing against. (The best current archeological thinking favors the Catholic view of the Holy Sepulchre as the most likely place for it to have existed historically.) The whole superstitious business of the Holy Sepulchre, epitomized by the annual spectacle of fairground spirituality that took place there at Easter in the ceremony of the Holy Fire (in which crowds thronged the church to witness a lamp over the tomb of Christ being lit by divine agency) "was to a Protestant painful and revolting," Robinson wrote.

Robinson's work was biblical geography, rather than biblical archeology, strictly speaking, since he only conducted a surface survey and carried out no excavations. His real accomplishment lay in the meticulous record he made of his survey, linking biblical place-names with their contemporary Arabic equivalents, without reference to legend. He favored local Palestinian folklore, seeing in it a more reliable, continuous tradition. By this method he correctly identified the site of Megiddo, for instance, an identification which formed the starting point for the later archeological study of that site.

Robinson was motivated by a strong Protestant attachment to the text of the Bible, which he took as literally true. In this he was violating an elementary principle of geography, articulated in antiquity by the second-century geographer and astronomer Ptolemy: that the landscape is more important than the map. Instead, Robinson saw the map (the Bible) as more important than the landscape. But his intellectual honesty is impressive for his time, and there is no obvious instance in the three volumes of his principal work that suggests he distorted anything he saw out of reverence for the Bible. His only shortcoming as an archeologist was his lack of interest in anything in the land and history of Palestine that didn't have to do with the Bible.

Robinson explained that his journey to the Holy Land was the fulfillment of a lifelong ambition, one that had emerged from his experience of growing up in New England. "As in the case of most of my countrymen, especially in New England, the scenes of the Bible had made a deep impression upon my mind from earliest childhood," he wrote. For the child growing up in the Puritan culture of New England in the early nineteenth century, "the names of Sinai, Jerusalem, Bethlehem, the Promised Land, became associated with his earliest recollections and holiest feelings." For Americans of a variety of backgrounds—for Robinson, for Albert Glock, and for millions of others—the sacred geography of the Holy Land was superimposed on the geography of North America. The notion of America as the new Israel, a God-fearing, perfect society set apart from the rest of mankind—"a city on a hill"—was imported with the first English settlers in the seventeenth century, and remains an essential part of America's idea of itself.

This sentiment gave rise in Edward Robinson to a "scientific" curiosity, a yearning to visit the country whose place-names were already so familiar to him. In exploring Palestine he was, in a sense, exploring New England: he was fathoming his own experience, his own identity. "In no country of the world, perhaps, is such a feeling more widely diffused than in New England," he wrote.

But this feeling was widely diffused in a number of places besides New England. The Palestine Exploration Fund (PEF) was established in London in 1865 with a purpose similar to Robinson's: to study, according to its original prospectus, the "archeology, manners and customs, topography, geology, natural sciences (botany, zoology, meteorology)" of the Holy Land, on the grounds that "no country should be of so much interest to us as that in which the documents of our Faith were written, and the momentous events they describe enacted." Founded by the great and the good of Victorian Britain, with Her Majesty the Queen herself as its patron, the PEF was launched amid great popular enthusiasm and combined the adventure of discovery with the high goals of scholarship, Christian piety, and the emotional appeal of national purpose and pride. Its aim was to send expeditions to Palestine that would be funded by public contributions. In its first general meeting, the Archbishop of York, who chaired the gathering, expressed the project's fundamental motivation.

"This country of Palestine belongs to *you* and to *me*, it is essentially ours. It was given to the Father of Israel in the words: 'Walk through the land in the length of it, and in the breadth of it, for I will give it unto thee.' *We* mean to walk through Palestine in the length and in the breadth of it, because that land has been given unto us. . . . It is the land to which we may look with as true a patriotism as we do this dear old England, which we love so much. (Cheers.)"

Thus does Palestine belong to the Englishman, as well as to the American. It also belongs, in one way or another, one discovers, to the French, the Russians, the Germans, the Armenians, the Ethiopians, the Jews, and the Muslims, and a few other groups as well. Each of these nations has a claim to the Holy Land that is exclusive and incompatible with the others. Since the beginning of the Christian era, Palestine has been the focus of a multitude of claims, originating in a variety of cultures, to produce an effect of what one might call negative cosmopolitanism. The usual sense of cosmopolitanism denotes an outlook in which a person from one place identifies with many other places. Negative cosmopolitanism means the opposite: the identification of people from many places with one place.

The Protestant attachment to the Holy Land was separate from the tradition of Helena, but it, too, was subject to imaginative conceptions of the holiness of the Holy Land. This was certainly true in Victorian England at the time of the founding of the Palestine Exploration Fund. In its first years, the subject that dominated the pages of the *Palestine Exploration Fund Quarterly Statement* was the location of the sites of the Crucifixion and the tomb of Christ. Reason required the rejection of the Holy Sepulchre as the historical location of these sites, but faith required an alternative, and one was soon found. The modern tourist can now visit a walled garden outside the old city, near the Palestinian bus station and the Damascus Gate, known as the Garden Tomb. It contains a pair of stone grottoes, which were probably once used as tombs. But Protestant tradition has settled on one of the grottoes as the likely tomb of Christ, and it has come to be invested with holiness. Its tranquil setting and physical simplicity compared to the hectic Holy Sepulchre reflect the more individualistic and unadorned character of Protestant spirituality. One of the reasons the nineteenth-century Protestant sensibility chose this site as the tomb of Christ was the physical resemblance of the rocky mound in which the tomb was cut to the dome of a human skull. The Bible uses the word *golgotha* to describe the place of the entombment: the place of the skull. Like Helena, the Victorian Protestants were seeing what they wanted to see, finding what they wanted to find.

In contrast to the Protestant and Catholic traditions, the Orthodox saw no need to identify the "true" sites of the events of the life of Christ. To Russian Orthodox pilgrims, whose liturgy retained the mysticism of an older form of Christianity, the Holy Sepulchre complex was not *supposed* to be historically realistic. This was a place where the cosmic realm penetrated the earthly. The tomb of Christ was a three-dimensional icon, a miraculous object possessing real supernatural power, not just representing it. If it looked like a normal tomb, or was held to be one, it could not be the tomb of the son of God, and it would not put the beholder in touch with the divine. In entering the Church of the Holy Sepulchre, the pilgrim was entering a zone of divinity, not a real place but something higher. He sought to be amazed, not reassured.

The Protestant Golgotha inspired the visionary imagination of one especially eminent Victorian: the British military hero General Charles Gordon, the martyr of Khartoum. Before he embarked on his doomed expedition to confront the rebel forces of the Mahdi in al-Sudan, and after his victorious campaign against a rebellion in China, Gordon spent a year in Jerusalem as a solitary mystic, studying the Bible and the topography of Jerusalem. His research led him to the conclusion that the sacred sites were set out on the landscape of Jerusalem in the form of a vast human skeleton. The skull-shaped hill, with two caves resembling eye sockets, was its head, Solomon's Quarries were its chest, the lower back lay on the Temple Mount, with the Dome of the Rock at its pelvis, the knees at the Dung Gate, and the feet some distance outside the Old City. Gordon propounded this theory in the *Palestine Exploration Fund Quarterly Statement* in 1885. Why a skeleton? Because it would represent sculpturally an enormous human sacrifice on the Temple Mount. The lunatic fringe of biblical archeology today, mainly American evangelicals who pursue such projects as searching for and finding Noah's ark, still embrace ideas like this.

Gordon's idea is a good example of the tendency toward biblical mysticism that thrived among members of the ruling class of Victorian England, and that motivated the work of the Palestine Exploration Fund, despite the "scientific" nature of its expeditions.

A more widespread notion, similar to one held by contemporary American fundamentalist Christians, was that the Jews should be "restored" to Palestine from their worldwide diaspora as the fulfillment of biblical prophecy, a development that would be followed by their conversion to the true (Anglican) Christian faith and the return of the Messiah as the leader of a thousand-year era on earth of peace and justice, before the end of the world. This belief—chiliasm—led to the establishment of missionary societies dedicated to the conversion of Jews in England and even in Palestine itself. Although the success rate of organizations like the London Society for Promoting Christianity among the Jews (established 1808) was dismal—making only about six or seven converts a year even after thirty years—its members remained optimistically active throughout the nineteenth century.

The best-known proponent of the chiliastic movement was the seventh Earl of Shaftesbury, Anthony Ashley Cooper, better known now for his campaigns for benevolent social legislation, such as the law limiting the working hours of factory workers. The same evangelical Christianity that inspired his social campaigning at home led him to work equally hard for the restoration of the Jews, and he became president of the "Jews' Society" in 1848. Although he saw little evidence that the mass conversion of the Jews had begun, as he hoped, the Earl of Shaftesbury had considerable success in influencing British foreign policy in line with his ideas. He persuaded the foreign secretary, Lord Palmerston, to establish a British consul in Jerusalem in 1838, charged with the protection of local Jewish interests, and granting Palestinian Jews British citizenship. A few years later, his lobbying bore fruit in the creation of an Anglican bishopric in Jerusalem, with a converted Jew as its first incumbent.

Eventually, in 1875, Shaftesbury became president of the Palestine Exploration Fund. In his first address to the PEF as its president, he called with undiminished enthusiasm for "the return [to Palestine] of its ancient possessors." His mystical belief in Britain's instrumental role in returning the Jews to Palestine—for the sake of Christianity rather than Judaism—was the ideological force behind Britain's increasing political involvement in Palestine throughout the nineteenth century. This involvement could be seen later in British support for Zionism, as expressed in the Balfour Declaration of 1917, and in Britain itself assuming control over Palestine in 1921 and holding it for nearly thirty years in the form of the Mandate. To understand politics, it is sometimes necessary to understand the power of irrational ideas.

For Albert Glock, such views represented "the difference between Palestine in the mind of the west and on the ground in the east," the consequence of which was "the virtual extinction of Arab Palestinian culture and population." Glock's critical reaction to the history of Western intervention in Palestine motivated his determination to create a new type of Palestinian archeology, and even to maintain the intemperate belief that "Christians were simply not able to live peaceably with another religion."

In its first years, the pages of the *Palestine Exploration Fund Quarterly Statement* were dominated by reports from the field dispatched by the leaders of the expeditions the fund had sponsored. These were eventually published as books, which have become the classics of early biblical archeology. Notable among these is the expedition of Charles Warren, a captain in the Royal Engineers, who used military mining techniques to excavate the tunnels and subterranean chambers under and around the Temple Mount in 1867. His account was published in 1876 as *Underground Jerusalem*. This was one of the first expeditions sponsored by the PEF, and it nearly bankrupted the fund, obliging this tireless officer to postpone excavation work for weeks at a time due to lack of money to pay laborers.

The object of Warren's exploration was the Temple of Solomon, and in his search for it he exemplifies the mystical tendency of Victorian Englishmen toward anything to do with the Holy Land. His search for the original temple of the biblical Israelites set in motion a popular obsession that persists to this day. Warren was motivated in his curiosity by his experience as a Freemason, a membership that was common among English military officers. (A number of the officers who assisted him were also Freemasons.) Freemasons consider themselves observers of an unbroken tradition of occult knowledge that begins with the builders of the First Temple and its founder, Solomon, whom biblical legend has given the character of an archetypal complete being, supreme in both power and wisdom. The rituals of Freemasonry, in which the individual ascends a hierarchy of esoteric lore through progressive initiation, are based on metaphors of the construction and architecture of the temple. To Freemasons, Solomon's Temple is a radiantly meaningful symbol, rich with associations of power and practical knowledge, deepened to a condition of mystical enlightenment, and held in the collective hands of a closed fraternal institution. Adding to the sum of knowledge of the temple would have been of enormous importance to Freemasonry, and masonic lodges donated regularly and generously to the Palestine Exploration Fund in the years Warren's reports were being published.

Warren, therefore, had a definite object in mind when he began his work. The image of the temple in his mind formed the template into which all of his discoveries fitted, and almost immediately his expectations were rewarded with results that confirmed them. He dug shafts along an exposed side of the Temple Mount, then tunneled under it. Illuminating his way with strips of burning magnesium, he discovered pottery fragments inscribed with the words for "the king" and markings in Phoenician characters on stones near the base of the structure that he took to have been made by the temple's original builders. He pronounced the area he was exploring to be the corner of the palace Solomon built for himself adjoining the temple, in fact a highly dubious attribution. If a temple built by Solomon ever existed, no trace of it has been found.

In the course of his exploration of the hidden part of the western wall of the Temple Mount, he found a long vault to which he gave the name the Secret Passage. He believed it to be a secret tunnel used by King David (Solomon's father, according to the Bible) to walk from his palace to his place of prayer on the Temple Mount, an idea originating in a fifteenth-century description of Jerusalem that Warren had read—and one based entirely on pious folklore. No such tunnel could have existed. ("This passage would have been revealed whenever anyone living on the street above installed a cistern beneath his house," the Israeli archeologist Dan Bahat wrote in 1991.)

Farther on, Warren found a large hall (which can be visited today as part of the controversial Western Wall Tunnel complex) that was part of a group of Herodian buildings. These were constructed at the time of the Second Temple, commissioned by Herod, nearly a thousand years after Solomon is thought to have lived. Warren dubbed it the Masons' Hall, a name that is still used. Its connection with the Masons of Solomon's Temple lay entirely in Warren's imagination, but within a few months of its discovery it had been adopted by Freemasons as their own, and a group of American Masons held an initiation ceremony in it.

Freemasonry came to identify even more closely with a cave that can be seen today near the Damascus Gate, which has come to be known as Solomon's Quarries. Masonic initiation ceremonies are now carried out inside it annually, and during the British Mandate stones were quarried from the rock inside and used as the cornerstones of Masonic lodges around the world. According to Masonic legend, the ritual implements used by the priests of the temple were hidden in it at the time of the Roman siege of the city.

Later on, Warren uncovered stones in which a long, straight groove had been cut. He took this to be a drain along which blood flowed from the sacrifices in the temple. His source for this was again a colorful legend that he found in his reading: in this case taken from the traditional Jewish text the *Mishnah*.

The mythic power of Warren's work, and the lively prose in which he described it, attracted enthusiastic public interest. Soon after the excavation began, *The Times* expressed its fascination with Warren's project of "the discovery of the true foundations of the Temple of the Holy City, of the ancient aqueducts, subterranean passages, and grandiose engineering projects of the Scriptural Monarchs." Warren's exploration of the irregular system of spaces, passages, watercourses, and cisterns under the Temple Mount—in the course of which, at one stage, he floated through a channel of sewage on an improvised raft made of wooden doors— contributed to the popular folklore of the Temple Mount as a maze of occult secrets, where a source of supernatural power lay hidden in inaccessible tunnels. The idea, of course, originates in Jewish tradition: the temple was the earthly seat of God. Jerusalem was the center of the world; at the center of Jerusalem was the temple; at the center of the temple was the Ark of the Covenant; at the center of the Ark of the Covenant, seated invisibly on a throne within it, was God. Warren's syntax falters with excitement when his exploration took him, so he thought, close to the divine point at the center of these concentric circles of power, the ark: "As we pursued our course along the wall to the north, and were opposite the end of the Birket Israil, we came upon a slit about eighteen inches wide and four inches high, formed by cutting away the upper and lower portions of two courses. Here was an exciting discovery: what might not be in this chamber in the wall? The ark and utensils secreted at the destruction of the Temple might here be hidden away." The Pyramids of Egypt hold a similar place in the popular imagination, with their systems of tunnels and supernatural secrets, but the Temple is in the Judeo-Christian religious tradition; the Pyramids are merely pagan.

Although Warren was certainly advancing the archeological knowledge of the structure of the Temple Mount, he was also adding to the corpus of folklore surrounding it, particularly the fascination with secret tunnels. The narrative of his book, *Underground Jerusalem*, as its title hints, is driven by the mythic power of his search for the secrets of the Temple Mount through tunnels. His exploration of underground Jerusalem is a search for esoteric knowledge, a gnostic adventure, and one that fully assorts with Masonic tradition.

Among one's own people, a tunnel is a marvel. Held by an enemy, a tunnel inspires fear and suspicion: it is a sinister thing, and evidence of a conspiracy. In September 1996, about seventy Palestinians were killed by Israeli soldiers in a riot that broke out in the Old City of Jerusalem after the Israeli authorities opened an exit to a connected series of chambers and passages that followed the length of the Western Wall. This was the same area explored by Charles Warren.

There is a charming legend in the Islamic tradition of the

holiness of the Holy Land, about a magical secret passage. According to a *hadith*, a saying of the Prophet Muhammad, the Prophet declared that there would be a man, a Muslim, who would enter Paradise on foot while still alive and return to tell the tale. This prophecy came true after the Prophet's death in the following way. During the caliphate of Omar, who captured Jerusalem and Islamized the Holy Land in the seventh century of the common era, a man named Shuraik ibn Hubashah came to Jerusalem with his tribe, the Banu Tamim. He went to the Temple Mount to fetch water from a well there. He lowered his bucket into the well, and the bucket fell in. So he climbed down into the well to retrieve it. At the bottom of the well he found a door. He opened it and found himself in the garden of Paradise, exactly as described in the Qur'an. He walked around, amazed at what he saw. The thought occurred to him that no one would believe him if he could not prove he had been there, so he plucked a leaf from a tree, put it behind his ear, and climbed up out of the well, with the bucket. The man showed the leaf to the governor of Jerusalem, who despatched a letter to Omar, the Commander of the Faithful, in Mecca, seeking advice on the marvel. Omar wrote back with the judgment that if the leaf really did come from Paradise, it would not wither or dry up.

The leaf stayed green. It was like the leaf of a peach tree, the size of the palm of a hand, and pointed at the top. Shuraik placed the leaf between the pages of his Qur'an, and when he died the Qur'an with the leaf in it was buried with him.

The legend refers to a cistern under the al-Aqsa mosque, which now bears the name Bir al-Waraqah, the well of the leaf. Other Islamic legends refer to miraculous channels of water running under the Temple Mount. According to another legend, the waters of the well Zamzam inside the sacred enclosure at Mecca flow into the spring of Siloam, in Jerusalem, on the night of Arafat, an Islamic holiday commemorating God's transmission of the text of the Qur'an to the Prophet. A further legend tells that the four rivers of Paradise—Sihon, Gihon, the Euphrates, and the Nile—originate from the base of the Rock on the Temple Mount. "The Prophet said, 'All the rivers and clouds and the winds come from under the

Rock of Jerusalem. . . . The sweet waters and rain-bearing winds issue from the base of the rock of Jerusalem.' "

These legends elaborate the fact that the Temple Mount contains a system for supplying water to the temple for ritual purposes. They Islamize the tunnels in the same way that Warren's tradition gnosticized them. They are separate, dreamlike responses to the same thing: the marvelousness of this massive structure.

Jerusalem was built by the Canaanites because it had three physical advantages: it was on a hill, which made it easy to defend; it was close to an established road to the Mediterranean coast; and it had a secure water supply, the Gihon Spring, which supplied the original Bronze Age city. (The site of this original city lies outside the familiar Ottoman walls of the Old City of Jerusalem.) The water supply allowed the city's survival. When the First Temple was built, water was channeled to it from Gihon for the purpose of ritual cleansing. The marvel of water had been turned into something sacred. Once captured by the Israelites, Jerusalem became their political and religious capital. Political and sacred power came to rest in the same place. The whole vast corpus of the contending traditions of the holiness of the Holy Land grows from this convergence.

The original attraction of a securely defended city with a safe water supply developed over the millennia into a tradition that generates new traditions, which, in turn, clash with one another, producing a spiritual swarm. Thus do Ethiopian Christians—to cite just one example—believe Jerusalem is theirs. They assert that the spiritual leadership of Israel under Solomon has passed to them. In the ancient Ethiopian text the *Kebra Negast*, Makeda, the Queen of Sheba, travels to Jerusalem to hear the famed wisdom of Solomon from the king's own lips. After entertaining her sumptuously, Solomon consummates his desire to have a son by her. That night, Solomon has a dream in which the sun, which by divine command had shone over Israel, "suddenly withdrew itself, and it flew away to the country of Ethiopia, and it shone there with exceeding great brightness for ever, for it willed to dwell there." Later tradition holds that it is in Ethiopia that the Ark of the Covenant, the seat of God, came to rest; such is the power of the sacredness of Jerusalem, the holiness of the Holy Land.

In the same fashion, the Islamic tradition builds on this original attraction of Jerusalem, creating a new idea of holiness. The Dome of the Rock, the city's most recognizable landmark, symbolizes the Islamic claim that the Qur'an and the religion it enjoins both absorbs and supersedes its two monotheistic predecessors, Judaism and Christianity. This ornate octagonal shrine topped with a golden dome that dominates the skyline of the Old City, the Dome of the Rock is the Temple of Solomon rebuilt. For a few years during the prophetic career of Muhammad, the earliest Muslims prayed toward Jerusalem. The rock over which the dome is built—an exposed natural outcrop upon which Abraham reputedly bound his son Isaac, and from which Muhammad is held to have risen to heaven—was circumambulated in the way that the Ka'ba, the central shrine at Mecca, is now. The Islamic holiness of the Holy Land has been taken up and developed in recent years by the Palestinian Islamist movement. Its activists argue that the whole of Palestine is an Islamic trust, occupation of which by modern Israel is a violation of religious law.

A seventh-century writer, Ibn al-Firkah, relates that God created Mecca, Medina, and Jerusalem a thousand years before the rest of the world, and that when the waters of the flood subsided, the first earthly thing to appear was the rock. The sweet waters of the earth originate from it, and hellfire is heated here. "Who gives alms to the amount of a loaf of bread in Jerusalem, it is as if he gave alms to the weight of earthly mountains, all of them gold. Who gives alms to the value of a dirham, it will be his redemption from the Fire. Who fasts a day in Jerusalem, it will mean his immunity from the Fire." Al-Firkah's translator notes that "Moslem reaction to the Crusades was a potent factor in the development of the Islamic literature on the 'merits' of Jerusalem and Palestine."

Charles Warren evoked a sense of kaleidoscopic dismay in a description of the discord of daily life in the holy city, where these multiple conflicting religious visions produced something ultimately absurd and meaningless.

An Anglican bishop guards the interests of the German church, a
Jew, converted by a miracle, adorns with images the walls of the

Latin church, whose altar is placed below the arch where Pontius Pilate exclaimed *Ecce Homo*. The Queen of Sheba's representatives have sold their birthright in Jerusalem for a daily dole of pottage. The Syrian bishop, feted in India, with a man-of-war at his disposal, here lives in a cellar. The Arab Protestant takes off his shoes in one English church and his turban in another.

The priest of one communion cannot marry; in another, priest's orders are not given until a son is born to him. German plans of the city show no English buildings thereon; they are all evangelical; but the German buildings are shown as German. The French consul acts for the Italian convents; an Italian consul acts for the Spaniards; a Spanish consul acts for the Mexicans, of whom there are none; the German consul is chairman of the English library. Russian Jews, after six months' residence in Jerusalem, become British subjects.

The passage produces an effect rather like motion sickness, where a multitude of images rush by too fast for the eye to settle.

ABOUT THE SAME TIME that the Earl of Shaftesbury was exulting in the establishment of an Anglican bishopric in Jerusalem, seeing it as the beginning of the fulfillment of biblical prophecy, a Russian foreign ministry report noted, "Jerusalem is the center of the world and our mission must be there." Contemporary with Shaftesbury's scheme of an Anglican New Jerusalem absorbing Jerusalem of old was an equally potent Russian belief in a divine role for Russia in Palestine. Proclaiming itself the successor to Byzantium as the world's Christian empire, imperial Russia encouraged its subjects, mostly poor peasants, to undertake grueling pilgrimages to Jerusalem and the sites around it. A Russian hospice and cathedral were built for the purpose. It was not difficult for anyone visiting Jerusalem at the time to see that there was a political aim behind this policy: the Russian spiritual claim to Palestine, expressed through its role as the traditional protector of the interests of the Orthodox Church, could without much adjustment be translated into an assertion of political rights. Under Czar Nicholas I, Russia demanded the Ottoman empire accept a

Russian protectorate over all its Orthodox subjects. Within a few years, the Crimean War began.

The Crimean War was a war of negative cosmopolitanism. Its nominal cause was a feud between the Catholic and Orthodox caretakers of the shrine of the Nativity in Bethlehem, the traditional birthplace of Christ. The combatants were priests and monks who in the past had fought one another with broomsticks over the right to adorn and maintain parts of the shrines associated with the life of Christ, mainly in the Church of the Holy Sepulchre and the Church of the Nativity. In 1847, an ornate silver star marking the traditional site of the birth of Christ was stolen. The Catholics blamed the Greeks. The conflict escalated. With its own mystical claim to the Holy Land, expressed in a claim to protection of Catholic interests in Palestine, France took the side of the Catholics. France and Russia needed a war for extraneous political reasons, and so war was joined over the Orthodox-Catholic conflict over control of the holy sites, with France, Britain, and the Ottoman empire on one side and Russia on the other. Russian public opinion viewed the war as a religious crusade.

The religious claims of the imperial states were the means of establishing political footholds in a geopolitically strategic corner of the crumbling Ottoman empire. Britain had established a consulate in 1838, as a result of the lobbying of the Earl of Shaftesbury, but with practical political interests underlying Shaftesbury's millenarian aspiration. Other powers did the same. Where the faith went, the flag soon followed.

Prussia, too, joined the competition for a political stake in Palestine. Like Britain a Protestant country with no indigenous coreligionists in Palestine, Prussians established a religious claim to the land by identifying themselves with the medieval Crusaders. The Prussian emperor, Frederick II, despatched a delegation to search for the tomb of King Frederick Barbarossa, the German Crusader, and other Crusader remains and encouraged religious colonies modeled on the Knights Templar. In 1898, the emperor consolidated diplomatic relations with the Ottoman state with a ceremonial visit to the Holy Land. An opening was cut in the wall of the City of Jerusalem, built nearly five hundred years earlier by

Sultan Suleiman, so that the imperial party could enter in full pomp, with the kaiser on horseback. The intended symbolism was that Frederick would enter the holy city like his earlier Crusader namesake. The day was the anniversary of Luther's protest against the papacy, and once inside the city, the kaiser inaugurated a church built on the site of an old Crusader hospice.

This religious-political involvement included the establishment of a Prussian archeological institution in Palestine: Prussia, too, sought to advance its knowledge of the land of the Bible. This was the Palästina Verein, founded in 1878. This organization sent vast amounts of antiquities back to the national museum in Berlin and established formidable archeological operations, which caused Britain in particular grave diplomatic and scholarly anxiety. The Verein's main project was the excavation of the biblical site of Taanach, an expedition conducted in 1902–1904 by the Austrian biblical scholar Ernst Sellin. Sixty years later, in a reexcavation of the site sponsored by the Lutheran Church, this was the place where a young and idealistic Albert Glock was to cut his teeth as an archeologist.

"By the end of the nineteenth century," the archeological historian Neil Silberman wrote, "all of the major powers had established permanent national archeological societies devoted to the exploration of the Holy Land." A short-lived American Palestine Exploration Society was established in 1870, and a French institution, the École Biblique et Archéologique, was founded in 1890, by the French Dominican order. A second American institution, which survives, the American School of Oriental Research, was founded in 1900. (The conspicuous exception was Russia: the Orthodox tradition did not emphasize the notion of the Bible as a sacred, yet historically infallible, text as the Protestants did, and consequently felt no compulsion to "prove" its veracity archeologically.)

These competing European archeological institutions were founded despite the fact that Palestine had poorer archeological remains than any of the countries surrounding it, or anywhere in the Near East. Even Cyprus, historically comparatively unimportant, existing on the fringes of successive empires, offers a fuller record of ancient life than Palestine. With the exception of the massive Herodian Temple Mount structure in Jerusalem, the area has no examples of monumental architecture to compare with the ancient structures of Egypt or Iraq. The documentary record, which augments the material remains obtained by archeologists, is dominated by the Bible, a religious text that is not a history at all.

The Palestine Exploration Fund was participating in imperial competition, as well as satisfying an atavistic need. The two imperatives were bound tightly together. The Survey of Western Palestine, conducted by Lieutenants Kitchener (later Lord Kitchener) and Conder of the Royal Engineers, had by 1881 established the boundaries that were used by Britain after the Great War to define the area it governed under the Mandate. To some extent these boundaries are still visible (altered by war and conquest) in the map of the State of Israel. The PEF defined Palestine as a geographical entity.

When the British took over Palestine from the defeated Ottoman empire in 1920, they established an antiquities authority as a branch of government. The articles of the Mandate, the terms of its rule, went into greater detail on the preservation of antiquities than on the legal status of the Palestinian Arab inhabitants. The control of archeological activity in the Holy Land became a symbol of authority in Palestine.

When the State of Israel was established in 1948, it inherited the British antiquities laws. While stewardship of the antiquities of the Holy Land added a dimension of Christian piety to Britain's imperial grandeur, for the modern State of Israel the ancient sites and ruins of the land of the Bible helped serve a political purpose. In the early decades of Israel's existence, the archeology of ancient Palestine broadcast three simple messages to the world: that the archeological sites of ancient Palestine told the story of ancient Israel, that ancient Israel was the predecessor of modern Israel, and that modern Israel was therefore the legitimate owner of the land—not a foreign transplant, but a restoration.

CHAPTER FOUR

"ARCHEOLOGY WITHOUT THE BIBLE is archeology without a soul." With this robust maxim, leading Israeli archeologist Adam Zertal of the University of Haifa defended the traditional approach of the old-fashioned biblical archeologist, with its confidence in the Bible as a true chronicle of history. Zertal's enthusiasm for this approach on occasion has had controversial results. In 1980 he began excavation at the summit of Mount Ebal, an arid mountain that overlooks the West Bank city of Nablus. Five years later, he published an article in an archeology magazine in which he claimed that a ruined stone structure he uncovered there, filled with ash and the remains of burnt animal bones, was the actual altar where the Bible says the Israelite commander Joshua offered a burnt sacrifice to God after his military conquest of Canaan. The claim was a triumph of enthusiasm over judgment, and he has since then adopted a more sober view. But the episode showed how enduring the biblical myths are in the minds of archeologists working in the Holy Land in our present age of scientific rationalism.

Zertal's traditionalism demonstrated that the religious enthusiasm for the land of the Bible, which motivated biblical archeology in the nineteenth century, has persisted into the present, surviving the challenge of a secular, rational worldview. As a medieval cosmology receded in other disciplines, the archeology of Palestine became a haven for those who took the Bible to be the true record of creation. Even among archeologists who professed a secular outlook, there was still a conspicuous tendency to go starry-eyed when digging in the Holy Land, to fall back on the images of the Bible stories of childhood, and to see in its strata of rock and time images of the familiar ancient myths they wanted or needed to see.

However, most university-based archeologists have undergone a kind of Copernican revolution in recent decades. Albert Glock was no exception. These revisionists strove to remove religious bias from their work. Joshua didn't fight the battle of Jericho, they announced; the walls didn't come tumbling down. Excavations conducted by British archeologist Kathleen Kenyon in the 1950s proved that the site was uninhabited when the Israelites would have been on the scene: Jericho and the Israelites were separated in time by about 150 years. The world was turned upside down. As the academic archeologists looked at the material remains of ancient Palestine with a gaze of ever-sharpening rational focus, the mythic images of biblical history faded and disappeared, leaving behind a complicated and inconclusive picture of settlement, commerce, and faint traces of ethnically unidentifiable people where earlier scholars had seen the simple story of the Israelite conquest of the Canaanites. Archeology began to show that there was no evidence to claim that Moses, Abraham, Joshua, Saul, David, Solomon, or their kingdoms ever existed. The state of the art of knowledge in the archeology of the region today, the cutting edge, is to profess that nothing is known with certainty: an agnostic's creed. The new map of ancient Palestine is marked "obscured by clouds."

There was intellectual comfort in this transformation for those of sufficient scholarship to understand it. But the best scholarship on the presence or absence of early Israel has become too difficult for all but a handful of people to comprehend. Biblical archeology has come to be dominated by the narrower field of Syro-Palestinian archeology, the dispassionate study of a small region with a complex history, situated on the periphery of successive empires. Just as modern cosmology isn't concerned with one's personal metaphysical feelings about the universe, the meanings it contains and one's conceptions of its maker, the new Syro-Palestinian archeology isn't interested in helping people to become better Christians by deepening knowledge of the Bible.

The Syro-Palestinian archeologists* are a small elite whose work is mostly written for an academic readership. They don't take the Bible literally, and they see Palestine as a place like any other, where thousands of years of human habitation have left behind a mass of data subject to countless contending hypotheses. Glock knew several of the leading lights in the field, and he respected their scholarship and their secular approach. But he kept his intellectual distance: they were, after all, still primarily interested in geographical Palestine as the land of the Bible.

Below the ivory tower, old-fashioned biblical archeology still attracts a multitude of adherents. Their beliefs form a wide spectrum, from scholarly Christian traditionalists to academic frauds to a lunatic fringe. From time to time, an intellectual is tempted away from his austere rationalism and persuaded to write articles for *Biblical Archeology Review,* the leading publication of the traditionalists, with its circulation of 200,000. But generally the two camps remain hostile. Without the institutional funding and support that sustains academic archeology, the unreformed biblical archeologists run shoestring operations, raising funds from church congregations and subscriptions to their self-published magazines.

A leading member of the popular fringe was Ron Wyatt, a hospital anesthetist from Gatlinburg, Tennessee, who died in 1999. In his spare time, Wyatt founded a biblical theme park outside Smoky Mountains National Park in the foothills of the Appalachian Mountains, and as an amateur biblical archeologist made an astonishing number of spectacular discoveries of original biblical sites.

Relying on nothing more than direct divine inspiration, Wyatt "found" the true site of the Crucifixion of Jesus, and Noah's ark atop Mount Ararat in eastern Turkey, on an expedition in which

---

*Prominent among them are William Dever of the University of Arizona and Thomas E. Levy at the University of California, San Diego, in the United States; Jonathan Tubb at the British Museum; Israel Finkelstein and David Ussishkin, both of Tel Aviv University; and Amnon Ben-Tor of the Hebrew University, Jerusalem.

he was accompanied by the Apollo astronaut James Irwin. He also found the route Moses and his followers took across the bed of the Red Sea, and the destroyed remains of Sodom and Gomorrah in the strangely shaped mounds of mineral deposits in the dried bed of the Dead Sea. Most spectacular of all, Wyatt located the Ark of the Covenant in a quarry near the Damascus Gate in Jerusalem (where it apparently remains to this day).

Further along the spectrum toward respectability stands Bryant Wood, founder and director of Associates for Biblical Research, an organization dedicated, according to its promotional literature, to "demonstrating through field work the historical reliability of the Scriptures." Dr. Wood uses archeology to prove the Bible, with a mental certainty that not even the pious explorers of the Victorian era would dare to assume.

Unlike Ron Wyatt, Bryant Wood has a foothold in serious archeology. Well known among American evangelicals as a leading "creationist archeologist," Wood has contributed to the *Israel Exploration Journal*, the publication of the Israel Exploration Society, founded in the 1920s as a Jewish national organization for archeology in Israel and one of the country's leading archeological institutions. This enables him to describe the Associates for Biblical Research as being in the vanguard of scientific archeology. Its promotional literature proclaims

> The modern science of archeology, which began in the mid-1800's, has revolutionized our knowledge of the ancient Biblical world. Many archeological discoveries relate directly to Scripture and confirm the historicity of the Biblical record. Other discoveries provide fascinating background material for the Biblical narratives. As people are made aware of these discoveries, the Bible suddenly comes alive and Bible study is made more interesting and meaningful. Today's technology has enabled archeological research and publication to be greatly accelerated. . . .

The organization offers readers *Bible and Spade,* "a 36-page nontechnical quarterly publication for members focusing on archaeological evidence and creation/evolution issues to show the historical reliability of Scripture. Themes regularly covered include: Old and New Testament archaeology, Current excavations, Dead Sea Scrolls, Bible customs, Current events and topics related to archaeology, Bible geography, Early church history and archeology, Creation/evolution issues, Dinosaurs, The Flood, The origin of the universe, earth and man."

Bryant Wood cultivates the appearance of a serious archeologist with a perfectly respectable scientific theory that the Bible is an infallibly accurate record of the history of ancient Palestine. He does this by casting archeological information so that it seems to prove whatever biblical story he is writing about. His methods include finding elasticity or vagueness in the archeological record and selecting small, discrete bits of data, stripped of context, that might demonstrate something quite different.

Wood's main project is to prove that the Israelite conquest of the Canaanite city-states in Palestine, led by Joshua, happened exactly as the Bible says it did. According to scripture, Joshua crossed into the land promised by God to Moses and captured Jericho. Moving to the west, he conquered the whole southern part of what is now Israel before turning northward and defeating the Canaanite armies wherever he encountered them. Twice a year, Bryant Wood brings a group of volunteers to excavate a site called Khirbet el-Maqatir in the West Bank. Wood believes that the site is the true site of the biblical city of Ai, one of the Canaanite cities Joshua conquered along with Jericho. His volunteers pay $2,600 each to work on the dig for two weeks.

Wood is undeterred by the UNESCO convention that prohibits excavation in occupied territory, which most archeologists (except Israelis) observe. He is perhaps the only foreign archeologist—other than Albert Glock—who applies for excavation permits from Itzak Magen, the staff officer for Archeology, Judaea and Samaria, the Israeli occupation's archeology authority in the West Bank. There is an obvious political significance in this. The biblical story of Joshua's conquest was very popular in Israel after the Israeli military victory over the Arabs in 1948. The same thing seemed to be happening again: the righteous Israelites routing the locals and conquering their territory. Christian fundamentalists like Bryant Wood favor this story, too, because in their view the reestablishment of the state of Israel precedes the Second Coming of Christ.

This conjunction of aspiration has created a strong link between Christian fundamentalists and militant Israeli Zionists. It expresses itself in a myriad of ways, from Pentacostalists who saw Benyamin Netanyahu, when he was prime minister of Israel, as the founder of the Third Temple, to the American religious right's unwavering support for Israel in American politics. In an article in the *Israel Exploration Journal*, an otherwise dry report of an excavation near Bir Zeit, Wood notes that his team was given accommodation and logistical support by Pesagot settlement. Pesagot, built on a hill overlooking Ramallah, is one of the more militant Israeli settlements in the Occupied Territories. In December 1991, in the weeks before Albert Glock's murder, two residents of a nearby settlement were shot as they drove through Bir Zeit. In response, residents of Pesagot went on a rampage in the town, smashing car and shop windows. Without some sense of kinship with the ideology of these settlers, it would be strange for a group of foreign archeologists to want to lodge in such a place, especially since it is not that close to Khirbet Nisya.

IN HIS LECTURES AT BIRZEIT, Albert Glock argued that this fascination with the Bible on the part of both foreign Christians and Israelis had the effect of disproportionately focusing the attention of archeologists on the search for the biblical Israel, to the exclusion of other periods. It has also had the effect of causing archeologists to look at the remains of human habitation in the Bronze and Iron Ages (the transitional period between 1200 and 600 B.C., in which biblical Israel was thought to have emerged), and to be overoptimistic in interpreting them as evidence of the ancient Israelites.

Glock criticized the tendency to interpret any Bronze/Iron Age site in the mountains of the West Bank—or what some Israelis call Judaea and Samaria—as "Israelite." He argued that this ethnic label was hung on people who are, in fact, ethnically unidentifiable. This habit went back to 1934, when the towering figure in biblical scholarship, W. F. Albright (who held the firm belief that nothing archeologists could find in Palestine would ever contradict the Bible), published an article associating the ancient Israelites with a type of house regularly found in excavations of Iron Age Palestine. This house had four rooms built around a courtyard. Because the Bible told that the Israelites settled in these hills in what is now called the Iron Age, Albright held, these houses must therefore be Israelite. Similarly, a type of large water jar found in these settlements, bearing a distinctive rim that looks like a collar, came to be seen, after Albright, as proof of Israelite habitation. (It would be equally absurd if archeologists two thousand years hence were to find the remains of a Sony cassette player, and declare the site to be Japanese.) In purely material terms, it is impossible to distinguish Israelites and Canaanites.

WHILE FOREIGN CHRISTIANS sought proof of the bible, for many Israeli archeologists the pursuit of biblical archeology was motivated by an exclusively nationalistic interest.

Although the founder of the Zionist movement, Theodore Herzl, was uninterested in digging up the ancient sites of Palestine, believing the citizens of a Jewish state should look to their future in the country rather than their past, the Jewish population of Palestine was fascinated by archeology in the years before and after the creation of the State of Israel. Quite obviously, biblical archeology showed—often spectacularly—that Jewish people had been in Palestine centuries earlier, and it was therefore right and natural that they should be there now. Jews were not migrating to Palestine, the archeology showed, they were returning to a land that had once been theirs. There was nothing religious in this belief: religious Jews were often opposed to archeology, seeing it as unnecessary and even impious if it risked disturbing the resting bones of Jewish dead.

Nothing demonstrated the nationalistic fervor archeology aroused in the early days of the State of Israel better than the ancient Hebrew texts known as the Dead Sea Scrolls. The scrolls were acquired, in a powerfully auspicious coincidence, on the very

EDWARD FOX

day the United Nations voted to acknowledge the State of Israel in 1948. The link between the ancient heritage of the land of Israel and the modern state was pointedly expressed by the scrolls' principal discoverer, Eleazar Sukenik, in an address to the Israel Exploration Society in the summer of 1948: "Here in the east," he declared, "there is only one people, the Jewish people, that has a connection to the past and to the antiquities that are being discovered every day. The archeological reality instils a feeling in the heart of the individual and the public that every inch of this country is ours and it is our obligation to defend and to fight for it. This science is our spiritual weapon and an important buttress for the State in its path to the future."

It was Sukenik's son, Yigael Yadin, who took these strident words as a manifesto and turned archeology into a national patriotic creed in Israel. Before he embarked on a career in archeology, Yadin had been one of Israel's most distinguished soldiers: chief of military operations in the Haganah, the Israeli military force that fought the first Arab–Israeli war in 1948, and later founder and chief of staff of the Israeli Defense Forces (IDF). In Yadin's life and career, archeology and military conquest were fused into a single endeavor. He established in Israeli society the archetype of the soldier-archeologist, for whom conquest of the land of Israel and exploration of the land were part of a single mission.

Yadin's first major dig after leaving the IDF was at Tell al-Qedah, a project potent with historical and military symbolism. This was a mound in the Upper Galilee region of Israel, near the Syrian border. It was reliably believed to be the location of Hazor, one of the Canaanite strongholds conquered by the biblical Joshua. Hazor was essential to the study of Israel's entry into Canaan at the end of the Bronze Age. The study of it would reveal the military strategy of the ancient Israelites, at a time when the modern Israelites were still flush with the glory of their own recent military success. Yadin thoroughly embodied this exciting typology of ancient and modern Israel: his doctoral dissertation was on warfare in the ancient Near East, with particular reference to the war plans of the Jewish sect that produced the Dead Sea Scrolls.

Hazor is a huge site, the largest "biblical" site in Israel; it covers more than two hundred acres and is now a national park. The excavation, which began in 1954, was a project of enormous prestige for Israeli archeology, rivaling the projects of the older foreign archeological institutions in Palestine. But its intended audience was the Israeli public, who would be presented with a impressive demonstration of their own history, and their own martial valor. Yadin gave archeology what the Israeli writer Amos Elon has called "a psycho-political role . . . in Israeli culture." A decade after Hazor, he excavated the legendary mountain stronghold of Masada, in the Judaean desert, which in his interpretation told a grand moral fable about Jewish bravery, endurance, and pride. His genius for imaginatively wedding ancient Israel to modern Israel gave the country its own national pageantry. He initiated the custom of holding torch-lit swearing-in ceremonies for IDF soldiers atop the fortress of Masada. He even hosted a fortnightly archeological quiz show on Israeli television.

Patriotic archeology in Israel reached its peak after the 1967 Six Day War. In their excitement at possessing once again the Old City and the Temple Mount, few Israelis cared that the excavations under Benjamin Mazar of the Herodian walls of the Temple Mount (or, to use its Arabic name, the Haram al-Sharif) violated the 1954 Hague Convention against digging in occupied territory, a transgression that caused an international outcry and led to Israel's expulsion from UNESCO. Yadin himself boasted in the foreword to a book on the Jerusalem excavations that "archaeological activity in Jerusalem between 1968 and 1974 revealed more of the city's past, within the Turkish walls, than did all the excavations in the same area in the last one hundred years."

Implicit in Yadin's statement was that this activity revealed more of Jerusalem's Jewish past. In the years that followed, Albert Glock would be haunted by the fact that the Islamic past was more than just ignored in all this patriotic elation; it was in some cases physically bulldozed away. Most notoriously, the Maghreb Quarter of the Old City, within a week of the Israeli victory in June 1967, was flattened to create the plaza in front of the Western Wall. The Maghreb Quarter contained some of the oldest houses in Jerusalem, including a religious school and two twelfth-century mosques, and was a protected historic site under the Jordanian administration. This excitement at regaining their biblical heritage not only led officials of the Israeli Ministry of Religious Affairs to destroy and neglect Islamic sites in Jerusalem, but also inspired them to commence their own independent excavation. They began work to open a tunnel alongside the portion of the Western Wall that lies underneath the centuries of later construction around the Temple Mount. The tunneling was carried out in secret by rabbis with no previous archeological or mining experience, and the work they did was so bad that it caused massive subsidence in the ground above the tunnel. The excavation severely damaged a number of medieval buildings that were the property of the Waqf, the Islamic trust that owns and controls the Temple Mount/Haram al-Sharif. The construction of the Western Wall Tunnel, as it is now known, was a prolonged fiasco that ended in tragedy: in 1996, when the tunnel was opened at its far end, to enable visitors to exit onto the Via Dolorosa rather than double back the way they had come, dozens of Palestinians were killed by Israeli soldiers in a riot over the violation of Waqf property. The Western Wall Tunnel Experience is now a flashy, high-tech tourist attraction: visitors are led through a complex of atmospheric subterranean stone chambers and halfway through their tour are shown an enormous model of the Second Temple that rises slowly out of the darkness, festooned with tiny electric lights. It resembles one of the secret underground rocket bases in James Bond movies.

Albert Glock came to see that for the Palestinians, archeology and conquest were indistinguishable: they were part of the process by which the land they live on had been taken away from them. This is especially evident in the close working relationship, established by Yadin, between archeology and the military. Yadin's own excavations were organized like military operations, and Yadin exploited his own military connections to mobilize IDF equipment and personnel to assist him on his digs. Even now, excavation reports in the *Israel Exploration Journal* often note that a dig received security or logistical support from the IDF. When Israel invaded Lebanon in 1982, two leading Israeli archeologists, Israel

Finkelstein and Rafael Frankel, conducted an archeological survey of the captured territory. The former head of the Israel Antiquities Authority (IAA), Amir Drori, is a retired IDF general. He assumed his post at the IAA in 1983 when he resigned from his military position in the aftermath of the massacre of Palestinian civilians in the Beirut refugee camps Sabra and Shatila by members of an Israeli-allied militia. In September 1991, a few months before Albert Glock's death, Drori launched Operation Scroll, a campaign in which archeologists of the Israel Antiquities Authority (some of them with great reluctance) were pressed into conducting a search for antiquities in the area around Jericho that was soon to be handed over to the Palestinian Authority. This military connection is especially conspicuous in the West Bank, where the staff officer for Archeology is part of the area's military administration. The current staff officer for Archeology in the West Bank, Itzak Magen, has used military force when necessary to extract artifacts from their Palestinian caretakers.

———

THE PALESTINIAN REGION can have a strange psychological effect on people. Many who spend time there acquire a sense of mission, a feeling that they have become protagonists in its history, promoting a view that must be borne like a battle standard. The area is no place for the urbane or the ironic. This sense of mission is what connects individuals as different as Ron Wyatt, Bryant Wood, Yigael Yadin, W. F. Albright, and Albert Glock. They all lie at specific points on a spectrum of belief, with credulity at one end and secular skepticism at the other.

If Ron Wyatt occupies the end of the spectrum associated with total credulity, the opposite end would be held by Keith Whitelam, who represents with the zeal of a Crusader a nihilistic skepticism about every aspect of the biblical tradition. He belongs to a movement within biblical studies that has come to be known as the Copenhagen school, because a number of its leading members teach at universities in the Danish capital. Whitelam is based at the University of Stirling in Scotland. He is the author of a vehement and bitter polemic entitled *The Invention of Ancient Israel: The Silencing of Palestinian History*, which argues that biblical history and archeology are hopelessly contaminated by the theological bias of Fundamentalist Christian archeologists, and, worst of all, serious scholars like W. F. Albright. He likewise condemns the political bias of Israeli archeologists like Yigael Yadin, and asserts that in their enduring obsession with ancient Israel both groups serve the political interests of the modern State of Israel and support its continuing oppression of the Palestinians. Unlike Albert Glock, who insisted on keeping his theoretical feet firmly planted in the practice of field archeology, Whitelam is a textual scholar with no archeological experience. *The Invention of Ancient Israel* was published after Glock's death, and if he had lived to read it, he would have probably recoiled from the whiff of its acrid polemic.

Nineteenth-century biblical historians, Whitelam argues, saw ancient Israel as resembling a militarized and centralized European nation-state. Twentieth-century biblical historians, in his view, tend to regard ancient Israel as something like the modern state of Israel: warlike, yet democratic. Both views projected onto their historiography Western versions of what they wanted to see, with negative consequences for the Palestinians. (By "Palestinians" he means everyone in the region not covered by the term Israel, conflating the ancient Canaanites with the modern Palestinians.)

Whitelam demolishes the work of W. F. Albright, who saw no contradiction between his own religious faith and the scientific results of his archeological work. Of all the regions of the earth, Albright believed, only in the Holy Land were faith and reason still in harmony in the twentieth century. Whitelam quotes accusingly the final paragraph of Albright's *The Archeology of Palestine*, a standard work of biblical archeology: "To one who believes in the historical mission of Palestine, its archeology possesses a value which raises it far above the level of the artifacts with which it must constantly deal, into a region where history and theology share a common faith in the eternal realities of existence."

Whitelam goes on to point out that the search for ancient Israel in the transition from Late Bronze Age to Iron Age is a futile undertaking, because no unambiguous evidence of biblical Israel has ever been found. He cites two pieces of extra-biblical evidence for the existence of ancient Israel: the Tel Dan inscription, an Aramaic fragment (discovered in northern Israel in 1993) that mentions "the house of dwd"—which *might* mean "the house of David"; and the Merneptah stele. The latter is an Egyptian inscription dated to 1207 B.C.E. that records the war campaign of the pharaoh Merneptah and lists the cities he has defeated. It includes the line "Israel is laid waste." Whitelam argues that these two texts tell us practically nothing, and that they are certainly not proof of the biblical narrative. Archeology does provide evidence of "settlement shifts" in the mountains of the West Bank, suggesting the possible emergence of Israel among the vaguely defined societies of ancient Palestine. But these shifts don't support the biblical narrative. Whitelam sees the Bible as a mythical and theological narrative, reflecting the political and religious concerns of Persian and Hellenistic periods; that is, of periods many centuries later than the events it claims to record.

Whitelam offers these examples because he wants to show that the search is hopeless, that what the biblical scholars and archeologists are looking for just isn't there. It is wrong to be looking for anything in archeology, he says, because that implies a prejudice on the part of the archeologist. The only sound position is to look at the archeological record, the sum total of the data collected, and to see no pattern in it at all. His approach is an act of postmodernist intellectual hara-kiri.

More stridently than Albert Glock, Whitelam was seeking to join the cultural front of the Israel-Palestine conflict on the side of the Palestinians. Yet the Palestinians themselves have had their own ideas about their relationship to archeology. It is a misunderstanding of human nature to expect people to approach archeology with no subjective motivation, as Whitelam prescribes. In this way the Palestinians have been like the Israelis: using archeology in the service of nationalism. One of the terms of the Oslo Agreement of 1993 was to allow the Palestinians to establish their own Antiquities Authority. This body quickly began to conduct excavations in the areas under its control, with an obvious preference for sites associated with Arab and Islamic history. Indeed, antiquities have been swiftly adopted as a source of national symbolism by the Palestinians: the first postage stamps the Palestinian Authority (PA) issued depicted an Umayyad-era site, Hisham's Palace outside Jericho, which had come into its jurisdiction.

The Palestinian Antiquities Authority has other duties as well. It restores traditional and vernacular Palestinian architecture, and has also cracked down on the illegal plundering and trade in antiquities in PA areas, for the sake of preserving a Palestinian cultural heritage that had already been massively depleted in the years of Israeli occupation.

The head of the Authority, the man chiefly responsible for establishing an official Palestinian national archeology to rival the Israeli version, is a former student of Albert Glock. His name is Hamdan Taha.

CHAPTER FIVE

Albert Glock made his first trip to the West Bank in the summer of 1962, seeing at last the country whose alluring image had formed in his mind as he grew up in the enclosed world of the Lutheran Midwest. He and a handful of other biblical scholars were to undergo a crash course in the techniques of archeological excavation at a site near Nablus called Tell Balata, under the direction of Harvard archeologist G. E. Wright, a student of W. F. Albright. There is nothing in Glock's correspondence to suggest he responded to his arrival in the Holy Land with anything like Edward Robinson's elated sense of at last reaching the Promised Land. For Glock, his trip was a natural development in his work, which was tending toward historical analysis of the Bible, a study to which archeology could contribute. It was also a chance to escape the claustrophobic theological controversies that were stifling the Missouri Synod back home.

This was the beginning of Glock's career as an archeologist. The following year, he joined the core staff of an expedition to excavate Tell Ti'innik. The excavation was sponsored by Concordia Seminary and the American School of Oriental Research, the leading American institution for biblical archeology, and was funded by an insurance company owned by the Lutheran Church, the Aid Association for Lutherans.

Tell Ti'innik was the site of the biblical Taanach. In recorded history, Taanach was first mentioned in the fifteenth century B.C.E., in an account carved on the walls of the Temple of Karnak of the military campaign of the Egyptian pharaoh Thutmose III. Taanach was one of the Canaanite cities that his forces captured. It appears later in the Bible in a list of thirty-one Canaanite city-kingdoms conquered by Joshua. It is mentioned again in the sanguinary Song of Deborah, in which the warlike Israelite prophetess bursts into a triumphant song to celebrate a victory over the Canaanites at a site near Taanach. ("The kings came and fought, then fought the kings of Canaan in Taanach by the waters of Megiddo; they took no gain of money." [Judges 5:19])

The Taanach dig was the first full-scale archeological excavation sponsored by the church. The Missouri Synod frowned on "higher criticism" of the Bible, but allowed "lower criticism," which meant biblical scholarship that did not contradict the church's doctrine of the historical infallibility of the Bible. Lower criticism "illuminated" the Bible; that is, it produced facts that confirmed the biblical text and strengthened the believer's faith. Biblical archeology served this purpose. (The church continued to fund the Taanach project until the Missouri Synod split irrevocably in 1972.) The dig was typical of expeditions in biblical archeology in that none of the members of the core staff, with the exception of its director, Paul Lapp, had previous field experience in archeology. They were biblical scholars first, archeologists second.

Albert Glock was nominated as the expedition's "publicity director," charged with explaining the aims of the dig in popular articles for church newspapers. "Since the 1930s," he wrote in one, "archeology has been responsible for a major increase in the scholarly estimate of the trustworthiness of the Bible as an accurate reflection of the ancient world from which it purports to come. Since the Bible is much more than this, archeology is an ancillary discipline for the Church's scholars." This was the sort of statement that Glock would have choked on if confronted with it twenty years later, when he had long since jettisoned biblical archeology in favor of the version of Palestinian archeology he came to develop at Birzeit.

Tell Ti'innik had been excavated sixty years earlier by Austrian theologian Ernst Sellin, in an era of imperial competition and the Protestant rediscovery of the land of the Bible. The trenches Sellin dug, using excavation techniques that would now be considered crude and unprofessional, are still visible, though covered over with a thick layer of coarse grass. The purpose of the Concordia-

ASOR excavation that began in 1963 was to explore the site using modern archeological techniques, and to find what Sellin had missed.

Tell Ti'innik was a strange place to excavate, and it gave Albert Glock an early immersion at the deep end of the grim complexities of the Arab-Israeli conflict. In 1963, the West Bank was under Jordanian control, having been annexed by the Kingdom of Jordan in the breakup of British-ruled Palestine that followed the 1948 Arab-Israeli war. Because it was so close to the border with Israel—on a clear day, you could see Nazareth from the summit of the *tell*—the surrounding country as far as Jenin was a military area, subject to the strict regulations of the Jordanian army. As foreigners, the archeologists had to have permits to enter and leave the area. And they were physically confined to the southwestern quarter of the *tell*. The northern side of the mound was occupied by a Jordanian army gun emplacement, which was sealed off from the rest of the *tell* by barbed wire. The archeologists were supervised by an official of the Jordanian Department of Antiquities, who oversaw the excavation, and by a Jordanian army lieutenant, who policed their movements. They were not supposed to raise their heads above the summit of the hill, lest they even glimpse the military installation on the other side. As the dig's designated photographer, Lois Glock was forbidden to take photos without supervision, and even then she was only allowed to photograph with the camera pointing downward.

The dig proceeded with war a handbreadth away at any moment. Powerful symbolism was provided by the presence on the other side of the Israeli border of Armageddon, known locally as Megiddo. At this time, Palestinian guerrilla groups led by the young Yassir Arafat were making audacious but militarily ineffective attacks into Israeli territory from bases in Jordan and the West Bank, provoking severe retaliation against Palestinian villages and refugee camps by the Israeli Defense Forces. A second season's dig, scheduled for 1965, had to be postponed because of the threat of a renewed outbreak of another multinational Arab-Israeli war.

The Taanach archeologists were a starry-eyed and unworldly bunch at first, still unaffected by the cumulatively depressing effect that the entrenched culture of conflict in Palestine can have on the human spirit. They had little knowledge of the politics of the conflict, or of the effect that the creation of the State of Israel had had on the Palestinian population. Their correspondence still radiated optimistic Christian cheeriness, and they still signed their letters to one another on archeological matters with expressions like "feet shod with the Gospel," "yours in Him," and "peace."

The exception was Paul Lapp, the director of the excavation, and from 1961 to 1965 the director of the Albright Institute. He too was a Lutheran minister, originally from California, but this fact was little known in the archeological community where he was regarded as one of the brightest young archeologists in the field (he was thirty-three in 1963). Lapp was an archeological radical; his critique of biblical archeology (a way of thinking to which Albert Glock gradually turned) argued that "too much of the structure of Palestinian archeology is an inflated fabrication," meaning it was distorted by the tendency of theologians-turned-archeologists to see their religious beliefs confirmed in their archeological results. He was not just a scholar; he had a missionary zeal for defending the weak, which meant a disposition toward helping the Palestinians. Before turning to archeology, he had worked for the American government aid agency USAID, in a project to help develop archeological sites on both sides of the Jordan River into tourist attractions. After the last season of excavation at Ti'innik he came close to accepting a job with an organization dedicated to aiding refugees.

In 1967, the inevitable war came. Arab forces led by Egypt massed in Syria and Jordan in readiness for an attack on Israel, but before they could act, Israel launched a massive preemptive strike on Egyptian air bases, wiping out Egyptian air power. Israel then secured a stunning victory over the Arab armies in 132 hours and 30 minutes altogether, less than six full days. The West Bank and the Jordanian sector of Jerusalem (including the Old City, with its sacred shrines) were in Israeli hands, as were the Gaza Strip and the Sinai Peninsula and the Golan Heights. Israel had achieved a victory so complete that its effects still dominate the politics of the

Near East. Israel was now clearly the region's dominant military power; since 1967, no Arab country has been able to negotiate with Israel from a position of strength, real or imaginary. Arab society was traumatized, its confidence shattered. In the war's immediate aftermath, Egypt's president, Gamal Abdel Nasser, announced that he would resign, in recognition of his responsibility for an Arab military effort that had been a fiasco, based on empty rhetoric and poor organization. Nasser stayed on, but he died three years later a heartbroken man.

The 1967 war exposed the Taanach scholars to the realities of the conflict as never before. Immediately after the Israeli capture of the Old City, Israeli archeologists began extensive excavations there, aimed at recovering a long-lost Jewish past. In 1968, the Israeli archeologist Benjamin Mazar began an ambitious excavation at the foot of the massive Herodian platform whose western wall is modern Judaism's most sacred site. Going against the main stream of Western opinion, which congratulated the Israelis on their conquest, Lapp published an angry article in 1968 criticizing the Israeli Department of Antiquities for allowing these digs, which were in contravention of a UNESCO code prohibiting excavation in occupied territory.

The 1967 war divided archeologists in Israel and the Occupied Territories along the chasm of the Arab-Israel conflict. Now that the Albright Institute, based in East Jerusalem, was in Israeli-controlled territory, its links with Israeli institutions strengthened, creating a vacuum for archeologists whose work was based in Jordan. In 1968, in response, a new, more Arab-oriented institution was formed in Amman, the American Center for Oriental Research. Meanwhile, in the summer of 1968, the third and final season of excavation at Tell Ti'innik took place, with the West Bank now under Israeli control. The Jordanian troops and their gun emplacement were gone, and the archeologists could move freely around the site and over the border into Israel proper.

The Israeli conquest put the archeologists in a dilemma: their permit to dig was from the Jordanian Department of Antiquities, but the new power in the West Bank, Israel, demanded under its military regulations that finds from the dig be deposited in an

Israeli museum. Now Glock and his colleagues encountered for the first time the hardball politics of archeology in the West Bank. The director of the Israeli Department of Antiquities, Avraham Biran, was demanding that the finds of the 1968 season be turned over to his department. These finds included a beautiful Canaanite clay altar, which was evidence of the indigenous religion that was flourishing in ancient Palestine at the time of the emergence of the Israelite religion: it was a coveted treasure for Israeli history. Paul Lapp's angry article had done nothing to establish good relations between the Taanach archeologists and the Israeli government, and Biran's demand was firm.

In a memorandum to his colleagues about how to deal with the problem, Glock wrote:

> The fact is . . . that according to the Hague [UNESCO] Convention the occupying power is merely a temporary manager of the cultural heritage of the occupied regions. It is also, according to the Convention (which Israel signed), illegal to carry such material across international boundaries without the express permission of the temporarily displaced political authority, which in this instance is Jordan. . . . On the face of it, at the present time, it would hardly seem reasonable to expect Jordan to grant our request.

In this way, this group of temperamentally conservative men, whose seminary training had taught them to "render unto Caesar" as a matter of instinct, were forced into a confrontation with the Israeli state, and compelled by their consciences to resist it. The result of their earnest deliberations over how to deal with the problem was to allow the Canaanite altar and other finds to be deposited in the Rockefeller Museum, the East Jerusalem antiquities museum that had been under Jordanian control until the museum and its contents were seized by Israel as the spoils of war. Their reasoning was that the Rockefeller Museum was not in Israel at all, but in Jordan. The Taanach altar has since been moved to the Israel Museum in West Jerusalem, across the former border.

THE DAY BEFORE Albert Glock wrote his memo, September 17, 1970, the thirty-five-year-old King Hussein of Jordan made a radio broadcast announcing the imposition of martial law in Jordan as part of his determined campaign to crush the Palestinian guerrilla forces that were threatening to overthrow his regime. Albert and Lois were living in Jerusalem at this time. When civil war broke out in Jordan they watched tensely from the sidelines, fully expecting the Hashemite state to fall at any time and a new Arab-Israeli war to break out in the ensuing chaos. Meanwhile, a new episode in Albert Glock's life had unexpectedly begun. It was to prove his life's work, and a burden that he would carry until his final day.

CHAPTER SIX

I N 1970, Paul Lapp drowned while swimming off the coast of northern Cyprus, near Kyrenia. Lapp was a strong swimmer, and his mysterious death combined with his outspoken opposition to Israel led many to concoct an implausible conspiracy theory that he had been murdered, a story that would have eerie parallels to the story of Albert Glock. Upon Lapp's death, Glock was appointed to take over as director of the Taanach dig and to see its results into publication. Glock was now the heir of Paul Lapp's unfinished project, and Glock's vision of the Holy Land was beginning its evolution from the simple view he had brought with him from Illinois to something much more ambiguous and complex.

The same year, Albert Glock was nominated as a research professor at the Albright Institute. His career was now totally dedicated to archeology; he had little contact with the Lutheran teaching college that had launched his career, and he was impatient to end the connection altogether. Glock had inherited from Paul Lapp the responsibility for an enormous collection of Bronze Age pottery fragments accumulated in the three seasons of excavation: twenty-five thousand shards, piled up in baskets in the Albright Institute's storerooms. He was faced with the task, which proved Sisyphean, of classifying this collection and compiling the definitive publication of the excavation's results.

Glock hit upon the idea of studying not just the design of the pottery, but the technique and technology used to make it. He devised a system of classifying the fragments according to their appearance, and then sliced them into thin sections to analyze their fabric. He made hundreds of these thin sections with the aid of a souvenir maker in Bethlehem, who cut them with a table-mounted saw used for cutting mother-of-pearl. This was slow, painstaking, narrowly focused work, and it replaced the entire human dimension of the archeological story with a meticulous accumulation of raw data and mathematical formulas about the chemistry and mineralogy of Bronze Age pottery. Glock was deeply discouraged when his archeological colleagues expressed skepticism. Not only was the project emotionally arid, as an experiment in quantitative history, it was unsuccessful: his system of classification didn't work. He never made a final publication of the results.

Glock had indeed come a long way, but now he found himself at a dead end. In 1976, however, things would change for the better. Still a research professor at the Albright Institute, he began teaching at Birzeit University once a week, driving the short distance from Jerusalem into the other world that lay across the Green Line, the 1967 border between Israel and the Occupied Territories. This was the beginning of his work on an archeology of Palestine that was of interest not to biblical scholars in the United States but to the Palestinian people themselves. Establishing this new Palestinian archeology involved Albert Glock in a radical intellectual and personal transformation, and a rejection of almost everything in his Lutheran past. Birzeit would give Glock a renewed sense of purpose. It began to fill an emotional and intellectual void.

———

ALBERT GLOCK KEPT DIARIES from about the time he began to teach at Birzeit in the mid-1970s until the end of his life. Writing them was probably a psychological necessity for a man who kept his thoughts and feelings so tightly under control. It's clear from the diaries that he suffered oppressive loneliness for much of his time in the West Bank, despite the sense of mission that had brought him there. In tiny, precise script, he recorded the daily events of his struggle to establish a Palestinian archeology, and they form a respectably coherent personal history. The reading of these hundreds of handwritten pages is guided, of course, by the knowledge of how they end.

Glock kept two types of diaries: small pocket diaries in which he noted appointments and made very brief entries, recording the occurrence of important events, but without describing them in detail; and larger notebooks containing long prose accounts of his days. When the diaries begin, Glock had been a research professor at the Albright Institute for seven years. In 1978, he became the Albright's director. He held this post, one of the most highly visible and prestigious jobs in the field, for two years, and in his diary entries he frequently expressed a feeling of impatience with the administrative responsibilities of the job. He and Lois had a pleasant apartment in the Albright building, a cool, green oasis in the center of hot and dusty east Jerusalem. The building was constructed in 1925, during the British Mandate, a fine example of colonial architecture, with its breezy colonnade around a shady veranda. Deep wicker armchairs faced gardens with palm trees and a babbling fountain: an adaptation, through the Western sensibility, of a classically Islamic style of comfort. The rooms had high ceilings, whitewashed walls, and cool tiled floors. In these grand surroundings Glock would have sherry with visiting archeologists and distinguished locally based scholars of a variety of nationalities. He mentions, among others, Kathleen Kenyon, excavator of Jericho, the American excavator of Ai, Joseph Calloway, and William Dever. (In later years Dever would undergo a transformation of outlook comparable to Glock's, arguing that biblical archeology should be replaced by a rationalist archeology of ancient Palestine that kept biblical fundamentalists at a safe distance.)

Any other archeologist would have been happy in this job, yet the fifty-two-year-old Glock felt restless. He carried out his duties without great enthusiasm and in a mood of critical detachment from the world that surrounded him. In his 1977 diary he wrote: "AIAR [Albright Institute for Archeological Research] work is very much a nuisance. I'm not sure why I do it, in part for the sentimental value, the contact w[ith a] great diversity of scholars and that the position has prestige value, yet one cannot get much else done, at least so it seems." Of Jerusalem he wrote, "One sees here the old and the ugly right next the beautiful and satisfying. There is no hiding—the crippled, the depressed, the decrepit and the crazy are all visible on the streets."

As director of the Albright, he was obliged to organize people, as well as to be an administrator and a manager. To be on top of the job required a personality like that of the conductor of an orchestra, an ability to coordinate the work of numerous others in a harmonious way. Glock was too absorbed in his own personal odyssey to be well suited to this. Even before he assumed the post of director, he was thinking of ways to get out of the Albright. He hoped that after one year the renamed American Schools of Oriental Research, which governed the Albright, might offer the job to someone else, enabling him to concentrate on his work on Taanach and on the work that was becoming increasingly important to him: teaching at Birzeit. Freed from his duties at the Albright Institute, which he saw as little more than dealing with correspondence, he would commence, he wrote, "a major shift."

Glock felt himself tiring of the security of the Albright and its comfortable environment of tenured academic careers and a worldview based on the solid cosmology of the Bible. Soon after he began teaching at Birzeit, he conceived the idea of establishing an archeology program there. The project was less a career move than a crusade, an adventure of conscience, which he undertook without regard for the consequences. His excitement with this idea fills the diaries. There was a vivid sense of purpose in the humble errands he carried out in his regular drives from Jerusalem to Birzeit. He recorded in his diary in 1980 that he brought "4 200w light bulbs, 3 desk lights, plastic for windows, weather strips, heaters, lamp," things that were taken for granted in Jerusalem, but vital supplies for that needy, forsaken institution in the occupied West Bank.

Glock came to believe that foreign archeological institutes in Jerusalem—the Albright, the British School of Archeology in Jerusalem, the (French) École Biblique—would diminish in importance in favor of national institutions. The institutes of archeology in Israel, preeminently that of Hebrew University in

Jerusalem, would be matched by the department of archeology he himself was establishing at Birzeit, which would be nothing less than the national archeological institute of Palestine. Certainly, this was the historical pattern in the Near East: as the countries of the region became independent of European imperial rule, control of the archeological institutes the foreign rulers had founded—in Egypt, Iraq, and Jordan—passed to local governments and local archeologists. He began to read books on Palestinian society and politics: he notes in his diary reading *Palestinians: From Peasants to Revolutionaries* by Rosemary Sayigh, a Birzeit lecturer. He became a member of the tight circle of committed people—which included a high proportion of idealistic foreigners—who ran the university. "At that time, we really felt we were building things at Birzeit," recalled Penny Johnson, a colleague of Glock's. On trips out of Israel that he was obliged to make every three months to renew his tourist visa, Glock would carry messages to Hanna Nasir in Amman, the exiled president of the university, who ran its fund-raising operation.

To his scholarly colleagues in Jerusalem, particularly members of the Albright board, Glock's migration to Birzeit seemed like an expression of contempt, of alienation. His desire to quit as the Albright director was fulfilled in 1980 when the board voted not to elect him to another term. By the fall of that year, he had burned his bridges. Reflecting on the future of the Albright in his diary, he wrote, "I think that by the end of the century it will be very weak and we at Birzeit will be very strong." By this time, he felt himself sufficiently integrated into the Birzeit community to begin lobbying for tenure as a professor.

There was something more motivating Glock to leave Jerusalem in favor of Birzeit than the mission to establish a department of archeology: the change satisfied his solitary, maverick nature. At Birzeit, he would be beholden to no one. While he was careful to maintain good and correct relations with the university administration, he did so to guarantee his own freedom. At Birzeit, he would be in charge of an institution of his own, without the need to involve himself—or so he thought—in academic politics.

He tried to explain his shift to an archeology of "Palestinian Palestine" in a long letter he wrote a decade later to his daughter, Alice, in 1990. By then, Alice, at thirty-seven, had a family of her own and was living in New Jersey. The emotional subtext of the letter was a father's explaining to his daughter why he was away so much of the time, why he had not ended his odyssey and returned home. The split in the church, he wrote, was the trauma that impelled him away from biblical studies and made him turn to archeology, which to him at that point still meant biblical archeology.

"After working on it for a bit," he wrote, "I discovered how flawed was this so-called sub-discipline." His unease about the fact that biblical archeology limited itself to the biblical period in Palestine grew into a conviction that the discipline had "virtually obliterated the Arab contribution to the cultural history of Palestine. I now thought I had found something that deserved attention."

IT WAS THE ARCHEOLOGY that mattered above all. Everything else was secondary. Lois would often be disturbed in the night by her husband waking up at two o'clock in the morning, his sleep interrupted by a nagging need to look something up in a book. He would dash into his study and work until sunrise. He would forget to eat; he would neglect his health; worst of all, he would neglect his family. For his three sons and daughter, Albert Glock was an absentee father for long periods of time, busy at Birzeit while the rest of the family was in America. As children, they had grown up with Middle Bronze Age potsherds strewn over the dining room floor. In later years, they lost him entirely to archeology, when it became clear that he would never return to America.

As they grew up, the children reacted to their father's absence in their own different ways. Albert Jr., stoical and most like his father in temperament, went his own way early on by joining the air force. Jeffrey, the youngest, spent the most time in Jerusalem, joining Lois as a member of Albert's archeological team, before returning to America as a young man. Peter, to his father's dismay, became a minister in the Lutheran Church–Missouri Synod, immune to his father's antipathy to the church that Glocks had belonged to for a century. When Peter was ordained in 1991 in North Dakota, his father at first claimed to be too busy to attend the ceremony, and changed his mind only with great reluctance in response to the entreaties and persuasion of Alice.

Albert Glock's relationship with Alice was the rockiest of all. For years they did not speak, as Alice was consumed by anger with her father's intellectual and emotional severity. For her the episode that symbolized the chasm between them was an encounter in an art gallery in New York, when Alice was studying art at New York University. She had helped organize an exhibition of Ottoman art, and her father came to the opening. Instead of adding a benign fatherly presence to the scene, he exploded in indignation. The exhibition showed only the property of the Ottoman elite, he complained to Alice's professor; it showed nothing of ordinary life. "I felt like the rug was taken out from under me," she remembered. "I was just blown away. I think his anger and my anger just exploded at that point." In the years that followed, Alice nursed their relationship back to health until she became the recipient of Albert's most confidential revelations.

All of this was loyally borne by Lois: Albert's absence, his severity, the intensity of his commitment to his work and to his mission. Lois Glock was a neat, serious, and precise woman. Over the years she had worked as her husband's patient and selfless assistant throughout the progressive stages of his career—sorting and arranging his pottery and his library, sharing his interest in students, accompanying him on digs, always preferring to remain quietly and dutifully in the background.

In his dedication to Birzeit, Albert had developed a heretical personal theology from which faith and hope had been stoically eliminated, and all that remained was an austere, angry, and self-sacrificing Christian love. His years of living in the land of the Bible had turned him into a dissident against the biblical God his Lutheran education had given him. He had discovered that what he had thought of in his younger days as the land of the Bible was in reality the land of the Arab–Israeli conflict, the scene of a century of hatred, injustice, and bloodshed. He could no longer believe what he used to believe. The Palestinian cause filled the void his change of heart had left in him.

His was a lonely position, and one that required him to rely, with little respite, on his own inner reserves of moral fortitude. He seemed to draw strength from the sheer difficulty of living in the midst of conflict, under military occupation, like the salamander of ancient belief, the creature that lives in fire. Yet the effort of will strained him gravely. A dark current of emotional turmoil and depression ran underneath the mental activity of his daily professional life.

Glock's inner turbulence made him appear, to casual acquaintances, a formidable figure. He had little time for small talk, and little patience for anyone who did not live at a comparable pitch of intensity. He looked out at the world through his large square-rimmed glasses and rarely smiled. At sixty-seven, he seemed younger than his years. His hair was gray, but still thick, with a fringe that swept off his forehead. His prominent, slightly cloven chin gave his features an air of fixity of purpose. It was the craggy face of a midwestern farmer, one that had seen hard winters and stony ground. A preference for dressing in biblical black added to the austerity of his appearance.

He didn't seek popularity at Birzeit, or the role of charismatic academic guru. He was little noticed on the campus, and he preferred to keep as low a profile as possible, a tactic that enabled him to go about his work with the minimum of disturbance.

Glock was too preoccupied to notice the many subtleties in the way human beings relate to one another. In the delicate daily negotiations of academic life, he was gruff and undiplomatic. In Arab society, where circumspect courtesy is an indispensable element of any transaction, he often caused offense. He didn't much like to listen to people. A conversation with Albert Glock tended to be a monologue in which Albert Glock spoke, compulsively and at length, about what he was interested in, and the person to whom he was delivering it listened.

But this blunt, flinty man was also capable of extraordinary acts of kindness. His trademark VW bus served as a kind of local taxi service, ferrying students and colleagues around the West Bank. "He wouldn't let his students use the lack of transportation as an excuse to miss class," his colleague Penny Johnson recalled.

Not many people at Birzeit knew that besides being an archeologist Albert Glock was also a Lutheran minister and a missionary. It was a fact that he preferred not to draw attention to. He didn't like people to know that while he was teaching archeology at Birzeit his salary was being paid by his church back in the United States, the Evangelical Lutheran Church of America. The word *missionary* oppressed him like a nightmare.

In the archeological thinking he developed at Birzeit, Glock retained the ethical essence of Christianity while rejecting anything in it that conflicted with the experience of the rational intellect. For a biblical archeologist, this was and still is a radical position. There are scholars at the Albright Institute who come from theological seminaries in the United States where they are required to sign statements of doctrinal obedience. It was part of Glock's odyssey of rebellion to view from the *outside* the discipline and the tradition that had shaped him. He began to reject the notion that there was anything holy about the Holy Land, and in doing this he demolished the last pillar of his medieval, religiously inspired worldview. The critique of biblical archeology which Glock undertook—and which he was not alone in making—was the unfinished business of the Copernican revolution. Biblical archeology began with a belief that a religious cosmology applied to one region of the earth and also contained a particularly Protestant idea that the Bible comprised the literal history of ancient Palestine. Glock replaced that with an archeology of Palestine whose purpose was starkly nonreligious and ethical: to serve the Palestinian Arabs, and to narrate a history of life in Palestine at its most ordinary. It was an archeology based on a belief in the beatitude of the downtrodden. He was following the Palestinian intellectual Edward Said's injunction to give the Palestinians their rightful place in the annals of history, and he sacrificed all intellectual comfort to take the losing side. "Archaeology, as everything else, is politics and my politics is not that of the winners but of the losers," he wrote to Alice.

Glock's readiest tool for establishing this new way of thinking about the archeology of Palestine was the identification of bias. In the courses he taught his Palestinian students (in English: he never mastered spoken Arabic), the first lessons were about stratigraphy, dating, classification, and how to identify the cultural bias of the observer, the prejudice he brings to the task. He explained the idea in an article entitled "Cultural Bias in Archaeology":

I should preface this discussion of the problem of bias with an autobiographical statement which will help you understand my interest in this problem. I live among people whose past as history and whose present as the remains of an ancient tradition [have] been of more interest to Christians and Jews in Europe and the Americas than [. . .] to themselves. Two forces have isolated Palestinians from anything other than a legendary past, prevented their development of a serious attempt to reconstruct their own past. The power centers that have attempted to control Palestine have for 4000 years either been elsewhere or in the hands of an immigrant population. Palestinians have therefore been forced either to flee into exile for fulfilment or bargain for survival with the foreign rulers. The development of an independent self-understanding based on the historical and archeological record would be perceived as either a threat or irrelevant. As a consequence there are seven foreign archeological schools in Jerusalem, many with long histories and impressive publication records while the Palestinians themselves have nothing. Since 1977 I have attempted to develop a Department of Archeology at Birzeit University, the only such department among the seven universities in the West Bank. Our purpose is to train archeologists and to encourage research in the complete archeological history of Palestine.

In attacking bias in the archeology of Palestine, Glock was attempting to overturn a monolith. Without bias, there would be no history of archeology. Every religious or national group that had excavated in Palestine brought its own set of beliefs to the undertaking, and each set was exclusive of the others: this was negative cosmopolitanism in action.

CHAPTER SEVEN

ALBERT GLOCK BEGAN the first of his excavations with
Birzeit students in 1977. Establishing Palestinian archeology was proving to be an uphill struggle for Glock. He
encountered innumerable difficulties in operating under military
occupation. In addition, when he began to excavate in the West
Bank, there was rarely a time when he did not face serious hostility and suspicion from local people—from Palestinians, the intended
beneficiaries of his work.

Glock's first Birzeit dig was the excavation of Tell Jenin, an
ancient mound in the center of the town of Jenin, in the northern
part of the West Bank. The main purpose of the dig was to enable
Palestinian students to have firsthand experience of excavating in
their own country. However, the Hague Convention of 1954 permits archeological excavation in occupied territory only in the
event of salvage excavation, that is, excavation for archeological
purposes of a site that is about to be built on or covered over (such
as the flooding of land for hydroelectric projects). All respectable
archeologists follow the Hague Convention and choose sites
within the 1948 borders of Israel rather than contravene it.

This presented Albert with a dilemma: as an ethical archeologist, and as an opponent of the occupation, he wanted to observe
the Hague Convention. But it was essential to his project of teaching Palestinians to uncover the history of their own country that
they should gain the experience of excavating it.

An opportunity that arose in 1977 enabled Glock to avoid
confronting this problem head-on. The site's owner had applied
for a permit to build on it, thus the Jenin dig would be a salvage
excavation. The site was a six-meter-high mound right in the

middle of the town of Jenin, overlooking the main bus and taxi station. Glock's excavation revealed that it had been inhabited, on and off, since Neolithic times. A Jordanian law, which the Israeli administration had adopted, required that an archeological survey be conducted before a building permit could be granted. In this case, the archeological department of the Israeli administration in the West Bank asked the Albright to carry out the excavation, and the Albright gave Glock the opportunity to direct it.

Without Glock's connection to the Albright, the dig could not have used Birzeit students. The permit was issued to Glock through the Albright, not through Birzeit. If the application for the permit had been made in the name of Birzeit, it would almost certainly have been turned down. Albert had to tread very carefully: he was doing something that went against the grain of Palestinian sensibilities and against the official policy of Birzeit. In receiving a permit from "the occupation," Glock could be seen to be contributing to the legitimization of it. To defuse potential conflict, Glock was careful also to obtain a purely hypothetical permit for the dig from the Jordanian Department of Antiquities, even though, as he deliberated on the problem in his diary, "The Jordanians have always insisted that we should not excavate in the West Bank . . . I suppose I cannot win but . . . I feel dedicated to the BZ students[.] I am willing to put myself on the line." Glock later discussed the issue of requesting permits from the occupation in exhaustive detail in a memo to Gabi Baramki. The memo is headed "confidential," reflecting its obvious political sensitivity.

Writing in 1980 about that summer's progress in the Jenin dig, which proceeded every summer until 1983, Glock made reference to the wary Palestinian response to the work. "It is clear that Jenin officially does not welcome us. Part of this is the fear [of] the occupation: they do not want the occupation to claim the *tell* as a historical site—whose history? I feel trapped because I do indeed see the problem of working or not working but how can our students grow if they do not participate in field work?" He would later describe active hostility to the excavations. Proving to Palestinians that archeology was in their interests was not going to happen overnight.

In 1982, he recorded a visit to a student's home in a village out-side Hebron. It was an old house and of interest to Glock for its traditional construction. "After tea in a room 50 years old, roofed with I-beams, we photographed a Tabun [a traditional outdoor oven] and nearby I noticed shards. It seems this area near the cemetery had Roman and Byzantine occupation. Najib's [i.e., the student's] mother was noticeably unhappy with this announce-ment and responded by saying they had recently broken a pot in the area—a clear untruth. There seems to be a felt threat to the prospect of the land containing antiquities." Too many Palestinians knew of or had experienced instances where Israeli archeologists had discovered antiquities in an area and then seized the land by military order. Landowners, such as the man on whose land Tell Jenin stood, often had to endure years of bureaucratic delay while excavation work proceeded, at a glacially slow rate.

The other common Palestinian attitude toward archeology was that it was the search for treasure. When the first digs began in Palestine in the nineteenth century, locals assumed that the for-eigners had come to plunder the land for valuables. Palestinians in rural areas still tend to consider antiquities to be an agricultural product: one aspect of the economic potential of their land, similar to its ability to produce marketable fruit. The boys who found the Dead Sea Scrolls did not discover them by accident: Palestinian shepherds were always looking out for things that could be sold on the antiquities market. Archeology by foreigners was an object of suspicion because it was comparable to poaching: the foreigners were stealing something valuable.

There was another way in which Glock's archeology went against the grain. In his mission to establish an inclusive history of Pales-tine through archeology, Glock settled firmly on the conviction that the way to this goal lay in ethnoarcheology, the archeology of everyday life. He believed that Palestinian archeology should not be limited to the study of the fine arts of the Islamic centuries, as some Palestinians instinctively wanted. This focus on Islamic antiquities and treasures, in Glock's view, was just as exclusive and incomplete as an emphasis on the brief period associated with the Bible: both were only short episodes in the long span of Palestinian prehistory and history. Some Palestinians wanted Palestinian archeology to provide a nationalistic alternative to Western- and Israeli-oriented narratives. They wanted archeology to tell of the splendors of Islamic Palestine, of the caliph Omar and the Dome of the Rock. Glock hotly refused to do this. He had argued bitterly at times with his daughter, Alice, over her study of Islamic art: he felt that the works she studied—the miniatures and mosaics—were luxuries of the rich that were now, to make matters worse, imprisoned in Western museums. These artifacts had been drained even further of meaning by being taken out of their social and historical context.

Instead, Glock hit upon a radical new approach. He introduced a program at Birzeit in 1982 in which he led students in the excavation of abandoned refugee camps. Glock had found a site outside Jericho called Ain al-Sultan. If one stands on Jericho's highest point, the ancient Tell al-Sultan, an expanse of crumbling, uninhabited mud-brick houses is visible beside the oasis town's banana groves. On first glance, the ruins look like some ancient settlement from an early era of the six-thousand-year occupation of this town, the oldest continuously inhabited place on earth. In fact, they are abandoned temporary dwellings built by refugees from the war of 1948. The people who built them and lived in them have long since moved on—probably to other refugee camps in the West Bank. Glock and his students studied a group of these ruined houses, collecting the material evidence that told how the refugees had lived.

It was a pedagogical exercise, but one relevant to Palestinian experience. Rather than use written sources for information about the movement of refugees, of the kind compiled by the United Nations Relief and Works Agency (UNRWA), the United Nations body responsible for Palestinian refugees, the students were to accumulate data about the inhabitants of the camp from what they had left behind. This meant "digging up their garbage, old sardine cans and plastic bags," as one Birzeit professor put it. The point of not using written sources was that such sources could, Glock told his students, introduce a bias into study of the material: one would be studying the remains as if they were a commentary on the documents, making the land fit the sources. Ultimately, this approach went back to Glock's postconversion suspicion of the influence of the Bible on Palestinian archeology. He was telling his students to look at the land without reference to any text, to be free of any preexisting knowledge, except, of course, the knowledge of what is relevant and meaningful to Palestinian experience.

Studying the camps in this way could lead to conclusions that differ from the officially published versions. For instance, the configuration of houses in a settlement could help one determine with a reasonable degree of certainty where the refugees in that settlement came from—either from within what is now Israel or elsewhere in the Occupied Territories—by judging the style of construction or the way they were arranged together to form a *hawsh*, a compound. The refugees had replicated the configuration of the houses of their home village.

Glock explained that the refugee camp would teach his students to look at how people abandon a domestic site, an important issue throughout Palestinian history. The physical evidence could show whether people left in a hurry, for instance. Applied to a site associated with biblical history, the method could potentially help answer controversial questions about whether people were forced to flee due to military conquest, or migrated for economic reasons. Hasty abandonment also produced a perfect snapshot of how life was lived at a precise moment in time. Glock found an ingenious method for proving that the inhabitants of Ain al-Sultan did indeed leave the camp in haste. He learned from people still living on the site that it was customary to store a cache of money inside the mud-brick wall of a house. When you needed to leave, the money was the first thing you took because it was the most valuable. You dug out the cache of money with a pickax. Glock concluded that people had been compelled to abandon the site in haste because of the crudeness with which the holes had been cut.

Albert Glock wasn't the first archeologist to study modern garbage, but in the West Bank it was a radical thing to do. As one of his students put it, "People thought this was very strange." Palestinians as well as many Israelis and foreign Christians thought that archeology meant the study of the glories of the past. One can even see this in the Arabic phrase for archeology, *ilm al-aathar*, which literally means the study or science of antiquities. For Palestinians, archeology meant the Phoenicians, the Canaanites, and Salah al-Din; not sardine cans, plastic bags, and burnt sheep bones, the sad tokens of the wretched existence of refugees.

THERE IS A POPULAR ASSUMPTION that diaries are the containers of the purest truth about a person, because in a diary the writer is writing solely for himself. Feelings are set down undiluted by social expediency: one can say what one really thinks without fear of the consequences. There is no need to hide or edit the truth in a diary, so a diary contains the final word on everything, the unvarnished truth; until it is read it remains a hidden treasure in a world of obscurity.

The weakness of this view is that it does not take into account a handful of human tendencies that reveal themselves in ungoverned writing: self-delusion, or the common inability to judge a situation while one is still in it, or the almost universal inclination of even fairly cheerful people to use a diary as a book of complaints about the daily grind of living.

Were Glock's students, therefore, really as he described them: disappointingly irresponsible, intellectually inadequate, lazy, untruthful? This was his attitude in practice toward his generation of Palestinian archeologists. Glock loved Palestine, but was less keen on Palestinians, it seemed.

There were exceptions. Glock's inner circle consisted of those few scholars whose abilities he had come to trust. His closest colleague was Maya el-Farabi, who was also his best student, most loyal disciple, friend, muse, tormentor. Another member of the circle was Maya's sister, Huda, a paleoethnobotanist, trained in making deductions about how ancient people lived—diet, agriculture, trading patterns—from the traces of grains, seeds, and other plant matter found at excavation sites. As a technical specialist, dedicated to producing detailed data about a specific aspect of the material record, she was just the kind of archeologist Glock liked.

He preferred people whose vision was narrowly focused, rather than masters of the big picture.

Glock also liked a teaching assistant named Hamed Salem, a gentle and quiet man whom Glock respected as "a good dirt archeologist." With the kind of single-minded seriousness that Glock favored, he was working toward a PhD on traditional Palestinian potters, studying a craft that had been continuously practiced in Palestine for five thousand years. Hamed's work was a perfect example of Glock's vision of Palestinian archeology in practice: it demonstrated in a technically precise way the continuous history of ordinary life over the centuries.

These were the people who had made the grade. They do not form a long list. One of the ironies of Glock's legacy lies in the number of former students dismissed in his correspondence as disappointing in one way or another who still work in archeology or related fields and speak of Glock as their inspiration. A generation of Palestinian archeologists did indeed come into existence. It just didn't emerge exactly as Glock insisted it should.

Among those in whom Glock was disappointed was Walid Sharif. He had been at the institute for ten years, from when it was still a fledgling department, and had worked on all its excavations and taught undergraduate courses. Glock was critical of Sharif's decision not to specialize in the technique of sediment analysis, as Glock had counseled. The two maintained a peppery relationship. Sharif took to heart Glock's principle that Palestinian students should go against their traditional respect for authority and engage their teachers in constructive argument, but he did so by dissenting with the autocratic way Glock ran the institute. Sharif was talented and ambitious, and he was uneasy with the fact that everything he knew about the discipline of archeology had been taught him by Albert Glock. He needed to stand back from his severe and demanding mentor, to preserve his individuality, so he could see things for himself. He is now an archeological officer in the Palestinian Authority's Ministry of Culture.

Of all the archeologists at Birzeit, none was to become more hostile to Glock than Hamdan Taha, whose differences with his

mentor exploded in the latter half of 1991. Taha came from Hal-
houl, a village outside Hebron, and was the first member of his
family to attend a university. One of his brothers had been killed
by Israeli soldiers. He was deceptive in appearance: beneath a diffident exterior lay a steely ambition to succeed. Taha had been a
student since Glock first began to teach courses at Birzeit, and
within a few years Glock gave him a job as a teaching assistant. In
1982, Glock appointed Taha site supervisor on the first excavation
he directed for Birzeit students, the salvage excavation in Jenin.

From the time Taha made his first appearance in Glock's diaries
and correspondence, it is clear that he was another of the "disap-
pointments." Nothing Hamdan ever did seemed to please his
teacher. "Still find his work shallow," he wrote. He commented
on the "lack of logical argumentation" in Taha's work, his "unde-
veloped thoughts" and "disconnected sentences." This went on
for years, and one can imagine the anger that built up in the younger
man's heart. When he secured a scholarship to study in Germany—
a triumph for a young man from a modest background—Glock
complained that the scholarship had not been organized through
the institute. As Taha proceeded with his PhD, Glock thought it
insufficiently scholarly. Yet the young student persisted and eventually earned a doctorate from the University of Berlin. His dissertation was about Middle Bronze Age burials at Taanach. It was
based on raw data that Glock had grudgingly given him.

"Hamdan was quite good, not outstanding, but quite good," a
Birzeit professor remembered. "Look: what outstanding scholar
can work under such terrible conditions, the restrictions, the curfews, the arrests, the lack of proper facilities? He should have been
given a chance. He was among the better people in the social sciences."

ONE READS THE NARRATIVE of Glock's life knowing what happens in the final chapter and looking for signals that foretell the
outcome. In a social and political pressure cooker like the Israeli-
occupied West Bank, these signals are not hard to find. Glock took
an almost masochistic pleasure in enduring life under military

occupation. It drained the spirit, it sapped the soul, yet the hardship fortified his sense of purpose.

In June 1982, Palestinian society underwent one of its periodic upheavals when Israel invaded Lebanon. Israel's purpose was to wipe out PLO guerrilla bases in the southern part of the country. The invasion sent a shock wave through life in the West Bank: as the Palestinian population rose up in outrage, the iron fist of the Israeli occupation fell even harder. The atmosphere became volatile, and especially so at Birzeit. At the time, Glock was trying to lead a group of students in an archeological dig. He now learned that there was no ivy-clad wall separating Birzeit students from the currents of Palestinian society; if anything, those currents flowed right through the campus. Birzeit was a crucible of Palestinian political life. It was here that the bond between society and politics was forged, where young Palestinians learned that everything they did as Palestinians was political and was to be expressed in political action and political speech.

Glock was caught between the Israelis and the Palestinians, and he felt under duress from both sides. From the Israelis, he faced the threat of deportation. The local military governor had issued an order requiring foreign staff at universities in the Occupied Territories—sixty-seven people altogether—to sign a declaration renouncing the PLO and all its works as a condition of their visas. Signing such a declaration was unthinkable to individuals who had already shown courage and tenacity in continuing to work at Birzeit despite the hardship of closures and curfews. The foreign staff defied the order en bloc, and nervously awaited a response.

Palestinians, for their part, thought Glock was a spy: at Birzeit, a mood of suspicion against foreigners, born out of nationalist feeling, would arise from time to time. "Caught as a foreigner, even an American in a highly sensitive nationalist community can be very uncomfortable," he wrote. His gruff manner and his tendency to be hard on his students didn't help. In wanting to establish a generation of archeologists who would rescue Palestinian history, he could not accept the shortcomings of the people who came forward to take part in this project.

The result was a gnawing unhappiness in Glock's heart, a dark cloud of depression that rarely broke. "I suppose the general situation is so depressing for me that it is affecting me physically and certainly psychologically. This is not necessarily bad but it sure is painful. Makes one even more alone. One fears what one does though nothing is by itself illegal or bad."

Again and again there are entries like this. "It is not at all clear to me how long I can stay here, the changes may be more than I can take. The deep emotional involvements are uncompromising and significant changes may rupture my ability to hold out." And "The internal strife is very great and cannot continue without some real change." "I do live in a personal vacuum." Yet the strife itself seemed to push him grimly forward.

But the worst torment of all was the self-destructive infatuation he had developed for Maya. Maya stood for everything Glock was striving for: she was his personal holy grail of Palestine and Palestinian archeology. She was culturally and politically aware, ardent, scholarly, serious, and formidably intelligent.

Like Glock himself, Maya, too, was something of a maverick. When Albert first met her in 1978, she was working as a draftsman for an engineering firm in Ramallah. She was twenty-two and had been thrown out of Birzeit twice for poor academic results. The report on her in the registrar's office noted a "rebellious nature." In the village of Bir Zeit, her fierce, passionate, confrontational personality had earned her the label of "Marxist," which in a socially conservative place like Bir Zeit was a way of marking someone as an outsider. But Albert saw potential and began to lobby the university administration to allow him to hire her in the archeology department as a draftsman and to readmit her as a student. "She lives nearby, has talent and wants to work," he wrote to Haifa Baramki, the registrar.

Having been rescued by Glock, Maya never looked back. She flourished academically. While working as a draftsman, she studied for a degree in archeology. After getting her BA, she worked as a teaching assistant in the department. With the help of Glock's references, constant guidance, and encouragement, she applied for and got a full scholarship to take a master's degree in anthropology and archeology at Washington University in St. Louis. This was followed in time by a place at the top of the academic heap: a UNESCO fellowship to work for a PhD in archeology at the University of Cambridge. Even if she had conceived such an ambition without Albert Glock's motive force, her family could not have supported her. The family's only income came from her father's Jordanian army pension and the irregular salary he had from carving olive-wood souvenirs for the Holy Land tourist trade.

Albert struggled with his feelings about Maya. Brooding over her in his diary, he would offer himself counsels of restraint: their relations must remain on a purely professional footing, he wrote. Elsewhere, he reflected that Maya was simply using him as a foothold to climb out of Bir Zeit and find a new life, including marriage—hardly surprising or reprehensible in a student. In 1983, he wrote, "I can hardly deny that I am deeply in love with her," and went on, "but I think she asks herself, what's the use of loving him?"

Maya blew hot and cold so unpredictably that Albert was kept in a constant state of emotional disorientation. He complained endlessly in his diaries about "difficulty communicating" with Maya, her angry moods, their standoffs and arguments. Albert was like an adolescent boy in his impossible desire: it existed only in a medium of frustration and turmoil. Love of this kind is painful because it as based on the pursuit of an illusion: a self-created image of the beloved in the mind of one person. Maya could sense this. She knew what she stood for in his eyes, resented it, yet stayed close to Glock because of their common cause of archeology. They needed each other too much to cut this tangled emotional knot. When Maya was at her most distant from him, he channeled his ardor into working for her academic and professional advancement. He wanted her but failing that (which was inevitable), he wanted to see her succeed, because her triumph would be Palestine's triumph.

———

A FEW WEEKS AFTER Israel invaded Lebanon, Glock resumed excavation at Jenin. The town was frequently under curfew, the streets were often blocked with burning tires and strewn with rubble, and there were general strikes throughout the West Bank. Two weeks into the dig, the students who were participating decided to join the strike: they didn't want to be seen to be working at a time when PLO bases and the surrounding Palestinian refugee camps in southern Lebanon were being pounded by Israeli forces.

One day a young man in Jenin stabbed an Israeli soldier in a patrol. The soldiers shot him dead, and the town was put under curfew to prevent a riot. That night, Glock wanted his students to join him in reading pottery, but the students had other ideas and held a meeting to discuss the situation. "The discussion grew quite heated," Glock wrote. As Birzeit students, they felt totally involved in the local turmoil, despite Glock's entreaty that they keep their minds on archeology. "I tried to say that it was necessary to balance the needs of the course, of the university, of the city and the country," he wrote. The plea fell on deaf ears.

Again and again, Glock learned the hard way about how different student life was in this strange world of military occupation. W. F. Albright, describing an earlier age of Palestinian archeology, wrote of the excavation leader's need to maintain a good atmosphere among the participants of a dig. "A very modest repertory of airs and songs will help to keep the younger—and older—members of a staff happy," he wrote. Glock's staff needed more than airs and songs. By 1983, six of the twenty-five students who had signed up for Glock's Jenin dig were in jail, victims of an Israeli policy in the Occupied Territories that grew ever more severe as the crisis in Lebanon worsened.

Glock learned that everything that happens in Palestinian society is expressed in the language of politics. At Birzeit University, student elections are taken as seriously as national elections in normal countries. Students form political parties and run them with zeal and impressive organizational competence. These parties mirror the political currents in the whole of the Occupied Territories, from the Islamic opposition to the factions of a variety of political hues that make up the PLO. The student "bloc" that prevails in these elections is treated within the university community as a genuinely formidable body: like the headman in the traditional Palestinian village, people will come to them to settle disputes.

This authority is the key to understanding a strange episode that disrupted the 1983 season of Glock's excavation at Jenin. One night, Glock returned to the apartment in which the student members of the dig were lodging. Three of the students had eaten a large quantity of meat intended for that night's dinner. Ibtisam el-Farabi, Maya's sister, who was part of the excavation staff, shouted at them angrily, adding (Glock wrote in his diary) "a curse on the Fatah because this was the party to which the students belonged." The result was a mutiny among the students, who boycotted dinner and demanded a meeting to discuss the dishonor they had suffered from Ibtisam's sharp tongue. They called her a "political problem" and vowed to report the matter to the student council. This uproar was not about the importance of Fatah, but it did show the anarchic power and self-importance of young men in Palestinian society, a power that would be unleashed with spectacular results during the *intifada* four years later. The authority of the student council was such that Glock wrote a separate report for them, giving his own version of events.

In 1985, Glock began the excavation that he hoped would establish the foundations of his radical new approach. In the reexcavation of Tell Ti'innik, the site to which he had first come as a biblical archeologist in 1963, all his ambitions were to be fulfilled: the dig would revolutionize Palestinian attitudes to archeology, he hoped, and in so doing would make ordinary Palestinian villagers understand that their survival as a people depended on preserving their culture. This was a new idea for people who had seen survival entirely as a matter of politics and warfare. Glock's approach would challenge the dominant narrative of biblical archeology, favored by Israeli and Western archeologists, by demonstrating the persistence of ordinary Palestinian life in Palestine throughout the ages of history. The dig would enable his prized generation of Palestinian archeologists to cut their teeth on a Palestinian site, give them the professional experience to carry on their work in the future, and establish a model of excavation that generations of archeologists could follow. Tell Ti'innik was Glock's grand project, and it would reflect the intellectual odyssey he had undergone in his progress from Lutheran minister to biblical scholar, and from biblical archeologist to Palestinian archeologist.

Glock intended to start the dig at the base of the *tell*, where the modern village of Ti'innik stands. This would reveal the evidence of the more recent human occupation at the site, and demonstrate the continuity of history from biblical Taanach to modern Ti'innik. The plan was that while Glock directed a stratigraphic excavation of Ottoman Ti'innik, Maya el-Farabi would carry out an ethno-archeological excavation, the study of the more recent material remains of life in the village built near the ancient site. Three years earlier, she had spent six months living in the village compiling an ethnographic survey and knew the village intimately. The way the villagers lived now would be the model for understanding what the excavation revealed about how villagers lived in the past.

Almost immediately, things began to go wrong. As ever, there was the problem of a permit. The dilemma of needing a permit from the Israeli Department of Antiquities—specifically, the branch that covered the West Bank—had not been resolved. The Tell Ti'innik dig was not to be a salvage excavation, the only type of dig allowed in occupied territory under the Hague Convention. For the Jenin digs, Glock had maneuvered around the problem by applying for a permit through the Albright Institute. When he attempted the same in 1985, the application was rejected.

The rejection came from Itzak Magen, the man in charge of the Archeological Department of the Civil Administration of Judaea and Samaria. It was Magen's view—and he had military orders to support him—that anything to do with archeology or antiquities in the West Bank was subject to his sovereign will. He controlled archeology in the West Bank—where there were four thousand registered archeological sites, more than within the pre-1967 borders of Israel—like a personal empire, even discouraging Israeli archeologists from working there. Although his department was nominally part of the Israeli Department of Antiquities (now renamed the Israel Antiquities Authority), in practice it was quite autonomous. Magen reported not to the head of the Department of Antiquities but to the deputy military governor of the West Bank, a soldier who had no interest in archeology. Magen's nickname among Israeli archeologists was "the bulldozer," not a flattering nickname for an archeologist. Magen had made enemies, many of whom envied his freedom to excavate without bureaucratic oversight. The nickname was a comment as well on his physical size—he weighed, by his own estimate, over three hundred pounds—and on his techniques of human relations. He had harried his predecessor into resigning and then took over his job, and he did not care what people thought about him. "There is hatred of me, and that isn't new," he once said. "I'm a hard man. There was disorder, and I came to impose order in Judaea and Samaria."

Magen also carried out his own ambitious excavations, for which he did not have to seek anyone's permission. His budget came from taxes levied on the Palestinian residents of the West Bank, who were effectively paying him to plunder their country of its movable archeological treasures and send them to the Israel Museum.

Before he came to the West Bank, Magen worked on Benjamin Mazar's controversial excavation of the base of the Temple Mount. Later, in 1977, he joined the West Bank archeological office and began to excavate immediately. He uncovered Samaritan burial grounds near Nablus, two *mikvahs* (Jewish ritual baths) near Jerusalem, and a huge Roman theater in Nablus. Magen also excavated a site at the summit of Jebel Gerezim, the mountain that overlooks the Palestinian town of Nablus. Jebel Gerezim is the holy mountain of the Samaritan people, and the location of the village where most of them live. An ancient Jewish sect, the Samaritans were separated from the main tradition of Judaism at the beginning of the common era. They take their religion from the five books of Moses exclusively, and reject the Talmud. Only about four hundred remain, most of whom live on Jebel Gerezim, where the effects of centuries of inbreeding (they traditionally marry only other Samaritans) are noticeable in the population. Their annual Passover ceremony, involving the sacrifice of sheep in a paved area that looks like a municipal basketball court, draws crowds of tourists.

Magen's finds in the Samaritan areas have been spectacular, and of radiant meaning for the Jewish heritage. He excavated an octagonal church that was built on the ruins of the Samaritan Temple by the Byzantine emperor Zeno in the fifth century: the Samaritan Temple is a primitive version of the larger temple at Jerusalem. At other sites in the vicinity of Nablus, Magen found a Samaritan synagogue of the fourth century B.C.E., which contained a fine mosaic from the Byzantine era depicting a menorah and the Ark of the Covenant. (This is now in the Israel Museum, despite UNESCO.) The 1993 Oslo Agreement, signed by the Israelis and Palestinians, contains an "Itzak clause," which allows him to continue his excavation at Jebel Gerezim, even though the area has come under the control of the Palestinian Authority. ("So what do they expect," Magen said, "that I'll excavate and then give it to someone else? The Samaritans are mine. No one can take [them] away from me.")

None of these finds have been formally published as archeological reports. Magen prefers excavation to scholarship. He is the last of the old generation of Israeli archeologist-adventurers. As an official of the Civil Administration, Magen has military authority, carries a gun in the field, and can mobilize soldiers when necessary. According to an affidavit taken by a human rights group in July 1987, Magen sent a man from his department accompanied by a large force of soldiers to the village of Sebastiyah, north of Nablus. Their mission was to seize a collection of Roman statuary—a statue of Salome and four busts—from the mosque where they had been stored during the period of Jordanian occupation. Knowing that the soldiers were coming, the keeper of the mosque locked himself in the room where the antiquities were kept and refused to open it when the soldiers knocked on the door. The soldiers broke down the door, restrained the keeper, and took the statues. The whereabouts of the statues are unknown to this day.

In the past, Glock had managed to keep his distance from Magen, maintaining the minimum of polite contact and trying to avoid attracting attention so that he could get on with his work at Birzeit unobserved and unhindered by the occupation. This time, it seemed, Glock needed to confront Magen. Glock was worried that Magen had refused the application because he wanted Glock to apply in the name of Birzeit, a step which he had studiously avoided until now as a matter of politics. If Birzeit applied for the permit, it would be "legitimising the occupation"—bending the knee. In a detailed memo to Gabi Baramki, acting president of the university, about the problem, Glock wrote, "I believe they are trying to force me to the surface; they now know that I teach at Birzeit and that Birzeit students participate in the excavation; I have consistently avoided publicity because I know the Israeli archeological community well enough to know that what we are doing could easily be perceived as a threat."

It is somewhat surprising that Glock's relations with Magen were not more sharply adversarial than they were. When asked about this by the archeological writer Neil Silberman, an early advocate of Glock's work and one of the few archeologists who quotes from Glock's slender corpus of published writings, Glock shrugged and said he had to work with Magen whether he liked him or not. "His tone surprised me," Silberman wrote later. "He was surprisingly nice in speaking about Magen. . . . There might just have been something about Magen's dominating character (certainly with his workers and employees) that Al found attractive." The two had one thing in common: later, during the *intifada*, they both continued to excavate while other archeologists stayed away in fear. At the height of the uprising Itzak Magen had the physical courage to turn his back on fifty Palestinian workers holding square-headed hoes.

Glock eventually got his permit, and it was in the name of the Albright Institute, not Birzeit. He had lobbied the Albright's governing body, the American Schools of Oriental Research, to approach Avi Eitan, the director of the Israeli Department of Antiquities, about authorizing Itzak Magen to issue the permit, which he did. Glock's cordial relations with "the bulldozer"— which he did not mention in his memo to the president of Birzeit—surely helped. Glock wrote in his diary, "I discovered later that one reason for the delay in issuing the permit was that last year an analysis had been done of Itzak's office and it concluded that he was too easy with permits. Therefore it was now routine for requests for permits to be more formal." In working with both sides, Glock was walking a solitary path in the no-man's-land between two irreconcilable worlds.

THE LESSON OF cultural survival through archeology that Glock was trying to teach the Palestinians was not easily conveyed to the inhabitants of Ti'innik, where Glock and Maya el-Farabi began to excavate in the summer of 1985.

The village of Ti'innik had 539 people living in it when Maya el-Farabi conducted her ethnographic study there three years earlier. It was an impoverished, isolated spot on the border of what had been Jordan and Israel. The village sits on the eastern slope of an ancient man-made mound that is visible for miles around in a fertile green plain called Marj ibn Amr in Arabic and Jezreel in Hebrew. The concrete bases onto which, until 1967, the guns of the Jordanian army had been bolted, pointing over the border into Israel, are still there, but the guns have gone. After Israel seized the West Bank from Jordan, the conquering state expropriated most of the hundreds of acres of land that the inhabitants of the village had farmed for generations. The villagers lived by subsistence farming on the little land they still possessed and by what they earned as construction workers in Israel. The village had one mosque, one school, one shop, and one paved road running through the middle of it. Electricity was supplied by generators. The flat summit of the mound was divided into rugged, rocky plots growing almond and olive trees.

At the base of the mound was a cluster of modest buildings, some made of concrete, some of traditional construction of mud-brick and stone, in varying degrees of dilapidation. Maya had written her master's dissertation on the way the buildings in Ti'innik had gradually sunk into disuse and crumbled, to become archeological layers. The shells of long-abandoned houses were used as rubbish dumps, with chickens and goats rummaging around on top of them. The village was a vivid example of the way Palestine was perpetually sinking into history.

Below the roots of the olive and almond trees, and under the soles of the feet of the people of Ti'innik, in layer upon layer of accumulated debris, lay five millennia of mute history. The modern village of Ti'innik was the latest phase in a history of occupation that went back to the early Bronze Age, circa five thousand years before the present. Early Bronze Age Taanach was a massively fortified town, surrounded by walls four meters thick. The shape of the *tell* is the product of centuries of rebuilding, abandonment, and decay.

In the sixteenth century, Ti'innik appears in Ottoman government records, described as a small village producing wheat, barley, grape syrup, goats, and honey, and paying one-third of the value of this produce in taxes. Then it lay abandoned for at least two hundred years. It was resettled in the 1860s, when four families from a neighboring village migrated to the *tell* in order to claim the agricultural land around it. The village began to be mentioned in the accounts of European and American explorers, who noted its connection with biblical Taanach. It was included in the 1882 *Survey of Western Palestine* by Kitchener and Conder. Their only observation about the village was that it lay near the tomb of a Muslim saint named Hajj Aleiyan, who, according to folklore, had been refused entry into mosques because of his ragged and filthy appearance. The legend tells that he spread his cloak on the sea and performed his prayers on it, a miracle of piety around which grew a local cult. In this way, Taanach had become Ti'innik, a Palestinian Muslim hamlet.

What would look to the unsympathetic outsider to be an untidy, ramshackle village, Maya el-Farabi meticulously studied as a model of "archeological site formation." There was meaning in every careless gesture of throwing something away. As the people of Ti'innik proceeded through the cycles of birth, marriage, and death, they left a trail of debris that told how they lived, and Maya carefully recorded everything she found. She listed and analyzed every new building that was built, every old building that fell into disuse. She recorded the furniture in the houses, the local diet (the residents lived mostly on bread baked in traditional ovens and sweet tea, drinking on average six cups per day), and the crops they grew. She tabulated all of the discarded objects she found in the rooms of abandoned buildings: "sack of charcoal, 6 glass bottles,

2 beehives, 6 tins, metal jerry can, copper lid, straw basket, metal tray, branch, grindstone, wooden box, metal pipe, 5 pottery vessels, manual sewing machine, concrete brick . . ." Elsewhere, she noted, "Soft drink and tomato paste cans are the most frequent artifacts found in the village garbage sites." These things were as much a part of the archeological history of Ti'innik/Taanach as the Bronze Age fortifications discovered by archeologists of an earlier era.

She lived in the village for six months, gathering this information, and lived in the house of the *mukhtar*, the mayor. What the people of Ti'innik thought about el-Farabi paying such close attention to the contents of their rubbish dumps is hard to tell, though she seems to have maintained good relations with everyone.

When el-Farabi returned with Glock and the team of Birzeit students in July 1985, the villagers were not as accommodating. The aim of this second dig, of which Glock and el-Farabi were joint directors, was to excavate the hitherto ignored Ottoman history of Ti'innik, the four centuries from the sixteenth to the early twentieth century. Glock proudly announced in letters to colleagues that it was to be the first complete excavation of an Ottoman village site in Palestine. This dig would uncover and study the layers of history that biblical archeologists customarily bulldozed away to get at the older layers that told of ancient Israel. The intellectual value of the project was substantial, as was the political significance that went with it. The Ottoman centuries in Palestine were the hidden history of the country, which European and Israeli accounts tended to dismiss in cursory paragraphs as a period of stagnation. In recent years, Palestinian historians had been developing an opposing view that sees the Ottoman period as being almost a golden age, when despite the exactions of the Ottoman tax authorities, and the turmoil of clan warfare, the inhabitants of Palestine were generally left to get on with their lives with a fair degree of political autonomy. The Ottoman period was the longest and most important chapter of the unwritten history of Palestine—much of the source material was handwritten in Ottoman Turkish and buried away in inaccessible archives in Istanbul. The Ti'innik dig would establish an approach to the excavation of Ottoman Palestine that would be part of the Palestinian struggle to write themselves back into history.

So instead of digging on the *tell*, as earlier archeologists, including Glock himself, had done, the group chose to dig in a field north of the village, on the slope of the *tell*. Glock recorded in his diary that the villagers were immediately suspicious. No one had ever excavated there. If these were real archeologists, they would dig where the archeologists had always dug. The inhabitants came to believe that the archeologists were looking for gold, or for buried treasure that would then be sold for profit; they doubted that the excavation could in any way benefit them. They feared that some ancient artifact might be found that would cause them to be expelled from their homes and the area taken over by the Department of Antiquities.

The dig also posed a threat because of the official attention it drew to the building plans of the owners of the land and their neighbors. In 1981, Glock had been a witness in the court case of a man from the village who had built a house (in the manner described so exactly by Maya in her dissertation) on land that contained Byzantine tombs. The house had been built without a permit, so the Israeli Department of Antiquities requested an order that it be demolished, and the order was carried out. Glock had been asked by the defendant's lawyer, in his status as the archeologist responsible for the site of Tell Ti'innik, to say that the archeological site was limited to the mound. Glock would not do so, because his idea of Palestinian archeology was wider than that. "Understandably," Glock wrote, "Hassan [the Ti'innik landowner in question] is no fan of archeologists."

Albert and Maya found themselves ensnared in intrigues among the main families of the village over legal and illegal building. Their plans for excavation involved digging on land owned by several families, two of whom were perennial rivals. Members of one family wanted an excavation, so they could legally apply for a building permit: under the Jordanian law the Israelis adopted, a building permit would only be granted for a plot of land after an archeological excavation had been conducted. Others were determined neither to allow an excavation nor to apply for a permit, and to build as they wished without either. "Resisting the occupation" was a modern way of expressing the Palestinian peasant's traditional contempt for government authority.

About two weeks into the dig, Albert recorded the first attack on the site: during the night, someone pulled up all the wooden stakes marking the excavation plots. The next day, Maya upbraided the landowner, insisting that he was responsible and that it should not happen again. Birzeit had a record of helping the villagers, she argued, and did not appreciate vandalism. "It was time they trusted us," Glock wrote in his diary.

Two days later, when the archeologists arrived at the site, they found it had been vandalized again: the stakes had been pulled up, large stones had been thrown into the excavated plot, and a wall that had been uncovered had been pushed over. Maya and Albert reported the incident to the *mukhtar*. With his familiar combination of plodding determination, Glock recorded it in his diary. "I suspect the people to the north as those attempting to discourage our work. We need to get past this problem."

Three days later, there was another attack, despite the fact that a boy from the village had been hired to guard the site. After the boy had been verbally chastised by Maya for his laxness, his mother sprang to his defense, insisting that the site was intact only three hours before Maya saw it.

One day when the archeologists were away, the *mukhtar* brought in a bulldozer and cleared an area of land for a new generator. When the Birzeit team returned the next day, they found human bones and skulls and pottery shards littering the surface of the bulldozed ground: the *mukhtar*'s hurried clearance job had uncovered a Byzantine burial ground.

When confronted by Maya about this, the frightened *mukhtar* admitted that he did not have a permit from the Department of Antiquities to bulldoze the site, but he pleaded that he had been given permission by the military governor to construct a building for the new generator. Emergency negotiations were conducted over tea. "We tried to make clear that we might be able to help them in such cases if they would tell us of their building plans," Albert wrote. The *mukhtar* was momentarily relieved when Albert and Maya told him that it was not their job to report such violations to the Department of Antiquities, thinking Glock would turn a blind eye, then was alarmed once again when they told him that "it *was* our job to prevent the destruction of the evidence required to uncover the 5000-year history of the village."

That night, Glock and el-Farabi were summoned to an urgent meeting. In a second-story room crowded with men (Maya was the only woman), the village elders tried to bluster their way out of the danger in which they saw themselves over the illegal bulldozing of the Byzantine cemetery. They professed their shame and outrage at the vandal's attacks on the excavation site and swore that it was the work of people from outside the village. They promised that they would protect the site and that there would be no more attacks in the future. This show of concern was presumably intended to mollify the archeologists so they would not report the incident to the Department of Antiquities.

Some days later an investigator from the Department of Antiquities in Nablus came to Ti'innik to look at a plot of land on which one of the villagers wanted to build a house. By chance, he passed the bulldozed Byzantine cemetery and noticed that an archeologically significant site had been destroyed. In a small village where nothing goes unnoticed, Glock's popularity in Ti'innik cannot have increased when he was seen accompanying the inspector, a Palestinian employee of the Civil Administration whom Glock had known for a long time. The inspector made it clear that he was unhappy about the damage and told the *mukhtar* that he would have to report it.

After this episode, the atmosphere deteriorated rapidly. At one point Albert and Maya went to a Ti'innik landowner to discuss the attacks on their excavation site and to ask permission to extend their excavation onto his land (an undiplomatic request at the time, one would have thought). The reaction was like a sword cast on the ground. "He swore so much that he saw nothing going on at our site that I'm quite sure he was the culprit," Glock wrote. "As far as the land was concerned, he proudly announced that he would be able to bribe whoever was necessary in order to build. He responded to nothing Maya said except in the most cynical fashion. He said that a neighbor got his permit for building by paying someone and our survey had nothing to do with the granting of a permit. In other words, he had money and with this he had power and to hell with all other interests."

There were no further attacks on the site for the next few weeks, but the idea of the dig being a Palestinian effort to reclaim Palestinian history was lost on the villagers. El-Farabi was told that, even though Glock was the only foreigner on the dig, the villagers thought the excavation party was not Palestinian at all, but American or Israeli, and that it was best to maintain this perception among them to guarantee respect. Persistently hopeful in the face of adversity, Glock wrote, "I disagree vehemently and hope we can find a way to change this."

The conflict with the villagers was largely the result of the clash of personalities. "I don't think he understood Palestinians very well," recalled Walid Sharif, who was working as a supervisor on the dig. "He was more interested in his work than in communicating with them. He would only talk to the villagers when he needed something," he said; in his view, a more attentive diplomacy would have yielded better results.

Since they were digging with a permit from the Israeli administration, Glock and his team were unable to do more than lobby the administration—that is, the autonomous antiquities office of Itzak Magen—in the villagers' interests. They were powerless to deliver the building permits they promised would follow once their excavations were completed. But even though Glock had a permit, the Birzeit students who took part had to have additional permits from the local military governor to stay overnight in the area, and the site was regularly visited by the military. Glock patiently showed the soldiers around. One day an officer visited the site. He was a Druze, a member of a heterodox Islamic sect, whose members in Israel serve in the Israeli military. The officer demanded a list of the names and identity card numbers of everyone working on the site. He came with a man in plain clothes: "probably from intelligence," Glock noted in his diary.

These events were a distraction from the dig itself, which was turning out to be a great success.

One of the goals that Glock and el-Farabi had set for the excavation at Ti'innik was to find the early Ottoman village that had once stood there. Historically, this was the village that had been abandoned at some point in the seventeenth century, leaving the site uninhabited for two hundred years, until it was resettled in the mid-nineteenth century. They were certain that there was a village there at this time because Maya had studied the sixteenth-century Ottoman tax records, which contained a wealth of detail about the population of the village, its property, and agricultural products. Nevertheless, there was no trace of building from this era to be seen on the surface.

There was one clue. The archeologists had conducted a surface survey of the village and noticed a field to the north, on the slope of the *tell*. It was a plowed field planted with almond trees and thickly scattered with pottery fragments that they judged (by comparison with examples from Jordan) to belong to the Mamluk or early Ottoman period of the thirteenth or fourteenth centuries. As they considered the field a possible site to excavate, they studied a plan of Ti'innik drawn for the original archeologist of the site, the Austrian biblical scholar Ernst Sellin, who dug there from 1902 to 1904. The area that had attracted their interest was labeled "ruins" on Sellin's plan, although whatever ruins Sellin had seen had since been plowed under in the need for agricultural land. Glock and el-Farabi decided to begin their search here, and within a few days of digging began to find traces of the early Ottoman village only twenty centimeters below the surface, under a layer of what turned out to be rubbish from the Jordanian army camp on the summit of the *tell* (old corned beef tins, plastic bags, and sheep bones). Glock wrote in his diary, "I truly believe that we hit the archeological bull's eye on the first try."

They excavated two plots in this field, working amid the buzz of cicadas under a tarpaulin sheet rigged up like a tent to shade them from the summer sun. The baskets of earth the students removed as the weeks went by uncovered a cluster of one-room houses built around a courtyard. The place they had chosen to dig was right in the middle of the Ottoman village. The archeological significance of this modest complex of houses was their similarity to the village's nineteenth-century buildings, several of which were still standing, if in somewhat dilapidated form. Both generations of buildings consisted of a single room divided into two floor levels, where the human inhabitants lived on the upper level while animals were housed on the lower level. It showed the continuity of ordinary life in Palestine over the centuries, the link between "the archeological past and the living present" that was the refrain and theme of Palestinian archeology.

Their other aim was to excavate the ruins of a nineteenth-century house in the middle of the modern village. This was a roofless shell consisting of three bays that had once been rooms and a courtyard. It had been built in the second half of the nine-teenth century by a branch of the notable Abd al-Hadi family of Nablus, who settled in Ti'innik as tax-collecting bureaucrats fol-lowing the Ottoman land reform law of 1858. The house was larger than most in the village, consisting of three rooms instead of the usual one. The Abd al-Hadis moved out in the 1920s, and the house fell gradually into disrepair, although it was twice reoccu-pied later. By 1968, after its last occupants (refugees from the 1967 war) had left, its roof had fallen in completely. Tufts of grass were growing from the chinks in the stone walls, and the rooms now contained a *tabun*, a traditional dome-shaped oven used for baking bread, a chicken coop, and storage for dried dung and firewood. The Abd al-Hadi family, who now lived in Jenin, still owned the house, and must have been delighted and surprised when this earnest pair from Birzeit University sought to rent the house from them for the purpose of archeology.

Glock and el-Farabi applied their thorough and meticulous approach to extracting every possible scrap of archeological infor-mation from this unremarkable heap of stones, so that they might build up a detailed picture of the reality of village life in the twelve decades or so of the house's existence. The middle of the three rooms contained the chicken coop, so they left that one alone, and excavated the two rooms on either side of it.

The dig determined the original architecture of the house, its traditional style, how it was rebuilt and altered, and how the rooms were used. Doorway, ledge for sitting, hearth for coffeepot, window, rebuilt wall, collapsed wall, archway, floor, pavement, step: these were the pieces of the puzzle. They studied the pieces; described, analyzed, measured, and classified them; and carefully assembled them into a narrative of the history of this ordinary three-room house. In one place in Maya's report, she describes a niche in a wall that she suggested was used for storing small things like "matches, oil lamps or other domestic items." A grainy snapshot of old Palestine emerges from the mass of tiny facts that they compiled, flashing glimpses of lost moments in unrecorded lives. They were salvaging the people of Ottoman Palestine from oblivion and fixing them in the pages of history.

The dig promised to fulfill Glock's ambition to establish a Palestinian archeology of Palestine. One can judge him to have been happy at this moment: even he, the granite-featured midwestern Lutheran pessimist who rarely smiled and had difficulty getting along with people. Certainly, complaints about being lonely or depressed appear rarely in his diary at this point. The promise of fulfilling an ambition, seen as a real possibility rather than a delusion, may have been better than the fulfillment itself.

On the second day of the excavation of the Abd al-Hadi house, a wall was revealed. It turned out to be secondary construction, that is, built later than the original house. Albert suggested to Maya that it was possibly the work of the refugees from the war of 1948 who had rebuilt one of the rooms of the house and inhabited it for a few years. Noting the conversation in his diary, he wrote, "I pointed out the analogy of the secondary walls of the Zealots on Masada in the casemate walls of the Herodian structure.

"Maya said, 'This is our Masada!' "

It is a powerfully meaningful remark, even if Maya meant it ironically. Certainly, there is no trace of irony in the way Albert recorded it, without additional comment, giving her the last word. Masada is one of the best-known archeological sites in Israel, and one of its most popular tourist attractions. A mountaintop fortress in the Jordan Valley near the Dead Sea, Masada was built by Herod, the Roman governor of Palestine, in case his subjects in Jerusalem should mount an effective uprising against him. In a spectacular episode (after Herod's time), recorded in an account by the Jewish historian Flavius Josephus, a group of Jewish rebels—the Zealots—seized the fortress in 74 C.E. and held out in it against the attacking Romans. (Glock's remark to el-Farabi was about the walls the Zealots built inside the Herodian fortress.) The Zealots defended themselves for as long as they could against the superior force; then, rather than face the ignominy of defeat, Josephus wrote, they committed mass suicide.

The Masada tradition is of dubious historicity but has persisted for its mythic force. The site was excavated from 1963 to 1965 by Yigael Yadin. He conducted the dig in a blaze of international publicity. The dig was jointly sponsored by the *Observer*, a Sunday newspaper in London, which carried regular reports, and it attracted a multitude of volunteers, who paid their own way to sweat under the desert sun and sleep in army tents. Archeologically, Yadin's interpretation of Masada is fanciful: he suggested that some bones he uncovered were those of the actual Zealots who had killed themselves, as described by Josephus. That the bones came from a later period and were incompatible with Josephus's account did not get in the way of a good story. In 1968, Yadin arranged for the bones to be removed and given the full state funeral accorded military heroes. The martyrs of Masada came to stand for the determination and martial values of the modern Israeli state. At Masada, archeology gave Israel a powerful nationalist myth.

If Ti'innik were to be the Palestinians' Masada, and if Glock and el-Farabi were to be its Yigael Yadin, the site would have to stand for something in the mythology of Palestinian nationalism. In one significant way, Ti'innik fulfilled this: it represented the tenacity, resilience, and persistence in the struggle for survival of the Palestinian peasant. The poets and politicians of the Palestinian national movement ceaselessly praised and idealized the Palestinian peasant since the loss of their country in 1948. In his stubborn, patient defiance of the oppressor, the peasant was the exemplar of the virtue of *sumud* (steadfastness). Through *sumud*, the Palestinians would survive, simply by staying put and refusing to leave, whatever hardships the enemy may impose. This quality was perfectly expressed in the narrative that Glock and el-Farabi were extracting from the ruined one-room houses at Ti'innik, a narrative of continued human occupation at Ti'innik over five thousand years. Glock believed that the archeology of Palestine must be relevant to "the Arab population of Palestine." It had to address itself to "the people in the villages," he wrote. This meant the *fellahin*, the heroic Palestinian peasants.

In Palestinian popular culture, the *fellahin* are idealized, not just as the exemplars of *sumud*, but as representatives of a way of life that most Palestinians have lost. This is the same idealization of the peasant that inspired Birzeit University to declare an annual Olive Picking Holiday, for example, or, more outlandishly, as they did one year, to construct on the campus a model Palestinian village out of Styrofoam.

In Glock's alternative history of Palestine, there were to be no victories, monuments, or great men. It was to be a history that concentrated on the way ordinary life was lived by everyone—not just the victors—and the economic and cultural forces that shaped it. For this reason, Glock was wary of publicizing Ti'innik. It had no potential as a tourist attraction. The plots in the field of almond trees have now been filled in; there is nothing to see. The Abd al-Hadi house is just a place for a chicken coop. He was afraid that publicity would attract the wrong type of interest: he was aware of the nationalistic significance of the work they were doing, yet if it drew too much attention his freedom to keep doing it could be endangered—by Israeli authorities who saw it as dangerous, or by Palestinians who saw it as too important a matter to be left in the hands of a foreigner.

———

THE ARCHEOLOGISTS EXCAVATED for three summers at Ti'innik, and by the third year, 1987, the excavation had reached the remains of extensive building in the Byzantine era. That season's dig reached a climax with the discovery, in the last few days, of a destruction level containing a wealth of objects of the Byzantine-Mamluk period, mostly pottery vessels, some of them whole, some broken but repairable, and hundreds of fragments. There were lamps, jars filled with grains and beans, pieces of broken and melted glass, and a few metal implements, including a plow. The patch turned out to be a storeroom for domestic utensils that had been destroyed in a fire. The fire had caused the roof to fall in, burying the contents and preserving them for centuries as a trove of artifacts from a long blank period in the archeological record. Albert Glock was working on the pottery from this room five years later on the day he was assassinated.

The problems with the villagers continued. One day one of the boys from the village who had been engaged as a laborer was caught pocketing a coin he uncovered while digging. Glock had been suspicious that something like this was going on since that season not a single coin had been found. The boy was told to hand over the coin, and then he was fired, along with another youth who had been "stirring things up with bad talk." That night, the excavation site was vandalized: the ropes holding the canvas canopy over the site were cut, and the screen on a sifter slashed. The site was vandalized this way again a week later, and yet again four days after that. Glock and el-Farabi complained to the *mukhtar*.

"If he knew who did it," Glock wrote, "he could not say." The *mukhtar* was an elderly rural headman, dignified and restrained in manner, whose neat black robe and ironed white headscarf suggested a preference for keeping up appearances. He told them to hire a guard, a measure they had avoided up to then, but this time they agreed to do it.

The local guard proved ineffective. The site was attacked again: another tent slashed. Albert and Maya realized that a man from the village was hardly likely to challenge one of his own neighbors, let alone report him. This time, Maya determined to go to the police, a very severe step. The only police in the West

Bank were Israeli, an institution of the occupation, even if at this time (before the *intifada*) there were still some Palestinian officers. To call on the police to settle a dispute was to align oneself with the occupation, virtually to proclaim oneself on the side of the enemy. In the rural West Bank, disputes were settled privately, typically by calling on the mediation of a more powerful outside party. But the archeologists were seen as outsiders and were unprotected by this traditional system and the village's umbrella of kinship.

Some policemen came from Jenin. They questioned the guard and the boy who had pocketed the coin. The boy confessed to damaging the tent and was charged. The following week, Gabi Baramki received an inflammatory letter from a group of people in Ti'innik. Translated from Arabic, it read:

> To the President of Birzeit University
> We find it necessary to co-operate with our academic institutions
> in order to protect this country, its reputation and future. There
> fore we would like to inform you about what is going on in our
> village by some individuals who reflect an unsatisfactory image of
> your institution. Your university is doing excavations under the
> supervision of an American Doctor, Abu Abid, and another girl
> calling herself Maya . . .

The letter complained that Maya "threatens to delay building permits for people who do not co-operate with her and curses our religion," and had falsely accused villagers of attacking the site. "Curses our religion" is a catchall insult, which can often be interpreted to mean "offends our sensibilities." The letter was signed by six members of the family of the boy who had been implicated in the attack on the excavation. From her thorough knowledge of the genealogies of the village, Maya knew who all the people were and how they were related. This family was a perennial rival of the family of the *mukhtar*. Glock was compelled to write a long explanation to Gabi Baramki.

"We have always over a long period attempted to befriend the village," he wrote. "It is clear that in the case of part of one of the major families we have not succeeded. However, I for one believe that the entire event helps us better understand the people to whom we must relate. Clearly, some, if not most, perceive of archeology as a dangerous enterprise."

It was going to get even more dangerous.

CHAPTER EIGHT

ON TUESDAY, December 8, 1987, a traffic accident took place in Gaza City. Then, as now, Gaza was a teeming, claustrophobic inferno, in which a million people lived like flies trapped in a bottle. The Gaza Strip served as a dormitory and reservoir of cheap labor for Israeli industry. Every day before dawn, a mass of men would pass through the bleak no-man's-land of concrete and barbed wire, and walk along a military defile a kilometer long to get to work. This checkpoint, known as the Erez Crossing, was at the time the only exit and entry point for the Gaza Strip. The rest of the territory was enclosed with barbed wire and watched by armed patrols.

At this time, before the pullout that attended the 1993 Oslo Agreement, Gaza City was still under active Israeli military occupation. Army patrols cruised through the dusty streets of the city and the surrounding refugee camps, keeping a weary and suspicious eye on a surly and downtrodden population. The army was not there to maintain law and order, merely to keep a lid on things. The traffic in Gaza skidded around chaotically; there had been plenty of collisions between Israeli trucks and the vehicles of Gazans in the past.

Just before dusk, an Israeli army tank-transport truck collided with a minibus carrying laborers returning home after a day's work in Israel. Seven of the laborers were injured, and four were killed. The crash scene, in the middle of a wide, busy avenue, attracted an angry crowd. The funeral that took place the following day turned into a violent confrontation with confused Israeli soldiers.

The anger spread like wildfire through the whole of the Gaza

Strip, borne on a wave of conflicting reports about what had actually happened. Within two days, the unrest reached the refugee camps of the West Bank, developing as it spread throughout the Occupied Territories into a general Palestinian revolt against the Israeli occupation. An Arabic name was given to the uprising: *intifada*, from a verb meaning to shake off, and a new word entered the lexicon of the Israel-Palestine conflict. In time, the *intifada* would energize the entire Palestinian population in the Occupied Territories and bring together in a common cause a people who were a mixture of often incompatible backgrounds and interests. In street battles with armed soldiers in towns and villages, Palestinian boys opposed live bullets with hurled stones.

In January 1988, a month after the initial spark of the uprising, the Israeli Civil Administration issued an order closing all the educational institutions—elementary and secondary schools, as well as universities—in the Occupied Territories, including Birzeit. Birzeit had already been closed four times in the 1986–1987 academic year, for periods ranging from one day to four months, in response to demonstrations or violent confrontations with soldiers. Schools were closed and reopened irregularly throughout the *intifada*, but Birzeit stayed closed for five years, and only reopened in 1992. The unstated reason for the closure, understood by all, was that the universities—Birzeit in particular—were seen by the Israeli authorities as the incubators of opposition, so that closing the universities was one way of suppressing the *intifada*.

The army enforced the closure by banning anyone but caretakers from entering the buildings on the university's two campuses, the old one in the town of Bir Zeit and the new one on a hill on the road to Ramallah. Army jeeps blocked the entrances. The Institute of Archeology was not located on either campus, but in a separate building in the town, so in previous years when the army closed the university, Glock would continue to work there, hoping the soldiers would not notice him.

The last season of excavation at Ti'innik had ended in the summer of 1987, and Glock was busy writing field reports on the results of the previous years, and dealing with the mass of data he and his students had collected. On days when the university was closed, and travel into Birzeit from the Glocks' home in Jerusalem was impeded by military roadblocks, he would rise at dawn to avoid them and get to his office before 7:00 A.M. There would be no students present, and Glock would work alone with the doors shut and the lights off in order not to attract attention.

The prolonged closure that began in January 1988 succeeded in stopping the normal functioning of the university, including Glock's teaching program at the Institute of Archeology. Before the *intifada*, the university had developed ways of continuing to operate during closures: classes were held off campus (which many called "going underground"), in Jerusalem, where the military order did not apply, or in secret in the homes of students and teachers. (This last tactic was illegal if the gatherings were of more than five people.) During the *intifada*, these methods helped Birzeit survive what seemed like an effort to drive it out of business for good. In 1988, teaching off campus, which was originally intended to help students who needed only a few more credits to graduate, increased as the *intifada* dragged on to involve some three hundred students, about a tenth of the undergraduate body. With the library and laboratories off-limits, teachers would smuggle laboratory equipment out; where the equipment was too big, the students were smuggled in.

The off-campus teaching program was merely a token of resistance. In reality the closure was a disaster for Birzeit. It meant that the university's income dropped, while the salaries of staff still had to be paid. Gabi Baramki was compelled to make frequent visits to PLO headquarters in Tunis to plead for funds to prevent the university's teaching staff from draining away to more secure jobs elsewhere, outside the Occupied Territories. Allowing staff to drain away would have accomplished what was seen as the Israelis' purpose in closing the universities: to undermine and weaken them so that they could not recover, and to make getting an education impossible for a young Palestinian, except outside the Occupied Territories.

The image of the "underground university" that Birzeit had acquired was impressive, but in reality little teaching or any other kind of work was done during the closure. Albert Glock was a conspicuous exception. He did his best not to let the closure, or any of the other hardships of the *intifada*, deflect him from his purpose of creating an edifice of scholarship, centered around the work on Ti'innik, that would be the foundation for Palestinian archeology. Although it was impossible now to begin any new research, and although only a handful of students were able to take his courses, Glock continued to teach. When his students couldn't get transportation he picked them up from their homes. Moreover, he did not relax the high standards he expected of them. This single-mindedness had made him seem an aloof figure at Birzeit, since he had been careful to keep himself apart from the political ferment of student life. His mission had not involved wearing a *kaffiyeh* and taking part in demonstrations. He instinctively saw his role as more serious than that.

The same fixity of purpose made him fearless. When his work obliged him to drive through an area where there was the risk of an Israeli bullet or a Palestinian rock coming through his windshield, he went anyway. When people remember Al Glock, they remember this. They connect his courage with his death.

Glock was almost boastful about the way he would carry on his business in the heat of the *intifada*. He seemed to relish the hardship it presented. The *intifada* challenged people and put them in situations that revealed their moral character. His rock-solid Lutheranism came alive during these months, when all the luxuries and embellishments of life were stripped away, leaving only the fundamentals. Ibtisam el-Farabi remembered that on strike days, Glock would arrive at their house with sugar and bread and milk, in case the family had not been able to stock up on these staples beforehand. The same devotion to the sacramental value of ordinary life could also be seen in his archeology.

Glock described his life during the first year of the *intifada* in a circular letter he sent to friends. It was dated August 1, 1988, and entitled "Between a Rock and a Hard Place."

Tomorrow I am going up to Ti'innik, our excavation site. I had planned to go on the western road but today a youth was killed in Qalqilya [refugee camp] by the army and the town is under curfew. I will have to take another road. Since I have a car with a black-on-yellow license plate (Israeli) and not the West Bank (black on blue), I can be mistaken for an Israeli and thus be a target for stone- and bomb-(molotov cocktails!) throwers. I drove up last Sunday, the first time in months, and had no trouble. The main road through the center of the West Bank is heavily patrolled by the army. At a check-point near Nablus the soldiers wore looking the other way so I simply drove through. In populated areas I am told to keep the left turn light blinking as a signal that I am an Arab. One can also spread a *kaffiyeh* on the dash, but if seen by the police one can be fined.

Birzeit stayed closed long after the other universities in the West Bank were allowed to reopen: the Civil Administration considered it to be the headquarters of the *intifada*. There was an element of truth in this, even though the *intifada* began and was directed from elsewhere. Gabi Baramki took pride in the perception, and did nothing to deny it. While Birzeit students, barred from their campus, threw stones at soldiers in the streets of Ramallah and in their home villages, there were two members of the Birzeit teaching faculty in the clandestine leadership of the uprising (Hanan Ashrawi and Sari Nusseibah, both of whom were friends of Glock) and Birzeit professors became its theorists. In the first year, a group of lecturers formed a kind of think tank to propose ideas that were included in the *bayanat*, the secretly printed circulars of the *intifada*.

The *bayanat* were the engine of the *intifada*. They announced strike days and boycotts, and pronounced and formed the opinion of the newly mobilized Palestinian masses. The bulletins were written in a stirring rhetoric, combining a highly wrought poetic language, usually in praise of the heroic actions of the people, with a militant political vocabulary. At their peak in the first year of the uprising, as many as six were published per month. Their authorship was always anonymous. Although they were written for Palestinian consumption and were printed and distributed in secret, these bulletins were also addressed to the Israelis, to communicate to them defiance, determination, and the formidable power of a movement with an inexhaustible membership.

The intensely political culture of Birzeit is impossible to miss. There are signs of it everywhere, especially in the weeks before student council elections, when the central plaza of the campus is festooned with banners and posters. Birzeit draws students from every quarter of Palestinian society, throwing together rich sophisticates whose fathers made money in the Gulf with the angry kids of the refugee camps. The university's policy is to allow them all the right to express themselves, however noisily. Sometimes the students rise up in protest against the university itself, as they did when the administration sought to raise the passing grade from sixty to seventy percent, but mostly their dissent was directed against the occupation, often with fatal results. The focal point of the campus is a monument, a granite slab set among myrtle bushes, dedicated to "the righteous martyrs of Birzeit University who were cut down on the road to freedom and independence." It lists a few dozen names, with the year of their death, beginning in the early 1980s.

———

GLOCK WOULD CONSCIENTIOUSLY organize his life around protests and demonstrations, which brought the West Bank to a virtual standstill, pragmatically minimizing the inconvenience to himself. News of every day's action was broadcast on a radio station that appeared on the airwaves in early 1988 named al-Quds—or Jerusalem—radio. Israeli intelligence identified its source after two weeks as southern Syria. It was the radio station of the Marxist Popular Front for the Liberation of Palestine. Al-Quds was the favored radio station of the *shabab* (youth) because it broadcast good music when it was not reporting on the *intifada* and megaphoning the instructions of its leaders. Its broadcasts began and ended with the slogan, "For the liberation of land and man."

Apart from the fact that it played better music, al-Quds radio was favored over the PLO radio station, broadcasting from Baghdad, because its message was more radical. Al-Quds broadcast the appeal of the Islamic resistance movement, Hamas, for a *jihad* to liberate the land. The station also regularly broadcast the names of individuals believed to be collaborating with the Israelis, and urged people to punish them.

This reflected the course the *intifada* was to take. After its initial peak, the *intifada* became routinized. Shopkeepers continued to slam down the shutters of their shops at noon every day, despite the efforts of the Israeli soldiers who enforced orders to keep them open by breaking the locks with blowtorches. But as the arrests of *shabab* continued, the strength of the movement was inevitably weakened. So many Birzeit students were arrested in demonstrations and stone-throwing skirmishes that pleading for his students in military court in Ramallah became a regular part of Glock's professional duties.

Observers speculated that if new forms of civil disobedience were not found, the *intifada* would turn violent. Previously the movement had carefully avoided the use of weapons. It gave the Palestinians the moral high ground that they were seen to be nonviolent by the eyes and ears of the world. But by early 1991, the year before Glock was killed, this began to change.

Besides being a rebellion against the occupation, the *intifada* became a rebellion of the young against the old. A young Palestinian could look at his father's and his grandfather's generations and their role in the history of Palestine and see a record of failure. In their inability to deal with Israel effectively, either politically or militarily, the older generation had turned the name of Palestine into a synonym for loss and dispossession and defeat. During the *intifada*, the traditional deference that the young showed the old broke down. Sons defied their fathers. The *intifada* was in the hands of the young, and young and old knew it.

The leadership of the young was both the strength and the weakness of the *intifada*. As a consequence of the Israeli strategy of arresting and in some cases shooting dead its leading activists, the movement came to be led by younger and younger people.

Besides having no respect for the authority of their elders, they had no patience with nonviolence. In Ramallah, teenagers ordered gray-haired merchants to close their shops, and vandalized the stores if they refused to comply. By 1990, young vigilante groups were on the scene, carrying out violent attacks on perceived collaborators. They had scary names, like the Black Panthers and the Veiled Lions. They frightened the Israelis as much as the Palestinians because they were unpredictable and impossible to infiltrate and had no links with the established Palestinian political parties. Previously the leadership was able to control the acts of violence against collaborators. Suspects were given verbal warnings and a chance to change their ways. But in the second half of the *intifada* hundreds of killings took place, many of which looked more like the settling of private scores. People began to call this phase of the uprising "the red *intifada*."

CHAPTER NINE

Y EARS LATER, Alice Glock recalled that her father was like "someone walking into his own death" in the last year of his life. He seemed to be aware of the danger that was gathering around him, but he did nothing to avoid it. What was her father doing in the last months of his life that was so dangerous?

The first stage in Glock's long walk into death began in the months leading up to the 1991 Gulf War. A climate of general danger had been steadily growing since the Iraqi invasion of Kuwait in August 1990. And on October 8, 1990, a massacre occurred on the Temple Mount/Haram al-Sharif. On that day, a group of Jewish extremists called the Temple Mount Faithful invaded the area intending to lay the foundation stone for a third Jewish temple— absolute anathema to the Islamic trust that holds the site on behalf of the Muslim world. The act caused a riot in which 18 Palestinians were killed and 150 were injured by Israeli soldiers. (The Islamic Museum at the corner of the complex now exhibits in its most prominent display cabinets not its rare manuscripts of the Qur'an but the bloody garments and framed photo portraits of the Palestinians who died in the massacre.) The incident provoked a spate of revenge attacks by Palestinians against Israelis, and a tightening of the military grip on life in the territories. Glock mentioned the episode and its aftermath in a letter to Alice:

Last week, following the massacre at al-Haram, we were stopped in our tracks for one solid week. Everything on our side of the city and country was closed down. In fact much of the WB [West Bank] was under a curfew. No public transport. Very few cars moving. Black flags flying everywhere. The army had also curfewed many towns. I did go to BZ [Birzeit] twice but people there said I should not travel. Nor was it easy to find food since all shops were closed. We survived but life is not normal, not that it ever is but now it's even less so.

The killings happened while the clouds of war were darkening the sky. The allied forces had issued a deadline to Iraq to withdraw from Kuwait by January 15, an ultimatum that Iraq showed no intention of obeying. As the deadline approached, Operation Desert Shield, the American-led military buildup in Saudi Arabia, prepared to turn into Operation Desert Storm, the high-tech war against Iraq. Even at this point, Glock was determined that he would stay when and if war broke out.

Life here is a bit tense and it is not quite right to run away—at least not until it is absolutely necessary and I doubt that, if there is war, there will be time for an escape. After all, the people I live and work with who will not be able to leave should not be served by someone who runs away when life becomes difficult. I hope you understand such a strange view of life.

Four days before the war started, he wrote letters to his sons Albert Jr. and Jeffrey. Now that the war was a virtual certainty, he sent them a package of essential personal papers. He wrote to Jeff,

Enclosed are copies of several documents that we would like you to keep on file, information that would be useful to one of us [that is, Albert or Lois] while visiting or in case of disaster, some basic data that you will find useful.

To Al Jr. he wrote, in partial explanation of this fatalistic fore-thought, "We are, after all, living directly below the headquarters of the IDF [Israel Defense Forces] central command." This was an Israeli army base on a hilltop at al-Ram near where the Glocks lived.

At the time Glock wrote this, Palestinians and Israelis were preparing themselves for an expected Iraqi chemical gas attack on

Israel. The Israeli public were issued gas masks. At first, the Palestinians in the territories were not, and gas masks were available only on the black market. Some people made improvised gas masks out of gauze stuffed with ground charcoal mixed with bicarbonate of soda, held onto the head with elastic bands. Eventually, the Israeli Supreme Court ruled that the residents of the territories had to be issued gas masks, too. In the last days before war broke out, both populations were preparing a single room in their homes to protect them from the expected chemical attack. The room was to be stocked with food, first-aid supplies, water, towels, candles, matches, bicarbonate of soda, and bleach. Shops in the West Bank and Gaza quickly sold out of their stocks of these items, as well as the adhesive tape for sealing the windows that the Palestinians called *luzaik Saddam*—Saddam's tape. The Glocks made the same preparations.

The day the war broke out, a total curfew was imposed on the Palestinian territories. The curfew was to last forty-five days, imprisoning the population in their homes. IDF soldiers were permitted to fire live rounds at anyone violating the curfew. Every third day, residents were allowed four hours to buy such food as was still available in the shops. The temporary lifting of the curfew was announced through loudspeakers on army jeeps cruising through the streets. One day, the wily Glock managed to get through the roadblocks and turned up at the el-Farabi house, to offer an astonished Ibtisam el-Farabi a box of essential groceries.

On the second day of the war, an Iraqi missile hit Tel Aviv. By this time, Saddam Hussein had declared that he would withdraw from Kuwait if Israel would withdraw from the West Bank and Gaza, a promise that no one except the Palestinians believed. This declaration roused Palestinian public opinion jubilantly and unanimously in favor of Iraq, a sentiment of desperation for which they were to be collectively punished after the war by the Israelis, the United States, and the rich countries of the Arab world who had been the benefactors of the PLO. Hanna Siniora, editor of the newspaper *al-Fajr*, explained the Palestinians' support for Iraq as follows: "When a drowning man is thrown a lifeline, he doesn't worry about the identity of the person who has thrown it." Once again, the Palestinians found themselves cast in the role of Cain, this time for what the rest of the world perceived as their support for the Iraqi dictator's invasion of Kuwait.

Imprisoned in their homes during the day, at night the people would stand on their roofs and cheer the Iraqi missiles streaking like fireworks across the sky toward Israel. At last, they said, someone seemed to be taking their side.

The same day Albert wrote the letters to his sons, he sent an angry letter to his sponsors in the United States, the Evangelical Lutheran Church in America (ELCA). He deplored their decision to order their missionaries, of which Glock was one, to leave the country for their own safety. "I do not think we can leave just now under any circumstances," he wrote. "We really do not wish the people we work with to think that we will run when the situation is threatening. It is precisely at these times when sticking with the job, the people, the problems that it counts most."

All the foreign institutions in Jerusalem and Amman had closed and sent their people home, including the Albright and other archeological institutions. Glock's stand was a lonely one, and he continued to explain it in a stream of letters, to his children back in the States, to friends, and to his employers, to whom he wrote with increasing intemperance. The officials in the Division of Global Missions of the ELCA cannot have enjoyed reading the protests of their awkward archeologist.

"Our credibility is at stake," he wrote in one of several missives he sent to the church, protesting the order to evacuate. "I have been here twenty years. It takes time to establish some kind of credibility among people who have suffered much at the hands of western governments. Leaving in the midst of crisis can destroy in a day what it has taken years to achieve."

In one of these letters he made a point that illuminated Alice's phrase about her father "walking into his own death." He was fully conscious of the precise type of danger that faced him, yet he chose to defy it. "If there is a war," he wrote four days before it started, "it is likely that being American will be a serious disadvantage. I understand this fully and agree with the anti-American attitudes. The double standard in foreign policy is all too obvious. If we experience a personal attack we have to take it."

He wrote this letter to his son Al Jr. It was a brave, principled stand, but to write this to his son, heedless of the filial anxiety it would provoke, showed the high price Glock was willing to pay to take the Palestinian side. Glock appears to have been willing to cut himself off from his family as a necessary part of being an honorary Palestinian.

He sought to feel as a Palestinian would feel. He joined his feelings with theirs as they watched the missiles of their expected deliverer streak toward the enemy metropolis: militarily, the Scuds were insignificant; their only power was emotional.

"On Friday when the air raid sirens sounded for the 16th time I went to the roof rather than the 'sealed room' to see and to listen," he wrote in a "war diary" he sent to a number of friends. "I was a few minutes too late to see the streaking missile which many in BZ regularly observe. But what I heard was the whistles and clapping of the Arab inhabitants of the Nuseibeh's flats, just below us across Nablus Rd to the west. The sound of gunshot was the answer of an Israeli patrol to this happy response of the Arab population. In BZ it is a shame not to be on the roof soon after the siren alerts to the approach of a missile."

The cheering Palestinians probably neither knew nor cared that when Saddam Hussein was warned by his own military advisers that the missiles his forces were launching might cause Palestinian casualties, he is reported to have said, "I'm not sorting lentils."

REMAINING IN PALESTINE after other foreigners had fled, Glock worked every day throughout the war. A new project that took up a great deal of his time and mental energy was a book on destroyed Arab villages in Israel entitled *All That Remains*. The book is a thick dictionary of detailed information about the 418 Palestinian villages that were destroyed, built over, or left to decay when the State of Israel was created in 1948. A collaborative effort, the book was compiled by a number of contributors, including Glock and, when she returned in the summer after completing her studies in England, Maya el-Farabi.

The book, published a few months after Glock's death, is unrelentingly bleak, with page after page of black-and-white photographs of what had once been houses, churches, mosques. Sometimes all that remained was a mound of rubble. In other cases, all traces had been obliterated, and what stood in their place was a neat playground or a stand of trees. Glock's contribution was to check this mass of detail. He did this in libraries and by making numerous trips inside the Green Line, across the border into Israel, to inspect sites, check facts and grid references, and write original descriptions. It was the kind of painstaking, meticulous work that suited him. And as a non-Arab foreigner he could travel inside Israel without hindrance and without attracting attention.

It turned out to be a larger project than he anticipated: he started working on it in February, and he and Maya were still doing so in August. The material was considered so politically sensitive that Glock would send each new batch of work to Washington, where it was published, via the diplomatic pouch of the UNESCO office in Jerusalem, with the help of a friend who worked there. Whether or not Israeli authorities would have seized this material if it was sent by ordinary mail is impossible to tell, but the precaution shows the paranoia that permeated life in the West Bank. Glock would often write in letters that he could not say more about a certain topic in writing, but would wait until he could see the person face-to-face.

Glock told no one in the Institute of Archeology about the project because of internal politics at Birzeit. Another department had been given the job, but had turned in results that were of an unacceptably low standard and asked for too much money. The Washington Institute for Palestine Studies, which was sponsoring the research, turned instead to Glock, who was willing to do it for nothing. During the course of the summer, Glock was absent so often from the institute on trips into Israel for *All That Remains* that his staff began to feel he was neglecting his duties. They had been kept in the dark about the real reason for Glock's absences.

With the campus closed and the university barely functioning, academic life at Birzeit had almost come to a halt. At the Institute of Archeology, a core of staff and faculty would still turn up at their offices when the conditions of the *intifada* permitted—that is, when there was no strike, or when travel was not made impossible by curfew or closure. But little work was done once people were at their desks; they came to work so they could continue to draw their salaries, as a matter of survival.

Glock was the exception, continuing with undiminished energy. Most of his effort went into preparing for publication the results of the Jenin and Ti'innik excavations. He also continued to teach a small number of students who were on the verge of graduating. He would get angry if the students used the occasion of a strike as an excuse to miss a class. In his view, the new Palestinian archeology was above politics. During and after the Gulf War, the Institute of Archeology became more than ever the personal project of Albert Glock.

As a result, Glock acquired a reputation for arrogance and secretiveness—a dangerous image for a foreigner to have at a time when Palestinian society was in a mood to challenge anything non Palestinian. Over the years he had discouraged his students from talking about their work at Ti'innik, for fear of attracting unwanted attention from the Israeli authorities, and he was careful not to publicize it himself. In the same spirit of caution, he even kept his political views to himself—except in private—though it was clear where his sympathies lay. By the time of the Gulf War, his circumspection was beginning to work against him in local opinion.

———

GLOCK'S FORMER TEACHING ASSISTANT Hamdan Taha returned to the West Bank from Germany in September 1990. His reappearance brought trouble that, in the highly charged atmosphere of the *intifada*, could not have come at a worse time.

Doctoral candidates at Birzeit sign a contract with the administration agreeing to accept a teaching contract at the university, if the university has an opening the candidate is suitable to fill. The purpose of the rule is to ensure that PhDs return to Birzeit to teach after graduating. In 1990, Taha arrived at Birzeit with a wife and a small child, moved into a house in Bir Zeit, and waited until a tenured job became available. For Taha, homecoming was a shock: he left a comfortable life in Germany to return to a country in the last desperate days of the *intifada*, a land of curfews, strikes, and violence, where the jeeps of a foreign occupation cruised the streets.

It would have been natural for Taha to get a permanent position in the Institute of Archeology, and this is what he wanted. The problem was that Glock did not want to give him one.

Glock wanted the institute to concentrate on research, specifically the publication of the Jenin and Ti'innik excavations as the base of scholarship on which the new Palestinian archeology would be built. He also wanted to reduce the institute's teaching load to a minimum until the project was finished. Hamdan, whose strength was in teaching, wanted the institute to concentrate on teaching. Even without a job, Taha made his presence felt. As a teaching assistant, he came to the institute every day and occupied a desk. Relations between Glock and Taha grew acrimonious. When Glock stopped appearing at the institute to avoid seeing Taha, the young scholar complained to the university administration that Glock wasn't doing any work.

Glock tried to solve the problem by finding Taha a job at al-Najah University in Nablus. But Taha didn't want to go to Nablus, where the archeology program wasn't as good; he preferred to stay at Birzeit. He appealed to the administration for support, and they viewed his case sympathetically. Glock dug in his heels and fired off long memos to the administration about why Taha should not be hired.

The conflict escalated. Taha enlisted the support of other staff members at the institute, mainly Walid Sharif and Hamed Salem, former students of Glock who were now his teaching assistants. The atmosphere became poisonous, as Taha and the others demanded that Glock attend staff meetings at which they challenged his direction of the institute. Taha and others were now trying to overthrow their leader. On August 29, 1991, they held a meeting of the governing body of the institute in Glock's absence and voted to nominate a deputy director who would do all the things they felt Glock was not doing. They condemned Glock's repeated absence from the institute, and the resulting "vacuum of administration." They also rejected "the distribution of teaching contracts for the coming term," that is, the fact that Glock was refusing to give Taha the contract he felt he deserved. Glock's Palestinian archeologists were turning against him.

None of what had happened up to this point—the summer of 1991—was unusual at Birzeit. Competition for faculty jobs was always fierce, and if an applicant didn't get a particular job, it was within Birzeit's culture of "democracy" to protest noisily and to attempt every kind of political maneuver. This is what Taha did.

He enlisted the aid of the Birzeit teachers' union, which increased the tension by another notch. The union sent Glock a very stiff letter, noting that he was disregarding university regulations in not hiring Taha, and in addition that he should resign from his position since he was past retirement age (he was sixty-seven). The letter ended with a peremptory demand: "We hope you do this quickly. Thank you."

Glock was already planning to retire. Since he had reached the age of sixty-five, the church had stopped paying his salary, and he and Lois were living on the small income he received from Birzeit. They were making ready to move to a smaller house in the Jerusalem area—on the Palestinian side, of course—where Glock would work on the final publication of the Jenin and Ti'innik excavations. Then el-Farabi would succeed him as director of the institute. It was a bitter irony that at the point in his life when he was making plans to bring his career at Birzeit to a close the institution that he had struggled to build from nothing had turned against him.

He wrote to Alice in September:

I am in some trouble because I have refused to renew someone's contract and for that I am getting all hell. This is not the first time but this time it is more difficult than the last. This time I will probably get a series of newspaper articles against me. This happened once before. But in my judgment the guy was just too mediocre, despite his recent Ph.D. from Germany. And I have known this person for more than ten years.

Glock disregarded the union's demand and continued to oppose hiring Taha. No one notices when an old man is depressed, least of all one like Glock who tended to say less the worse things became, but the conflict was a heavy burden on him. His health worsened: eczema, tension in his shoulders and arms, rheumatoid arthritis, which kept him in constant pain, and fainting spells. He would wake at 2:00 A.M., and not be able to go back to sleep. "Every single night," Lois later recalled, "he would say, 'I've got to take a sleeping pill.'" He would stay up and work on *All That Remains* until morning, then go to the institute where he would have difficulty concentrating. The atmosphere inside the institute must have been awful, judging by the memoranda that Glock kept in his files. His teaching assistants, Walid Sharif and Hamed Salem, barely spoke to Glock and instead communicated with him by memo and in tense, formal meetings, in which they demanded that Glock relinquish what they saw as his autocratic control over the institute. Glock would agree to some of these meetings but duck others.

It may be that in his depressed state of mind he was unable to judge the situation effectively, for his stubborn opposition to hiring Taha verged dangerously on folly. He failed to take into account the supremely important matter of how his attitude was being perceived in the tense and embattled Bir Zeit community. Bir Zeit, and the West Bank, is like an aquarium, in which everyone is visible to everyone else at all times. To be, in Palestine, is to be perceived. Al Glock did not bother to treat this fact with the consideration it demanded, and this was to prove a tragic mistake. "He was unquestionably a top-notch scholar, but he didn't have much modesty," recalled Albert Aghazarian, Birzeit's public relations director. "As far as he was concerned, he was the sole pillar of the archeological institute. It was his turf, his territory, and he was calling the shots—no one else."

As the conflict dragged on, the perception inevitably began to circulate that Glock, a foreigner, was denying a job to a Palestinian in a department whose work was politically sensitive to Palestinians: his efforts over the years to make Palestinians see the importance of archeology to their cultural survival were now turning against him. Glock's insistence on his own high standards had already been translated into a perception at Birzeit that he had fired a lot of people, all of them Palestinians, and even that he was *against* the development of Palestinian archeology because he was not interested in the fine arts of Islamic civilization: most people saw archeology exclusively as the study of antiquities—the art treasures of Palestine, not the garbage of refugee camps.

Glock likened his situation to a scene in a Greek tragedy where ungrateful offspring destroy their father. He should have seen that it looked very bad to let this particular perception take hold in the fourth year of the *intifada*, in which Palestinians were trying to shake off everything that was foreign and build their own institutions. A year earlier, describing in a letter his frustration with Walid Sharif, he wrote, "Firing people during the *intifada* has become taboo." He was perceptive enough a year earlier; why didn't he follow his own advice now?

The teachers' union had been careful not to express the dispute as a matter of a foreigner denying a job to a Palestinian, but once the politically powerful students' union took it up, they saw it as precisely that. By this time the administration had appointed a committee to arbitrate the dispute. Taha's students demonstrated outside the trustees' building in Ramallah when the committee was meeting, to show their support for their teacher. Inside the trustees' building, Glock continued to insist in his wheedling midwestern accent that Taha was not up to the standard the institute required.

"Did you see his PhD? It's totally worthless!" he is reported to have said. One of the committee members pleaded with him, "Al, why don't you just let him teach one course?" Still Glock refused to budge. Then someone said, "Al, look out the window." The students sitting in front of the building in support of their teacher could be seen on the steps. But Glock would not give in. Glock and el-Farabi later wrongly accused Taha of organizing the demonstration.

The university was to open, with a new semester, in November— later than usual, but in the latter days of the *intifada* the normal academic calendar had long since been abandoned. Until this point, the conflict had remained an internal dispute over hiring. But when the semester began, the issue took a further, dangerous turn.

Fathiya Nasru, a professor in the Education Department, published a strident article in the Jerusalem newspaper *al-Quds* that took the dispute out of the confines of the university and into the Palestinian street, the larger domain of public opinion. Nasru had a reputation as a firebrand who affected an air of professorial gravitas, and had persistently and noisily criticized the Birzeit administration for its policy of hiring foreign teaching staff. This was despite the fact that the small group of Europeans and Americans who taught at Birzeit were among the most loyal members of the Birzeit faculty, and the majority had been at the university for many years. They were politically active and were always ready to defend the university when it was under threat by the Israelis. The administration supported them because they were loyal and offered students diverse intellectual perspectives. Critics like Nasru argued that the foreigners were hired because they were more tractable as employees than Palestinians.

Now people were talking about the hiring dispute in the backseats of shared taxis, in coffee shops, in houses where groups of women met to do embroidery. No one outside Birzeit had ever heard of Albert Glock until this point, and all they knew about him now was that he was a villain, a foreigner who was denying a qualified Palestinian a job and breaking university rules. Glock himself had written to a friend some months earlier that at Birzeit there was no boundary between the university and the rest of the West Bank, that the politics of Birzeit and the politics of Palestine merged indistinguishably together. In a social climate where people were eyeing the *intifada*'s enemies with vengeful intent, Glock was now in an exposed, lonely, and vulnerable position. After one particularly heated meeting of the teachers' union, in which Glock was attacked by speaker after speaker, his loyal graduate student Hamed Salem stopped him outside the el-Farabi house and warned him of the danger he was now in. Glock had, in the jargon of Palestinian political science, lost the street.

The day the article appeared, November 15, 1991, Glock wrote a letter to Huda el-Farabi, Maya's younger sister. He mentioned the situation, but only after a longer discussion of his trials with his laptop computer. "Classes are beginning. But the problem of Hamdan Taha remains. It should be solved one way or the other this weekend. But problems here seem rarely to be truly 'solved.' I must also add that this affair has brought to the surface feelings that have long lain hidden and are now in the open and those feelings are disappointing in the extreme. If Hamdan is hired and assigned to the Institute I will probably resign. If he is put elsewhere, OK, at least for now."

What Glock meant by "it should be solved one way or the other this weekend" was that he had, at last, succumbed to the pressure of his academic colleagues and very reluctantly agreed to a compromise whereby Taha would be given a contract to teach courses in history at the institute. By this time, though, it may have been too late.

MEANWHILE, the social atmosphere in the Occupied Territories was turning violent. An autumn of strife was turning into a winter of knives, guns, and Molotov cocktails, in addition to the familiar stones. Young men were now running out of control, independent of the political leadership of the uprising. Unpredictable vigilante units—made up of youths who shared a violent, adolescent idea of justice and a morbid enthusiasm for bodybuilding and kung fu—had seized the leadership of the *intifada*. In response, the Israeli army had become paranoically trigger-happy, making increasing use of live ammunition in the daily confrontations. On November 15, the day Fathiya Nasru's article appeared in *al-Quds*, which was also the day the semester began at Birzeit, IDF soldiers shot dead a masked youth, one of a group painting slogans on a wall in the Old City of Jerusalem. Similar reports had become a daily occurrence.

In the midst of all this, Glock went about his business, driving his familiar blue VW van along his usual routes, from Beit Hanina through Ramallah to Bir Zeit. Many people had come know the vehicle and the eccentric professor behind the wheel.

Two weeks after Birzeit resumed classes, a military order was issued closing the university once again, and until further notice.

———

AT THE BEGINNING OF DECEMBER an incident took place that was typical of this time for its violence and for the harshness of the Israeli response. Both sides were weary with the *intifada*, and their blows against the other grew increasingly vicious as their frustration with the conflict reached the point of exhaustion. On December 1, two Israeli settlers from the settlement of Ofrah, north of Ramallah, were driving through al-Bireh, a town contiguous to Ramallah, when their car was shot at. One of the bullets hit the driver, who was seriously injured in the head. He later died in the hospital.

The Israeli response was severe. Ramallah and all Palestinian villages within a wide radius were immediately put under curfew, with an order that anyone on the street be shot on sight. Determined to find those responsible for the attack, the security forces fell heavily, conducting house-to-house searches that had the effect of collective punishment on the entire population of the Ramallah area. Few people could remember a heavier curfew. There were military roadblocks at every crossroads. Soldiers burst into houses, throwing furniture into the streets, shooting randomly into the air, arresting dozens of people. The soldiers were accompanied by plainclothes General Security Services (GSS) officers, who thoroughly interrogated the occupants of every house they entered, demanding information about who lived there, where they worked, whom they knew, and checking identity cards. According to some estimates, 150 people were arrested and taken to the police headquarters in Ramallah where they were interrogated further and held for three to five days.

Meanwhile, Israeli settlers in the area took the law into their own hands, rampaging through the streets of Ramallah, smashing car windshields and shop windows, and scattering a crudely worded but threatening leaflet in Arabic that read, "To the residents of Ramallah and al-Bireh: Following the recent dangerous incident here, we, the Jews living in this area, will not allow Jewish blood to be shed. We will not be prevented from doing what we have to do."

The curfew lasted well into the new year. Palestinians were not allowed to leave their houses, no trucks were allowed to bring fresh food to markets, and UNWRA employees were barred from going to work. Even ambulances were stopped. Eventually, five people were arrested—four men and a woman—members of the leftist Palestinian Front for the Liberation of Palestine. One of them died under interrogation, in all likelihood tortured or beaten to death. The rest were sentenced to life imprisonment.

As ever, Albert Glock observed and recorded what was going on. His VW van continued to ply the roads of the Judaean highlands, and when roadblocks were in place, Glock took his usual sly pride in navigating his way around and past them.

"As you may know," he wrote Maya el-Farabi, who was in America at the time, "here we are in prison. Ramallah has been under an unusually tight curfew for the past two weeks. It may be lifted on Friday but that is mere rumor. This of course means that the University has not been able to function." Glock goes on to describe his efforts to drive to Birzeit during a particularly severe thunderstorm:

At Rantis there was a checkpoint but the boys [soldiers] were so surprised to see me that I merely drove through. When I reached BZ the road in was blocked by a large military vehicle. . . . The entrance to Jalazun was guarded by a heavy contingent of military. . . . It was so foggy I could hardly see. I assumed there would be a checkpoint but it was my last and only hope. Sure enough, it popped out of the fog. On the right was a plastic shelter in which three soldiers shivered. They yelled at me to stop. One came to the window on the driver's side. It was raining so hard that when I showed him my passport, neither of us could say much. He let me go. Why, I do not know. So I got to BZ, delivered some vital supplies and left. It took 100 kms to drive the usual 20 kms.

That winter, Glock knew he was a potential target for violence, but it is impossible to know if he suspected danger from a particular quarter. Lois recalled that he began to take precautions with his van, which was always parked in plain view outside their house in Beit Hanina. He would check it carefully before getting into it, looking underneath as if he feared someone might have planted an explosive, although car bombs were never a feature of the *intifada*. He and Lois had a feeling they were under surveillance. They became conscious in a way they had not been before of the young men who sat at the bus stop across the street from their house, or who out of curiosity came up the driveway to look through Glock's study windows. He began to vary his usual routes.

Christmas came and went, and in the new year Glock resumed work at the institute. He was still deeply depressed over the Taha issue. On January 12, he wrote three letters to Gabi Baramki about the dispute. In one of them he wrote, "If Hamdan is hired, I will probably resign." He never sent the letter. Perhaps he had come to terms with the arrangement. No one will ever know. A week later, on a cold and rainy afternoon, Albert Glock made another routine journey from Jerusalem to Bir Zeit. He stopped at the el-Farabi house, parking his van outside. As he walked down the driveway, a man with his face wrapped in a *kaffiyeh* appeared behind him and shot him three times.

PART
II

"As in all good science
we do not favor one answer or the other."
—ALBERT E. GLOCK

CHAPTER TEN

TWO YEARS AFTER Albert Glock was murdered, I came across an article in an academic publication, the *Journal of Palestine Studies*, entitled "Archeology as Cultural Survival: The Future of the Palestinian Past." The article attracted my attention because it was unusual for the *Journal* to publish on archeology: its usual concerns were political science and history, and detailed accounts of the latest diplomatic convolutions in the never-ending struggle for the place known variously as the Occupied Territories or Palestine, a subject which had alternately fascinated and repelled me over the years. I had never heard of the author, and I turned to the biographical footnote, which took up most of the first page. It stunned me.

Albert Glock, an American archeologist and educator who was killed by an unidentified gunman in Bir Zeit, the West Bank, on 19 January 1992, wrote this essay in 1990. . . .

Dr. Glock spent seventeen years in Jerusalem and the West Bank, first as director of the Albright Institute for Archeology and then as head of the archeology department of Birzeit University, where he helped found the Archeology Institute.

A brief review of the facts connected with his unsolved murder is in order. Dr. Glock was shot at close range (twice in the back of the head and neck and once in the heart from the front) by a masked man using an Israeli army gun who was driven away in a car with Israeli license plates. It took the Israeli authorities, who were nearby, three hours to get to the scene. Apart from giving a ten-minute statement, Dr. Glock's widow was never asked about his activities, entries in his diary, possible enemies, and so on. The lack of Israeli investigation into the murder of an American citizen is perhaps the most unusual feature of the case. . . .

Finally, the U.S. authorities, including the FBI, have not responded to repeated requests by the Glock family to look into the assassination or to ask the Israelis to do so. Prospects for solving the case thus appear remote.

The footnote contained volumes of subtext. The way it was written—in a tone of muted outrage—suggested that Glock was killed by some sort of Israeli hit squad (the gun, the license plates, the lack of investigation). But why would an Israeli hit squad want to kill an archeologist?—especially an *American* archeologist, even one with obvious Palestinian sympathies? Why, for that matter, would *anyone* want to kill an archeologist?

I read the footnote again. What did the writer mean by "the lack of Israeli investigation"? Was there no Israeli investigation at all—or that there was no *successful* Israeli investigation? Above all, who was Albert Glock? Why was the former director of the prestigious Albright Institute teaching at Birzeit University, a chronically underfunded and embattled Palestinian university? A foreigner would be teaching there only if he had a serious commitment to the Palestinian cause: one would hardly consider it a place one went to advance a career. What had brought Albert Glock to Bir Zeit? I wondered.

Three years after reading the article, in September 1997, the footnote brought me to Bir Zeit. I enrolled as a foreign student at the university, in the hope that I might penetrate the mystery of Glock's death by being inside the institution where he taught. With the university's help, I rented an apartment in the town from a Birzeit professor, Munir Nasir. A few weeks later, my partner, Emma, and our three-month-old son, Theodore, joined me. The three of us would bounce back and forth on the road between Bir Zeit, Ramallah, and Jerusalem squeezed into shared taxis, with Theo strapped to my chest in a baby carrier. We carried him about with a little black-and-white-checked Palestinian *kaffiyeh*, given to us by Munir Nasir, wrapped around his neck.

Our apartment overlooked the route that Glock took on his last day, from the institute to the el-Farabi house. To my left, as I stood on the balcony, and just outside my field of vision, was the old town of Bir Zeit, the old campus, the Institute of Archeology, and the Greek Orthodox church where a funeral had taken place on the day of the murder. Closer was the stretch of pavement onto which Glock pulled over and waited to allow the procession to pass by. Before me, and occupying most of the view, was a vista of rocky hills. In the distance, on the opposite hill, were the refugee camp of Jalazun, and above it the Israeli settlement Beit El, and to the right of them, on the horizon, the blinking radio masts of Ramallah. Below, across the street, was a municipal trash Dumpster that at night attracted feral cats and by day jangled the nerves as people banged its metal doors open and shut. Behind it was a group of neglected olive trees standing in a clutter of soda bottles.

Still unpacked, but lying open on the tiled floor in the hall, was a suitcase containing a stack of papers: Glock's correspondence, published and unpublished articles, the available documentation of his life, his work, and his death. On a trip to the United States six months earlier, my first step in investigating the shooting, I had been to see Luis Glock, and she had let me copy the papers and computer disks in her late husband's enormous personal archive.

In the evenings I would sit on the balcony, eating grilled chicken from the restaurant across the street, looking out over the activity in the street below, and think that I was attempting the impossible. All societies have secrets that an outsider will never penetrate, and the secret of Glock's death was one held by no more than a handful of people. The headlights of passing cars— the Mercedes taxis and battered pickup trucks—would illuminate me for a moment where I sat. The town looked peaceful enough, yet just down the road, outside the post office where I bought my first Yassir Arafat postage stamps, there were terrible scenes during the *intifada*, scenes of people of all ages getting beaten, shot, and teargased. Now in the same place there were a couple of young Palestinian Authority policemen who had nothing better to do than check the licenses of the taxis that plied the two kilometers to the Birzeit campus. Four years after the murder, and three years after the Oslo accords, the turmoil of the *intifada* had been replaced by a superficial calm. The moment of the murder was lost and buried; it was now ancient history.

———

WITH THE HELP of Lois's notes and interviews I conducted with people who were there, I pieced together an account of what happened in that gray, drizzly January twilight.

Inside the house, in the moments before Albert Glock was shot in their driveway, the el-Farabis were entertaining visitors: an aunt and her two-year-old daughter. Maya and Ibtisam el-Farabi were at home with their parents, Umm Adnan and Abu Adnan. The two sisters were busy trying to keep the toddler amused, while their parents sat on the sofa and looked on. Maya had returned from the dentist earlier and had just come indoors from the garden with the little girl, and Ibtisam was in the basement, looking for a music cassette to play for her. Then they heard the shots.

Ibtisam stopped, listened, and thought, "the soldiers are in the village." But she continued to look for the cassette. After four years, the *intifada* had fallen into a familiar pattern of conflict, in Bir Zeit at least: boys would throw stones at the army jeeps patrolling the town, and the soldiers would shoot in response, either live rounds into the air, or plastic-coated bullets. It was her family's practice to wait for a few minutes after the shooting had stopped before venturing outside to look. The last thought in her mind before she heard the shots was to notice that there were fifteen minutes until the start of a radio program she wanted to hear. So she was sure that the shooting took place at about 3:15 P.M.

When her sister Maya heard the shots, she rushed outside and saw Albert lying on his back on the concrete, his chest spattered with blood. She dashed back indoors, shouting to the little girl to stay inside. Then she ran to the kitchen, where the window faces the driveway, and now saw a figure walking slowly and calmly up the drive toward the gate, then disappear from view: a young man wearing jeans, a leather jacket, and masked with a *kaffiyeh*.

A neighbor in the house across the street said later that she saw a white Subaru with yellow Israeli license plates waiting up on the road near Glock's van. Seconds after the shots were fired, a man with a leather jacket got into the van, followed by another man who was standing nearby, possibly acting as lookout. The car drove off toward Ramallah.

Ibtisam was in the basement for seven minutes. When she came upstairs with the cassette in her hand, she heard her sister say, "They killed him." For a long moment, Ibtisam couldn't comprehend what Maya was saying. Everything seemed unreal. Everyone froze.

Ibtisam—who was wearing pajamas—went outside to the supine body of Dr. Glock, lifted his hand, searched for a pulse, but felt nothing. The skin on his hand was pale, and the nails were blue. There were bloody wounds in his chest and under his right ear, and cuts on his nose and chin. He was lying with his arms outstretched. She pinched his face and called his name, but there was no response. A plastic bag with a partly eaten *ka'ak simsim* lay beside him. Light rain was falling. She went in and fetched a blanket, covered Glock's body with it, and ran out to get help. (The el-Farabis had applied for a telephone seven years earlier and were still waiting.) Still wearing only her pajamas, she stood in the road and tried to flag down a passing car to take her into town so she could telephone for help, but although a few cars passed, none would stop. So she walked down the road to a cousin's family's house, where there was a telephone, and there she made a stream of frantic calls, as if Glock was not already dead and might still be saved.

She dialed a hospital in Ramallah, but there was no answer. She called two other hospitals, and still no one answered. Finally she called Gabi Baramki, who was taking a nap at home. Glock was expected at their house in about half an hour. Instead, Ibtisam told Baramki that Dr. Glock had been shot and asked him to come immediately.

"Get me an ambulance and a doctor," she said.

Ibtisam hurried outside again, through the drizzle, and got a ride in a shared taxi to a pharmacy in the center of Bir Zeit. The pharmacist, Musa Alloush, was well known in the town for his knowledge of the town's families and as a collector of local history. He left her alone in the shop while he set off in his car to get a doctor.

Ibtisam sat alone in the pharmacy, shivering in her pajamas, and waited for as long as she could bear to. After about forty-five minutes, she returned to the house, where she saw a lot of people coming and going, and noticed that a municipal ambulance had arrived. By this time it was dark and raining more insistently, and the body was still lying on the concrete driveway, covered with a blanket.

AT THE GREEK ORTHODOX CHURCH, the funeral procession had arrived, and the ceremony was in progress. The deceased was a member of the Nasir clan, a large, old, respected family in Bir Zeit, who could trace their ancestry back to the settlement of the town by Christians in the sixteenth century. With backing from the Anglican church in Jerusalem, the Nasir family founded what is now Birzeit University in 1924 as a school for local children, and it grew over the decades from a secondary school to a teacher-training college and finally into a university. The congregation attending the funeral was so big that people spilled out of the church and into the road in front of it.

Munir Nasir (who would later be my landlord) was one of those who couldn't fit into the church, and was standing outside as the service proceeded, with its grave, mystical Byzantine music. Munir was a biology professor at Birzeit. He and his wife, Sumaya, were well known in the university and in the town. When the military administration closed all Palestinian schools as a way of breaking the *intifada*, Munir and Sumaya organized improvised primary schools with volunteer teachers.

A few years earlier, Munir Nasir and Glock had worked together on a project to survey, document, and restore the Ottoman buildings of the old city of Bir Zeit. Nasir had represented the university in negotiating with the owners of some of the traditional courtyard-centered houses in the old city to rent and renovate them. The project was never completed—the inhabitants lacked the academics' enthusiasm for the old buildings—but Glock continued to use the survey of the old city in his courses for undergraduates.

Nasir was standing with another member of the clan, Yusuf Khoury, an engineer. A teacher Nasir knew jostled up to him in the crowd. Before he spoke, Nasir noticed the expression of agitation and anxiety on the man's face.

"Don't you know?" he said. "Dr. Glock has been killed."

"Really?" he demanded. "Where? What happened? When?" Nasir was reminded of the moment of alarm sometime earlier when he heard that his son had been shot. At first, he didn't believe it.

"But it's true," the messenger said. "I just heard it a few minutes ago from someone who passed the el-Farabi house. There's a big crowd outside."

Nasir glanced at his cousin, and the two of them left the church and drove to the el-Farabi house. They arrived five minutes later, and saw the body lying cruciform at the bottom of the concrete ramp, covered in a blanket.

Gabi Baramki was there, stooping over the supine body of Albert Glock, with his hand against his neck, attempting in vain to feel a trace of a pulse. He and Haifa had driven to the house as soon as he had finished talking on the telephone with Ibtisam.

"I think I can feel something," Baramki said.

"Let me try," Nasir said.

Baramki stepped back, and Nasir crouched down and felt the dead man's neck. It was still warm. The eyes were closed, the mouth partly open, the hands loosely clenched. The skin was still the same color it would have been in life.

"There is no pulse," Nasir said.

"I am sure I felt something," Baramki insisted.

Munir put his hand back and held it there for a moment. Then he said, "It was your own pulse you were feeling."

———

WHEN GABI AND HAIFA BARAMKI HAD ARRIVED at the el-Farabi house, they found an ambulance waiting, with the mayor of Bir Zeit, Yaqub Ziadeh, and the driver standing glumly beside it. The mayor had called the military governor in Ramallah as soon as Ibtisam had called him, and the military governor told him that the body must not be moved until an army unit arrived at the scene. A firearm had been used in a Palestinian area. This raised the attack from an ordinary crime to a matter of "security."

As soon as they heard this, the Baramkis argued with the mayor and the driver of the ambulance. "At least take him to the army," Gabi Baramki pleaded. "Take him to Ramallah." But they feared the consequences of disobeying and forlornly stood their ground.

A doctor came, pronounced Glock dead, and left. But since Glock had not yet been transported to the hospital, the group gathered around him acted as if his life could still be saved, which by now was merely a gesture of piety. Munir Nasir whispered in the dead man's ear, "It's all right, Al. This is Munir, you are with friends. We will soon get you to a hospital."

Nasir returned home and telephoned all the doctors he knew to try to get one to come to the scene. The doctor who had attended briefly and pronounced him dead refused to return. "There is no use," he said. Another doctor was not at home, but a third agreed, and came to the body, and confirmed what they already knew, that there were no signs of life.

By this time, a crowd of students from the men's dormitory across the road had gathered at the gate, and Nasir tried to enlist a couple of them to help carry Glock into the ambulance. But one student fainted when he saw the body, and another said he could not touch a dead person.

After attending church in Jerusalem, Lois had returned to her house in Beit Hanina and went back to work packing the household things into boxes for the move into a smaller house nearby. Around five o'clock, as it was getting dark, the telephone rang. The caller was Samia Khoury, a friend of Lois's. She had been attending the funeral at the Greek Orthodox church when she heard the news, and the task of notifying Lois had fallen to her. Khoury asked Lois to come immediately to her house near the university's new campus. "I could tell from her tone of voice that it was something important," Lois said.

"Why don't I come straight to Birzeit?" she asked. That was where Albert was working, after all.

"No," Khoury said. "It won't do any good."

In that short conversation, Lois slowly began to comprehend Albert was dead. There was nothing for her to do. Samia confirmed that Albert was dead, that he had been shot, and that the police were coming. So Lois stayed where she was; in a daze she called the children in America.

MEANWHILE, Gabi Baramki called the American consulate in East Jerusalem, thinking that someone from there should come to the place where one of their citizens had been shot, if only to observe the police investigation. Baramki may have been thinking that an official American presence would put pressure on the Israeli authorities to give the shooting some degree of special attention. But it was a Sunday, and the weekend of the Martin Luther King holiday. None of the consular staff was available, and it was not consular policy to do what Baramki was asking.

Gabi Baramki was trying to take charge, as the el-Farabis had retreated into the house, too shocked to do anything. He saw Glock's glasses lying beside the body on the concrete. He picked them up and brought them into the house, where he put them on top of the television set. The glasses later disappeared, turning up again at the autopsy. He also noticed that the lights of Glock's VW van were still on, so he turned them off and took the keys from the ignition. He waited for the army to arrive.

Baramki expected to hear the army jeeps within minutes. He knew, with every other Palestinian in the West Bank, that the Israelis took gunfire in the territories very seriously. They would descend like a hammer, declare a closed military area, and impose a curfew. Then there would be house-to-house searches; the young men would be rounded up and interrogated, ordered to stand in lines by the road. This was the pattern during the *intifada*. It had happened the week before, near Ain Sinya, a village a few kilometers north of Bir Zeit, when shots were fired at a bus carrying Israeli settlers, which was an escalation from the usual attack with stones. The response was swift and severe. In these latter days of the uprising, the soldiers' nerves were frayed and their patience was exhausted, and the Israeli public was clamoring for an end to it all, one way or another.

But now, nothing. Hours were passing, and yet there was no trace of the army, even though Baramki had seen jeeps at the checkpoint when he drove in from Ramallah. What were they doing? He got into his car and drove past the new campus, and halfway to Ramallah, but there were no patrols on the road, so he turned back.

By this time it was dark, and the blanket covering Glock's body was damp with rain, but no one was allowed to move it.

The smell of blood attracted cats and dogs. Ibtisam shooed them away, just as she was shooing away the crowds of rubber-necking students who had gathered at the gate. She was shocked by the students' mood: they knew that it was Dr. Albert Glock who had been shot, yet they regarded his dead body with what seemed like fascination rather than grief.

Word of the shooting spread quickly into the town and beyond. Old people rushed back indoors for safety. The response of young men was the opposite: to get out of their homes and go down into the rocky valley so they would not be in their houses when the Israelis came.

Gabi Baramki went home to telephone the Birzeit Public Relations Department, to dictate a press release. The shooting had already been snapped up by the news media, and at least one Israeli TV station was planning to put the story on its main evening news program. It was important to get Birzeit's version out quickly. (The first journalist to arrive at the el-Farabi house was a local stringer for an Arabic newspaper, a student at Birzeit. She tried to force her way into the house, determined to take a photograph, but Ibtisam kept her out.) Baramki then drove back toward Birzeit, to look out for the army. At about six o'clock, he saw a convoy of military vehicles near the junction that led to the new campus. He stopped alongside the vehicle at the head of the convoy and rolled down his window.

"It's high time you came," Baramki said to the commanding officer, sitting in the passenger seat of the first vehicle. He addressed him in English. Baramki had deliberately never learned Hebrew, and he spoke to soldiers in either English or Arabic. It was strange to be almost pleading with the soldiers to come; and yet on this extraordinary occasion when he did want them, they had taken three hours to arrive.

"Do you know where we are supposed to go?" the officer said. Baramki turned his car around and led them to the house.

There were two vehicles; one from the Israeli police, one from the IDF. The police never went into potentially dangerous areas without an army escort.

About twenty soldiers and police officers spilled out of the vehicles. Half of them stayed up on the road, keeping watch. The other half came into the house. An army captain from the Civil Administration headquarters took charge. He sent away the gawkers at the gate and anyone else who didn't seem to have any business there.

THE CAPTAIN ORDERED the members of the el-Farabi family back into the house while the police investigators examined the scene of the murder. The el-Farabis couldn't see what happened next, although it seemed that the soldiers were operating a robot around the body, to check it for explosives in case it were booby-trapped. Then the investigators took photographs of the body where it lay. Inside the house, the family could hear the popping of flashbulbs.

Because it was dark now, the police officers examining the body took a lamp from the house. They spread out plastic sheeting around the body. Looking through the window, Abu Adnan saw a footprint on Glock's back when they turned him over. He also saw the officer reach into Glock's mouth and remove a bullet.

The officers cut Glock's clothes off him, and put them into plastic bags, and wrapped the body in a blanket. They took his wallet and the contents of his pockets: 250 Israeli shekels and a bunch of keys. Two or three 9 mm bullet casings lay on the right-hand side of the body. The police picked them up and put them into plastic bags.

Meanwhile, each member of the family present during the shooting was taken aside separately and questioned. They asked Ibtisam where she worked, what she had seen. She told them she no longer worked at the institute and now worked for the United Nations in Jerusalem. She explained that she'd been in the basement when the shots were fired.

The army brought with them a doctor (a civilian on reserve

duty), who made the official pronouncement of death. Sometime after seven o'clock, the army captain allowed the body to be taken away. The ambulance that finally took Glock's body was from the Ramallah Fire Brigade. It took him directly to Abu Kabir, the Israeli forensic laboratory near Tel Aviv, where all the fatalities of the *intifada* ended up.

After they had been questioned, the family members were allowed out of the house. Abu Adnan went outside and asked the army captain if he was going to impose a curfew.

"There is no need," the officer said.

Later Abu Adnan overheard two of the soldiers talking. One of the soldiers was a Russian immigrant. The native Israeli was explaining to the Russian the differences among military pistols. "There are two types. With one type, the empty shells eject from the top of the gun, like this. The other type ejects the shells sideways, to the right. That's the kind that was used here." Abu Adnan recalled the exchange because it suggested to him that an Israeli weapon had been used.

The captain approached Yaqub Ziadeh and spoke to him in Arabic.

"You have nothing to fear," he said. "You will be okay here in Bir Zeit," meaning there would be no collective punishment on the town because of the shooting.

They left after eight o'clock. Gabi Baramki remembered one of the policemen saying to him as he was leaving, "If you find any more shell casings, let us know."

After the police and the soldiers had gone, an el-Farabi cousin came to the house and washed the blood off the concrete with a hose, to keep the cats and dogs away.

GLOCK'S BODY WAS TAKEN to the Greenberg Institute for Judicial Medicine at Abu Kabir and kept on ice overnight. Glock had been dressed in gray trousers, blue underwear, brown shoes, and dark blue socks, the pathologist noted. One lens of the victim's glasses was missing, and his stomach contained a porridgy material: the *ka'ak simsim* he'd partly eaten earlier that day. The body showed the wear and tear that would be expected of a man of Glock's age.

His heart was in good condition. His lungs were a bit gray from smoking.

One bullet had entered the back through the right shoulder, passed through the right lung, the heart, and the liver, and exited through the lower ribs on the left-hand side. Another bullet entered under the right cheekbone (zygomatic bone), passed through the skull and the brain, and came out on the left-hand side of the neck. The paths of both bullets sloped downward, which indicated that the gunman had fired from a position higher than his victim. This made sense: Glock was walking down a slope at the time, and the gunman fired from the top of the slope. A third bullet entered his right shoulder from the front and emerged at the back of the body. This third bullet was fired from below to above, indicating it was shot at a different angle, that the body was in a different position when this bullet entered. The entry and exit wounds were clean— "no marks of powder burn, soot and/or fire effect"—which shows that the gunman was not using hollow-point bullets. Hollow-point bullets expand on impact and leave messy wounds as they pass through. They tend to be used by police officers because they bring the victim down quickly. The absence of these markings suggests that a military (rather than police) weapon was used: military weapons fire solid bullets, which leave clean exit and entry wounds.

It is hard to tell for sure which bullet was fired first, but the gunman may have fired first at Glock's back, as he was walking down the concrete slope. This shot—which entered the right shoulder— then turned him around so that the bullet fired the next instant hit his right cheek. Glock fell forward, onto his face, onto the concrete, wounding his nose and forehead. Then—and this depends on how much time elapsed between the first two shots and the last—Glock turned over where he lay, with his feet toward the gunman and his head away from him. The killer fired a final bullet into Glock's right shoulder before he made his escape in the waiting car. Whether Glock turned over in a spasm, or was turned by the gunman before the last shot, is unclear. In any event, Glock was found lying on his back, face upward, with grazes on his face.

The pathologist estimated that the bullets were fired from a distance "of about one meter."

HAMDAN TAHA WAS in his house in Bir Zeit that afternoon when someone came to tell him that Glock had been shot. When he heard the news, he did something unusual. He performed *yultum*, the traditional expression of grief: wailing and beating himself. It is something that only women do.

OF ALL THE MEMBERS of the el-Farabi family who experienced the events of that day, it was Maya who was to be most deeply affected by the murder. She had seen her mentor shot dead on her doorstep, the professor who in the past fifteen years had guided her transformation from academic lost cause at Birzeit to a PhD from Cambridge University, to the position of his chosen successor as director of the Institute of Archeology. Together, the two of them had labored to establish an independent discipline of Palestinian archeology, an intellectual edifice that would now remain essentially unfinished. The emotional interdependence between them and the shared intellectual outlook that made this work possible were now shattered. A few weeks later, she would take her annual leave from the university, go to England, then to America, and resolve never to return.

The family spent the rest of the night sitting in silence around the gas fire.

CHAPTER ELEVEN

INVESTIGATING A MURDER is like archeology: an archeological excavation presents the investigator with a sparse assembly of mute facts, which he then pieces together to form a convincing and coherent narrative. The same set of facts viewed differently can produce a completely different narrative. The problem with the Glock case was the same one that thoroughly suffused Palestinian archeology: people tended to see what they wanted to see in the facts available, depending on where they stood.

The problem of investigating the murder had an eerie connection with one of Glock's own articles, published in a special issue of the *Birzeit Research Review* in 1987. The issue was a collection of writings by Glock and his team of archeologists and represented the manifesto of Glock's vision of Palestinian archeology. Glock wrote, "The process of excavation is analogous to an autopsy (*post mortem*) in which the pathologist attempts to determine the cause of death and the effects of disease." He continued, "Assume for a moment that there was either objection to performing a *post mortem* or simply that this process had never been done and the culture never produced a trained pathologist. The facts of death, particularly if violent, would become an unverified story, perhaps growing to a legend." That is exactly what happened to Albert Glock: the cause of death—apart from the bare facts of the story—remained undiscovered, and out of this event grew the legend that Albert Glock, the radical archeologist who served a dangerous version of the truth, was killed on the front line of the Israel-Palestine conflict. The legend grew in the void of all that was unknown and unknowable about the circumstances of his death.

IN THE WEST BANK, exploring the world of the murdered man, I found myself surrounded by archeology, practically buried in it. The town of Bir Zeit and its environs were visibly crumbling into oblivion. This was probably mostly due, Palestinians would insist, to the penury into which the Occupied Territories were locked in their status as a land of the conquered. But no amount of prosperity would erase the impression the landscape gave of one era after another of human habitation being present simultaneously, each piled up on top of the other, their level rising rapidly and threatening to bury the present.

Walking downhill from Bir Zeit to the next village, for instance, I passed a number of dilapidated, decaying stone houses, some of them virtual heaps of rubble. Half the buildings seemed to be in this condition. Their roofs had collapsed so they were open shells. They were of an ornate style of construction that I guessed meant they were built around the turn of the last century, with arched doorways and decorative ironwork on the windows. Yet they were ruins, empty and abandoned. Buildings in this condition were a common sight in the West Bank. They may have been the result of the massive earthquake that hit the country on July 11, 1927, with Nablus at its epicenter. It registered 6.4 on the Richter scale, a release of energy approximately equal to a megaton of dynamite. The geological rift that Israel and Palestine straddle has given Western civilization its biblical myths of divine judgment and destruction.

Every village in the locality has an ancient site outside it—a *khirbah*—that an archeologist could declare to be an earlier settlement of the village, part of a continuous pattern of settlement. Usually, they were thickly scattered with potsherds. These are fragments of pottery, which fortunately don't decay. They thus redeem their status as humble objects, the rubbish of the past, by a second life of service, helping archeologists to attach a date to a site. These ruins tend to be used as quarries by villagers living nearby. In a folkloric version of local history, the Bir Zeit pharmacist Musa Alloush (the same pharmacist to whose shop Ibtisam el-Farabi had fled the day Albert Glock was shot) told me that, in the nineteenth century and before, when Palestinian society was torn by the notorious feuds between the Qais and Yaman clans, villages were often destroyed in warfare, and their inhabitants were forced to relocate. It was practical to settle near a *khirbah* because it was a convenient source of stone for building. In this way was the past recycled, and part of the fabric of life. The Palestinians of the hills of the West Bank were surrounded by ancient history, but they were trapped in it, unable to stand outside it and understand it.

Bir Zeit's *khirbah* stood at the summit of a rocky hill that overlooked the village and campus. The hill was topped by a concrete water tower painted with the red, white, green, and black of the Palestinian flag and the name of the Palestinian People's Party. One day I walked up there with a faculty member from the Institute of Archeology, a Palestinian woman named Faida Abu Ghazaleh. From the top of the hill you could see about ten villages or refugee camps, and at least two Israeli settlements. This is the region mentioned in the perennial arguments about the emergence of ancient Israel. Archeologists disagree over how the earliest Israelite settlements appeared, whether by the conquest of the Canaanites (the biblical version, and the popular Israeli version) or by a gradual integration into the local population (the contemporary academic version).

The landscape is one of the most intensively used, inhabited, altered, cultivated, and written about human environments in the world. Today it looks nervous and exhausted, like a mass of dissolving sculpture: every slope graduated by crumbling stone terraces that formed arid little agricultural plots on which olive trees grew in inconsistent densities. There was not one hill in the panorama we surveyed that had not been recorded in someone's history. Ghazaleh told me that some of these terraces were first built in the Iron Age: they were thousands of years old. The new terraces were built the same way, right on top of or parallel to the old ones, in a continuous tradition of building. The oldest ones merged into the dry, rocky, rubbly soil to become indistinguishable from it. It was hard to discern the ancient man-made terracing from the geological layering the limestone naturally produces: archeology merged into geology. This was Albert Glock's stomping ground, the landscape he saw every day.

Faida described the ruins at first as a *khan*, a sort of inn traditional to Islamic societies, built around a central courtyard, where traders could stay with their goods and animals. But as she took me around the site, it became clear what a confusing hodgepodge it was, and that to call it a *khan* was a matter of cultural preference. The hilltop location had attracted one phase of construction and human use after another, possibly since Iron Age times. The latest and most conspicuous was the concrete water tower that also served as a billboard for a political party.

There were tombs hewn into the rock that may have been Iron Age; there were more formally carved tombs, with separate chambers for burial gifts, which may have been Roman. There were reservoirs, two "watchtowers," as she called them, windows, and the traces of regular stone foundations, which indicated separate buildings. These could have been Crusader, Mamluk, or Ottoman in origin. What construction was still standing was gradually collapsing into the ground. Every two months or so another chunk of the arch of the vaulted ceiling of the *khan* falls off.

The latest layers of history attached to the site were modern. Most of the rooms of the ancient structure—low rectangles of rubbly stone enclosing patches of ground—had been plowed by the site's owner into little plots of soil in which the odd fig or olive tree was growing. In one place there was a flat, grassy area that Faida Abu Ghazaleh didn't want to walk on: beneath were the graves of some Jordanian soldiers who had died in a battle here during the 1967 Six Day War and had been buried where they fell. On the other side of the site was a separate stone building that had been filled in with rocks. During the *intifada*, Faida said, it was hollow and had been used as a cache for weapons for a time, but the villagers had filled it in with stones to prevent it from being used for a purpose that would bring them severe punishment from the Israeli military.

The *khan* could have been a church; it had a vaulted roof that had fallen in. It could have been a merchant's house. Its local name was *al-boubaria*, which was suggestive of the Old French word *bouverie*, meaning cowshed. This apparently European name would indicate a Crusader origin. There were shards of Roman pottery lying scattered about in the soil: thin and fired at a high temperature; and of Ottoman pottery: cruder, chunkier, fired at a lower temperature.

There was even a link to the period of the Maccabees, the Jewish dynasty of the second century B.C.E. The site is thought to be mentioned by the Jewish historian Flavius Josephus in his account of the war between Judas Maccabeus and the forces of the Seleucids, the Hellenistic empire that dominated the Near East, in about 165 B.C.E. The Jewish warrior is said to have died here in a battle in which he was greatly outnumbered by the Seleucid forces. The tradition is probably based on a misreading by Josephus of the text of the First Book of Maccabees, an error of scholarship that came to be absorbed into the historical record, and endlessly repeated by later writers.

Faida knew the names of all of the Israeli settlements that we could see, but she would never get any closer to them than we were now, looking at them from a distance. They were completely separate, sovereign city-states, as hostile as warring city-states in the biblical archeologists' vision of Iron Age Palestine. It was, I thought, a landscape as old as murder itself.

POLICE REPORTERS KNOW that most murder victims are familiar with the person who murders them. Most murders are solved within twenty-four hours and occur within the family: husband killing wife, wife killing husband, mother or father killing child (the most common type of murder of all). This death wasn't solved because it wasn't the ordinary type of murder. There was no one close to Glock who would have wanted to kill him, and he wasn't shot in a robbery. Glock's killing was an assassination; one way or another he was killed for what he stood for.

It seemed to me that this made it theoretically possible to unravel the mystery of who did it. By looking at the political thinking of the groups that were violently active in the West Bank at that time, one could make a judgment about the probability of the killing originating in a particular quarter, and for a particular reason. Glock's involvement in a hiring dispute at Birzeit had exposed him publicly in a place and at a time in which political violence was endemic.

The first problem I had to face was that the intended message of this assassination was ambiguous: on one hand, it was a blow to Birzeit, to Palestinian archeology and its implicit claim to the land, to the Palestinians, and to the *intifada*. On the other hand, it was also a strike against a foreign professor who had made himself unpopular at a dangerous time, and whose name, however ironic the misinterpretation, had come to stand for opposing Palestinian aspirations. As an assassination, therefore, the death was a failure: it did not send a clear message to anyone, only a garbled signal.

Still, there was a handful of possible suspects. Their names had been blowing around in the currents of rumor that followed the killing, and each was plausible enough to be taken seriously. I knew I had to assess the data and put forward the best hypothesis, as in archeology. If my hypothesis was convincing, it would withstand criticism. It was time to excavate the final layer: what archeologists call the destruction layer.

CHAPTER TWELVE

IN THE MONTHS that followed, using the information in my
Glock archive and what I gleaned from interviews, I pieced
together an account of what happened in the immediate aftermath of the shooting.

Once Glock's body had been taken to the forensic laboratory
near Tel Aviv, the action shifted to the Birzeit Public Relations
Department, which had to act quickly to manage the almost
immediate influx of reporters. The department's two senior staff
members, who were well accustomed to the task of communicating the university's outrage at the regular shooting and arrest of its
students by the Israeli military, were both out of the country. The
job of announcing the university's official reaction fell to a young
Canadian aid worker, Mark Taylor.

Taylor was at a friend's house in Ramallah when Gabi
Baramki called him. They discussed the reports that had already
been broadcast on the Israeli radio station, Kol Yisrael, which
stated, as if it were a known fact, that Glock had been killed by a
Palestinian, either in a personal conflict or as a result of the dispute at the university. Gabi Baramki wanted to get across that
there was no certainty at that point about who killed Albert
Glock. It was inconceivable to Baramki that a Palestinian could
have done it. He dictated to Mark Taylor the approximate word-
ing and let Taylor do the rest.

The press release that was circulated read, after announcing
the fact of the murder and giving a short biography of Glock,
"According to Israeli news reports, Dr. Glock was shot to death
late this afternoon near the village of Bir Zeit. To the university's
knowledge, there were no witnesses to the attack on Dr. Glock.

The university condemns this act in the strongest possible terms. It further holds that such acts are totally uncharacteristic of the spirit of the Palestinian community, and could only have been perpetrated by enemies of the Palestinian people." The last sentence, carefully vague, directed suspicion toward the Israelis, while allowing that a Palestinian could have been responsible.

The killing made it into the following day's *Jerusalem Post*. This story included speculation about who might have been responsible. "Palestinian sources," the paper reported, "said last night they suspected Glock was slain by Hamas terrorists trying to stop the peace process." Israeli–Arab peace talks were under way in Washington, and the Islamic party Hamas had declared its total opposition to the negotiations, which they considered capitulation to the enemy.

The theories followed a predictable pattern: each side blamed the other. In response to the suggestion that Hamas was responsible, Gabi Baramki told the *Jerusalem Post*, "This man has been with us for sixteen years and has been working with all his strength to serve our people. A nationalist murder? That's impossible."

The *Jerusalem Post* went into greater detail in the subsequent story it published. This one widened the field of suspicion but set it squarely on the Palestinian side. "Two motives for the crime are being discussed around campus [figuratively speaking: the campus had been closed for four years]. The first, say Arab sources, is that Glock was killed either by Hamas or Popular Front activists in order to disrupt the peace process. They also link the timing of this killing to the fact that he was an American citizen and this is the anniversary of the Gulf War." (Glock was actually killed three days after the Gulf War's third anniversary.)

"The second version is that the murder was part of a power struggle among the archeology faculty, one of whom was fired recently. Birzeit president Gabi Baramki denies this emphatically." The Israeli police spokesman persistently lobbed the teargas canister of suspicion into the Palestinian yard: "We're looking at the power games at Birzeit theory," she said.

In turn, Birzeit lobbed the canister back. "We are all in shock about this. He had been with us for many years and was well respected," Mark Taylor said. "I have no doubt that this does not come from the Palestinians."

THREE DAYS AFTER the killing, the PLO broadcast a statement on its Algiers radio station, Voice of Palestine. The statement placed the murder at the forefront of the Israel-Palestine conflict. Glock, the broadcast stated, was the victim of a political assassination because of the political potency of his archeological work. Israel, the report said, was responsible.

> The PLO denounces most strongly the ugly crime of the assassination of the U.S. professor Dr. Albert Glock, head of the Palestinian antiquities department at Birzeit University, where he contributed with his technical research to the refutation of the Zionist claims over Palestine. Zionist hands were not far away from this ugly crime, in view of the pioneering role which this professor played in standing up to the Zionist arguments. This crime provides new proof of Israel's attempts to tarnish the reputation and position of the Palestinian people in American and international public opinion. The PLO extends its most heartfelt condolences to the family and sons [sic] of the deceased, who are residents in Palestine, and to the Birzeit University family.

The PLO statement was one of a flurry of denunciations of the murder that were published in days immediately following the shooting. The clandestine leadership of the *intifada*, the Unified National Leadership, included one in its first bulletin after the incident.

> The Unified Leadership denounces strongly the assassination of Dr. Albert Glock, the head of the archeology department at Birzeit University, who was attacked and killed unjustly. It holds the secret agencies of the Zionist enemy responsible for the killing of Dr. Glock, who gave invaluable services to the Palestinian community, and gives its deepest sympathies to the family of the deceased.

Even Hamas issued a denial, eight days after the killing, in a statement whose main point was to contradict the *Jerusalem Post* report.

These announcements do not represent a considered view. They were verbal gunfire against the enemy. The only kernel of rational suspicion they contained was the nature of Glock's archeological work—"his technical research" in "the refutation of the Zionist claims over Palestine," as the PLO statement put it—and the fact that as a professor at Birzeit he was an honorary member of the Palestinian population.

Gabi Baramki was one of those who felt instinctively that the hand behind the killing was Israeli. He based his suspicion on the length of time the army took to arrive at the scene.

I met him in his house outside Ramallah, the one Glock had visited on his last afternoon. Baramki, a tall, courteous Palestinian patrician, with a thoughtful, donnish manner, was about the same age as Glock. "Israel has a very efficient and effective system of policing. But to come three hours late!" he said. The killing happened at about 3:15. The army didn't arrive until some time after 6:00. Yet when the Israeli police gave a terse list of official answers about the incident to the American consulate a year later, at the request of the Glock family, they claimed that the IDF patrol arrived at 4:05, a discrepancy of two hours. I asked Baramki why the Israelis would want to kill Albert Glock. He answered cryptically, "The Israelis always like to kill a hundred birds with one stone."

He meant, I think, that the killing was intended to create fear among the Palestinian population, to damage Birzeit's reputation, and to create an excuse to close the university permanently. The murder might also serve to frighten the remaining foreign teaching staff at Birzeit into leaving, to spread discord and suspicion, and to weaken Palestinian morale. Above all it removed from the scene a troublesome intellectual who was literally digging up facts potentially embarrassing to the Israelis.

On the last point, digging up the past, an educated Palestinian like Gabi Baramki would have some knowledge to back up his suspicion. Since the occupation of the West Bank began in 1967, Israeli censors had maintained a hawk-eyed vigil for anything that contained a Palestinian version of the history of the country. Hundreds of books had been banned. Recording the Palestinian past was considered an act of sedition.

"But what was the *purpose* of the delay?" I asked Baramki.

"They wanted to give the person who did the shooting time to run away."

From his point of view, given how few facts were known, this was the best explanation available.

It was also strange that the army did not impose a curfew. In the previous month, two severe curfews had been imposed in the Bir Zeit area in response to incidents where guns had been used by Palestinians against Israelis.

Glock himself referred to an incident in one of his last letters: "The curfew on Ramallah was very tight for two weeks and effectively shut down the university. The night-time curfew that has since been imposed, from 5 p.m. to 4 a.m., was lifted for 3 nights, 24–26 December. Then came the order not to use the roof of your house unless to hang washing and then use it for only 2 hours in a day."

Soon after the murder, Baramki "got in touch with the PLO outside. Just to check if they knew anything, to see if it had anything to do with any of the [Palestinian] factions. Because we wanted to know."

Gabi Baramki was a regular visitor to PLO headquarters in Tunis. He would go there to plead for funds for the university. Until the PLO's treasury was depleted by the loss of gifts from the oil-rich Arab states of the Gulf, in retaliation for the Palestinians' support for Iraq in the Gulf War, Birzeit had been funded almost entirely by the Tunis headquarters. Gabi Baramki himself was a mainstream PLO man, aligned with no particular faction but supporting it—like most Palestinians did—as his representative in world politics.

PLO headquarters in Tunis told Baramki they knew nothing about the murder. But they did not let the matter rest, and urged a Palestinian investigation. Baramki organized a committee of inquiry. At the head was a local Fatah politician, businessman, and Arafat loyalist named Jamil al-Tarifi, later to become a member of the Palestinian Legislative Council and Minister of Civil Affairs in the Palestinian Authority. The other members were Mursi al-Hajjir, a lawyer and an associate of al-Tarifi, and two journalists, Izzat al-Bidwan and Nabhan Khrayshah. Most of the work was done by the journalists, and the report itself was written by Nabhan Khrayshah.

The report can best be described as a work of crepuscular forensics. Unable to establish any substantial facts, because the conventions of the conflict prevented the committee from seeking information from the Israeli police, he deduced a suspect— Israel—from the pattern of meaning he discerned in the common knowledge about the case. The report is mainly of interest as a record of the prevailing currents of gossip and rivalry inside Birzeit. Otherwise, it was such a whitewash (and in its English translation, such a muddle to read), that I wondered if Khrayshah knew more than he dared to write.

I called Khrayshah and arranged to meet him one evening in Ramallah. His English was lucid, and his style salesmanlike and shrewd. But he liked to talk, and he was particularly interested in this case. "I accept the weakness of this report," he said. "The purpose of it was so that Arafat could have something in his briefcase to show people on his plane, especially Americans. The report was to clear the Palestinians, so he could say, 'Look, here is this matter of an American citizen who was killed in the West Bank and we are taking it seriously while the Israelis are not. It was a political report."

The report was kept confidential for about two months.

It did not tell Yassir Arafat who killed Albert Glock. As Khrayshah said, it was a political report, intended to supply Tunis with the available knowledge, and to suggest a line for the PLO to take. That was all it could be. Khrayshah didn't find out who committed the murder, and he couldn't even make a convincing guess. No one could. Applying the usual political logic failed to produce a suspect. It was hard to tell what message was being sent by the murder, and who was sending it. If it was a political murder, no one had followed the convention of political murders and "claimed responsibility."

The report was doomed from the start as an impartial evaluation of the available facts. Khrayshah recalled, "We sat down and discussed who might have done it. I said, 'We should look at Hamas and the PFLP. The PFLP was in the union that had been campaigning against Glock.' The others in the committee said, 'No, we cannot do that: these are our people.'

"I said, 'Well if they turn out to be innocent, then they are in the clear. And if they are not, it is not a problem for us. We are the mainstream. It is no problem for us if we investigate extremists.' "

The Fatah loyalists on the committee, led by the politically powerful Jamil al-Tarifi, overruled him. Both radical groups were rumored to have had political justification to assassinate Glock—lately proclaimed a public enemy—in the name of the *intifada*. It was well known at Birzeit that the teachers' union was led by active members of the PFLP, and Hamas by this time had recently entered the business of anticollaborator killings. So the order to avoid looking where something might be found, in the purely political interest of defending the honor of two kindred groups, fatally undermined the credibility of the investigation.

Khrayshah gives an account of the statements that were issued from within Birzeit by the teachers' union, the student council, and the administration, and concludes with the widespread Palestinian view that Glock was murdered because of the political potency of his archeological work, which was intended, as Khrayshah put it, to contradict an Israeli version of the archeology of Palestine.

This Palestinian suspicion, he wrote, was supported by the fact that the PFLP and Hamas both denied the killing. The professionalism with which the killing was carried out, and the fact that the police and their army escort took three hours to arrive at the scene, led him to conclude that, in the absence of any hard facts to the contrary, the Israelis must somehow be responsible. Israel benefited from the killing; Palestinian interests were gravely harmed by it. In closing, Khrayshah was careful to point out that the committee did not approach "the occupation" for information "because it does not recognize the occupation and its various authorities." And besides, the Israelis wouldn't have helped them even if they'd asked.

The only material of any substance is an account of the conflict within the Institute of Archeology, with Albert Glock at the center of it. Khrayshah considers rumors that Glock was killed because he had been responsible for firing qualified Palestinians from the institute. The report recounts campus gossip and other material gleaned in interviews with institute staff and others at the university who knew the dead man. It describes Glock as a "tyrant" in his running of the institute, and records a view that he "worked systematically to kick out all qualified Palestinian academicians in the field of archeology." In fact, Glock did not actually fire many people. But his colleagues and students included several who failed to meet his high standards and who were not appointed to positions they had sought. Among them was Hamdan Taha.

Nabhan Khrayshah's report said that some people thought Glock was a spy for the CIA. This is a canard that every American in an Arab country hears sooner or later. There is no reason that it be taken seriously. (But it points to a powerful irony: that a man who had sacrificed so much to develop a Palestinian-oriented approach to archeology was looked upon with suspicion and dislike by the very people he sought to help.)

Khrayshah's report was a kind of moral fable, concluding that Albert Glock's killing was the natural consequence of fatal flaws in his personality. "Glock was a person who tried to live the life of an individualist—the American dream—in an open society, and you cannot do that here," Khrayshah explained. "That was why he was unpopular." Glock tried to build walls around himself, he said. Khrayshah thought he had an insight into Glock's character and thinking, because he had once taken a course of Glock's at Birzeit and had read a few of Glock's articles. He wrote in the report that Dr. Glock was "mysterious," that "he never liked to appear in public. . . . He never wanted to go public or face the press with his views and [he] always encouraged his assistants not to go into details regarding what discoveries they found. . . . It is natural that this kind of behavior would arouse suspicion among Palestinians."

I asked if this climate of suspicion that had developed around

Glock, especially when he had become unpopular for not hiring Dr. Taha, could have led to his being killed by a Palestinian.

"It could not have been a Palestinian killing," he insisted, in a tone of flat certainty.

"Why not?" I asked.

His gaze drilled into me. "It was too professional. There were two fatal shots, one to the head, one to the heart. The Palestinians don't do it like that. When a Palestinian shoots someone, he just points the gun and goes *bang bang bang bang*."

I suggested that a hotheaded young man, perhaps with brothers who had died in jail, who was acting in the rage of despair, might have killed Glock independently as an anti-American gesture.

"But why would he kill Albert Glock?" he responded. "There are plenty of other blue-eyed people around. And bullets are precious and expensive and hard to get hold of for Palestinians."

He told me one detail I hadn't heard before. Witnesses in houses across the street from the el-Farabi home said the gunman was wearing white sneakers, which were the trademark of both the Israeli General Security Services and the *shabab*, the young fighters of the *intifada*. Sometimes the two sides can't be told apart.

Khrayshah concluded his account of the report by apologizing for it. He couldn't do a decent job, he explained, because the Israelis wouldn't give him the autopsy results and because he was unable to speak to the key people involved in the case. Maya el-Farabi had fallen to pieces during the interview. And Mrs. Glock had left the country, or so he thought (she hadn't). He could not identify the killer, because "there were no clues."

"Look to the archeology," Khrayshah kept saying: that was where the answer lay. The Israelis did it, or ordered it done, he said, because of the danger his work posed to a state so dependent on archeology for its ideological justification. Many Palestinians believe this theory, even though Glock had been in the West Bank on a tourist visa, which he had to renew every three months. If the Israelis hadn't wanted him in the country, all they had to do was reject his visa application. They wouldn't have to give a reason. They didn't need to shoot him.

This Palestinian view of the political potency of Glock's archeological work was darkly reflected in a rumor that began to circulate soon after the murder. The rumor was that Glock was working on an archeological excavation near Nablus, and that he had discovered something big and important, which would somehow undermine the whole Israeli historic claim to Jerusalem. The Israelis killed him to prevent him from revealing his discovery. The story is garbled: Glock never excavated near Nablus, and his work had little or no relevance to Jerusalem. But it showed that, in death, Albert Glock's life had attained the power of myth.

As we left the café, Khrayshah repeated the point he had been emphasizing throughout our conversation, and which to him was the key to the whole thing.

"Remember," he said. "Look at the archeology."

INVESTIGATING THE MURDER was the responsibility of the Israel National Police, but their inquiries ground to a standstill within a few days of the killing. At her daughter's house in New Jersey, Lois Glock had told me of the efforts she had made to press the Israeli police to make some sort of progress. She applied the same quiet conscientiousness that she had brought to helping her husband in his life to the task of politely and persistently lobbying the police and anyone else who might know something about the murder. Motivated by grief and the emotional vacuum of lack of certainty and conclusion, she had waged a patient and unrelenting crusade. Only when she had learned the truth, she said, could she achieve "closure."

Three months after the murder, in April 1992, her son Jeffrey traveled to the West Bank to look into the investigation. The family believed that if Albert Glock had been assassinated in any other Arab country, there would have been stories on it all over the newspapers and television. But Albert Glock was killed in a zone of embarrassing ambiguity for the American and Israeli governments. Through the American consulate, Jeff Glock arranged a meeting with the Israeli police. He met with a foreign liaison officer and the police captain who was in charge of the investigation. They told Jeff that a ballistics test on the bullets recovered from the scene showed, from their markings, that they came from the same gun that had been used three months earlier in a shooting in Ramallah.

The victim of this shooting was a woman, a lawyer named Rasmiyah Quran, they said. Somehow she had fallen afoul of Hamas, who had marked her as a collaborator. (The word Hamas usually used in these cases was "prostitute," which in the sexually paranoiac view of Islamic radicalism was a pejorative label for any woman who had, in their view, transgressed.)

The policemen told Jeff they had recovered that bullet, and that the distinctive rifling marks on it, made as the bullet emerges from the barrel, showed that it came from the same gun that was used to kill his father. The gun was a 9 mm pistol, but they would say no more about it than that. When that gun was used again, and someone was caught, they would make a breakthrough in the Glock investigation. That seemed encouraging at the time, but six years later the police were still waiting for the gun to be used again.

IN THE WEST BANK five years after the killing, I reckoned that if anyone could tell me anything concrete, it would have to be someone from al-Haq, the human rights organization in Ramallah. Throughout the *intifada*, its handful of staff members, mostly lawyers, diligently collected detailed records of incidents of human rights abuse in the Occupied Territories by anyone, Palestinian or Israeli. Since law and order were virtually nonexistent in the West Bank and Gaza, their work was often the only legal defense available to Palestinians. Their offices on Ramallah's main street, in a crumbling building, behind a reinforced steel door, contain an archive of files documenting thousands of individual cases of shootings, killings, arrests, beatings, house demolitions, denials of permits. Whenever a boy was shot in the street during a confrontation with the army, an al-Haq field-worker would try to track down the victim and take affidavits from him and from witnesses, if any were willing to come forward. The data were categorized and quantified. If al-Haq couldn't bring legal actions in defense of the victims of human rights abuses, which it usually could not, it could at least collect information about those abuses and publish the results. The group was at its most active during the *intifada*. Its office was bound to have a record of the Glock case.

I TURNED UP at the office one morning without an appointment and spoke to one of the top officials of the organization, Hussein Deifallah. He was vaguely familiar with the case, but I knew more about it than he did, and he listened intently. After I had finished, he said emphatically and with angry certainty, "This has all the characteristics of an undercover unit killing."

The undercover units were special units of the IDF and the Border Police that were ordered to track down and kill Palestinian activists who were believed to be responsible for acts of violence against Israelis and fellow Palestinians. The units were well known for their knowledge of Palestinian areas, for audacious killings in daylight, and for lying in ambush for their victims. Deifallah's certainty that the killing was the work of an undercover unit emanated from his perception as a Palestinian of total Israeli ruthlessness and of an invisible web of orders, plans, and sinister intentions.

The units first began to make their shadowy appearances in 1988, the first full year of the *intifada*. Their activity increased steadily every year, peaking in 1992, the year of Glock's death. Their method of operation was cunning yet bold. They would dress in a variety of disguises: as masked Palestinian activists, veiled women, day laborers, beggars, even as TV crews and Orthodox Jewish settlers. Some units were trained by actors from professional theater companies. Operating on intelligence supplied by the GSS, members of the unit would identify their target and study his movements. When the "wanted" man was in position—in the street, typically—they would drive up close to him, jump out of their vehicles, surround him, and shoot him at close range. Sometimes they would use cars with yellow Israeli license plates, and sometimes they would use cars with blue Palestinian license plates. Support vehicles—a jeep with soldiers for backup, an ambulance—would be present some distance away. The gunmen would aim for the heart and the head, and they would usually use more than one bullet. The object was to liquidate wanted Palestinians as quickly and efficiently as possible. By avoiding the cumbersome trappings of justice and taking direct military action against the hard core of the *intifada*, the uprising could be defeated and brought to an end, or so they hoped. By the end of 1992, undercover units had killed over 120 Palestinians, half of them in that year alone.

The undercover units were a secret at first: IDF press spokesmen repeatedly denied their existence. Their activities contravened IDF rules of engagement, and too often they shot the wrong man. In November 1991, the policy changed. Israeli authorities began to realize their psychological value: the units were feared, and that fear was a deterrence to violent action by Palestinians. So IDF spokesmen were allowed to acknowledge the existence of the units, but remained secretive about exactly what they did. The fact that Palestinians thought Glock was killed by an undercover unit showed how successful the units had been in creating a mystique of their own effectiveness.

The undercover units were a law unto themselves, acting free from official oversight and accountability. By 1993, there had been only two convictions of soldiers who served in them. In the institutional culture of the units, there was strong pressure on soldiers to produce results, to eliminate suspects as quickly as possible and cross names off their lists. According to a report by Middle East Watch, a sergeant in one unit said that his regional commander would send them a bottle of champagne every time they killed a suspect. "We had five bottles during the time that I was a sergeant," the sergeant said. It all reflected a desperate Israeli frustration to end the *intifada*, whatever the cost.

Certainly, there were a number of coincidences with the Glock case. The gunmen were dressed as Palestinians, and masked with *kaffiyeh*s. They were driving a car with Israeli license plates (although this did not mean much: Palestinian residents of Jerusalem also have yellow license plates, and the border between Jerusalem and the West Bank was easily crossed at that time). The method of shooting was like that used by an undercover unit: at close range, with bullets aimed at the heart and the head. The killing was fast and efficient, and the gunmen made a quick departure. It was chillingly professional.

The mysterious delay of the army and police in arriving at the scene supported this hypothesis. A slow response on their part would avoid the embarrassment of the gunmen confronting the authorities on their own side, and would allow their smooth escape. Someone would have to have given an order to this effect.

Information about the killing later released by the Israeli police to me and to the Glocks was scant and ambiguous—which, to be fair, is usual practice in an open investigation. The police would say only that the empty shells collected at the scene of the murder were of the 9 mm Parabellum type, a bullet casing so common, used in so many types of gun—including those issued to IDF soldiers—as to be the ballistic equivalent of a Bic pen.

"But why would an undercover unit want to murder an American professor, a man in his sixties who was about to retire?" I asked Hussein Deifallah.

"Look. The Israelis had been trying for years to close down Birzeit. But they never had a reason to do so that would be publicly acceptable, especially in America, and internationally. It would be no secret to the Israelis that there had been demonstrations against Glock on the campus: all they had to do was read the Arabic newspapers and listen to their informers. Then when they decided to act it would look like the work of a Palestinian. Anyone who thinks it was a Palestinian is thinking what the Israelis want them to think."

Deifallah denied the hypothesis that the act had been an anti-collaborator killing, carried out by someone who knew about the campaign against Glock, and decided that in not giving Hamdan his job he was an enemy of the Palestinians. It must have looked that way to a hotheaded young man: here was a secretive American whom no one knew much about (and who was therefore a spy), a foreigner who tried to hold back a qualified Palestinian in the highly politicized field of archeology. Glock was preventing the Palestinians from laying claim to their own history. He was therefore part of the Zionist plot, a collaborator who ought to be eliminated. It was not a hypothesis a Palestinian wanted to hear, but it made sense.

"The killing was too tidy," Deifallah said, "too professional.

These anticollaborator attacks are messy. They use axes, for one thing, or knives. Secondly, the people who carry them out usually give a warning to the person first, telling them to desist from whatever they are doing, which usually means cooperating with the Israelis or giving them information." If a warning does not have the desired effect, he explained, a physical attack would follow, and if that didn't work, and the crime of which the collaborator was suspected was grave enough, then someone would take it upon himself to kill him. That was the pattern, at least, and according to al-Haq's statistics, about seven hundred such killings had taken place in the four years of the *intifada,* and they increased in number every year, reaching a peak in 1992.

The Palestinian view, as Deifallah argued it, was that the killing of Glock was part of the Israeli policy of ending the *intifada* by undermining it. As one Palestinian expressed it to me, "'This would be a warning to Americans not to come here to help the Palestinians or see what the Israelis are doing to the Palestinian population—the oppression, beatings, killings, humiliation, and so on. Al was witness to all of this and there weren't too many people that were." There was also the idea that his archeological work was so politically potent, so intellectually effective in challenging the Israeli claim to the land, that he had to be eliminated. All that added up to an Israeli motive.

Deifallah's hypothesis was promising. He had assured me that the archives of al-Haq would provide ample material to demonstrate that Glock was killed by an undercover unit. But it turned out that al-Haq didn't have a file on the Albert Glock case; or if they did, no one could find it. It was like a mirage: a glittering object that vanished as soon as I approached.

FOR WEEKS I COULD get no further with the hypothesis of the undercover units. In al-Haq's entire archive of human rights abuses carried out during the *intifada*, there was no strong evidence to support it, however many files the office staff pulled or databases they consulted. I made two more fruitless visits to al-Haq's offices before I learned that the field-worker who had been responsible for the Bir Zeit area at the time of the murder had gone to work for another organization, taking the institutional memory of al-Haq with him. His name was Khalid Batrawi.

Batrawi worked for an organization a few blocks away from al-Haq in Ramallah called the Mandela Institute for Political Prisoners. It was located in a typically grim Ramallah office building, a door off a concrete stairwell, blasted with a visual din of spray-painted graffiti: red slogans, simplified maps of the whole of historical Palestine, ragged flyers. The secretary smiled and said quietly, "He is here. Wait."

I could hear someone talking on the telephone in the next room. Then the call ended, and Batrawi emerged, wearing jeans and a checked flannel shirt. He was an engineer by profession and did not spend much time in this office. Some Palestinians affect a pompous grandeur once they are in a position of responsibility. They get a large desk and a Mercedes, then do very little work. Batrawi was not of this type. I had come on the chance that I could arrange an appointment; instead, he led me to a bare office with a desk and two chairs.

He said, to begin with, that there was indeed a file on the Glock case at al-Haq. They weren't able to find it because it was in a special category of "open files," meaning unsolved cases. The major part of al-Haq's mandate was to investigate abuses of authority by the occupying power, but since this case could not be proven as an abuse of authority by the occupying power, it fell into a gray area. "We are not sure who the perpetrators are," he said.

"It is one of the more disturbing cases that I have dealt with," he went on. He was the first person who discussed the murder with me without putting any political spin on it.

In a logical, methodical way, as if he were describing an engineering problem, he drew a row of boxes on a piece of paper, and then drew a line between them, dividing the boxes, which represented possible perpetrators, into Israelis and Palestinians. The first box was marked IDF.

"Whether the IDF was responsible or not depends on the level of the investigation. In cases involving the use of firearms, the level of investigation is high. If two Palestinian factions were fighting each other and guns were used—as far as the Israelis were concerned—the gun might be used later against Israelis. So they want to know the source of the gun, who has it now, what kind of gun it is, how much ammunition they have, how many guns. They carry out a big investigation."

He continued: "What if a Palestinian collaborator who is armed by the Israelis, and has a gun license, kills a Palestinian but doesn't report it to the Israelis? The Israelis would announce a curfew, and investigate until they found who was responsible for the incident.

"But if the collaborator shoots someone, and the Israelis know about it, the level of investigation is low. In the same way, if an Israeli soldier shoots someone, the level of investigation is low."

In the Glock case, Batrawi said, "the level of investigation was high." There was an intensive investigation at the site. "On the positive side, they surrounded the area, investigated the same day, and brought in experts. On the negative side, they took no further measures, which means they *might* know who did it: we have that impression, but we can't confirm it."

Batrawi then turned to the Palestinian possibility, and began with the political groups that were active in the *intifada*. "The groups would always claim responsibility when they killed someone.

It made them look heroic. All the political groups denounced and condemned the Glock killing very quickly. But this doesn't mean they didn't do it. At the time, the United Leadership was still functioning. They condemned it, and they would have been able to reach the truth if it was done from within their own organization." But they came up with nothing.

And here Batrawi began to state, sadly and reluctantly, his own judgment of the case. "One can say about this case that the Israelis were not directly involved," he said. I asked him about Rasmiyah Quran, the Ramallah lawyer who was the victim of attempted murder. The Israeli police had told Lois and Jeff Glock they strongly suspected that the same gun was used in the shooting as in Albert's killing, and that Hamas was implicated in both cases.

"Quran was involved in moral problems," Batrawi said euphemistically, which assorts with the report that Hamas attempted to kill her because she was a "prostitute," whatever that meant. The logic of the anticollaborator movement at the time was that immoral conduct was one step away from collaboration with the Israelis. He said there had been three attempts on this unfortunate woman's life.

I brought up the undercover units, and he answered with his words falling into the same deliberate tread of judicious certainty. "Their priority was their own safety," he said. For this reason, there was always a jeep or an ambulance in the vicinity at the time of an undercover unit operation. No one reported seeing a jeep or an ambulance anywhere near the el-Farabi house at the time of the shooting.

Batrawi was spiraling in on the more plausible theory of the uncontrolled local vigilante groups, who could be better described as gangs. "During the *intifada*, there were two types of groups. There were the ordinary groups affiliated to larger organizations, like Hamas. The Israelis were not afraid of these local organizations. They could infiltrate them with collaborators. But they were afraid of local groups not affiliated to anyone. These were [nothing more than] groups of teenagers."

The killing could have been carried out by members of such a group. When I protested that this could not be the case, since the killing was so professional, he disagreed. Unlike other Palestinians I spoke to, he did not regard Glock's murder as particularly professional. "It was an ordinary killing." He shrugged.

Al-Haq concluded, he said, that it was a Palestinian act, but whether it was by a "patriotic" group or a collaborator was not known. (This was different from what Hussein Deifallah had told me.) "The Unified Leadership was not controlling everyone," he said. The likely perpetrators were an uncontrolled group of young men, acting independently of the authority of a political party. It was a very scary time, he said. Young men were out of control. To make his point, he cited an al-Haq figure of 721 inter-Palestinian killings during the *intifada*.

"We have this problem with our young men," he concluded. "Since the *intifada*, they think they have sovereignty. Some of the stone-throwing *shabab* of the *intifada* went on to join the Palestinian police when the PA was established, but many of them did not, and they still hold sway in their villages.

"Lois [Glock] is careful not to believe this, that Palestinians were responsible, but it hurts me more than it hurts her," he said. His face was open and sad, his gaze firm and honest.

STILL, I could not let go of the hypothesis about the undercover units: it had the virtue of simplicity. A few days later, I made a trip to Jerusalem to test it. I crossed the border into a country that seemed a continent away, a journey that a Palestinian from the West Bank could not make now without a permit. In an office in a lovely leafy neighborhood that was more like Europe than the Middle East, I talked to Yuval Ginbar of the Israeli human rights group Btselem. He was the joint author of a report on the activity of the Israeli undercover units in the Occupied Territories during the *intifada*. He spoke in that combination of seriousness and casualness that I took as distinctly Israeli. Ginbar didn't think much of my idea.

"It's too far-fetched," he said. The undercover units acted in a recognizable way, and not like the gunmen in the Glock case as I had described it to him. For one thing, they always had backup vehicles a few hundred meters from the site of the killing. And I already knew there was no report of any military vehicles being in the area when Glock was shot.

An undercover unit would not kill an American citizen, he told me, and risk the consequences of a rift with the United States. The units had other priorities, and these priorities were wanted men with blood on their hands. Apart from their rare mistakes, the units had not deviated from that assignment into wider realms of policy.

"They're evil," he said, "but they're not stupid."

It was a short interview. A too-neat theory had just bitten the dust, I thought as I left the Btselem office. I had to admit that what he said made sense, in the clear light of day. But I was glad to be out of the West Bank for a few hours, at least. I went across the street to a café and ordered a bagel with cream cheese and lox, feeling guilty and self-conscious in my enjoyment of this familiar delicacy.

A NAGGING QUESTION that remained was why the army took so long to arrive at the scene. This was one of the reasons for the Palestinian suspicion that Glock's killing was the work of an undercover unit. Why had the IDF taken three hours to arrive, when usually they would descend in force within minutes after receiving a report that a gun had been fired in a Palestinian area? In so doing, they were giving the gunmen plenty of time to make an easy escape. To Palestinians, it looked like part of a plan.

The official Israeli version was that the army didn't take three hours to arrive. In a written answer to a question posed by Glock's son Peter, the Investigation Division of the Israeli police replied, "Notification of the incident was received by the Civil Administration through a local resident and they informed the IDF. Army forces reached the scene at 16:05, the incident having occurred at 15:15." But the el-Farabi family, Gabi Baramki, and everyone else who was on the scene that day all dispute that. They are all consistent in claiming that the IDF arrived at about ten minutes past six, nearly three hours after the shooting.

The delay remains a mystery. One can only imagine the communication that went on behind the scenes after Ibtisam el-Farabi raised the alarm, as the police and the IDF decided how to deal with the incident. Since it was a foreigner who had been shot, and not a Palestinian or an Israeli, the shooting was not likely to flare up into a military confrontation, so there was no need for a rapid response. Common sense advises that soldiers—many of whom were, by this time, sick and tired of serving in the territories—would be disinclined to expose themselves to censure for reporting that it had taken nearly three hours to drive to a crime scene. It looked better to say they had arrived within an hour.

The police and the IDF must have spent some of this time coordinating their arrival. In a civil society, including Israel itself, responding to a report of a shooting would be the responsibility of the police. But in the Occupied Territories things were different. The police would enter an area only after it had been militarily secured. The army arrived at the scene, and only then did they call the police station in Ramallah to have them take over the investigation. As a result, the police were completely dependent on the army for their ability to operate in the Palestinian territories, and the army seems to have judged this a low priority militarily. The police may have been late because the army felt there was no hurry.

An incident of this kind would not have been a high priority for the police either, as a matter of institutional policy. The two main objectives of the police in the Occupied Territories were, according to their 1975 annual report, "to prevent the organizing of cells for hostile activity against the administration, such as distribution of leaflets, daubing hostile slogans on the walls, trade strikes, or demonstrations," and "to prevent the smuggling of stolen property from Israel into the administered areas."

Murder was personal; it wasn't "hostile activity against the administration." After a couple of months in the West Bank, it became clear enough to me that Glock's killing was not by any means the only unsolved murder in the Occupied Territories. One of the best known was the killing in 1985 of Aziz Shehadeh, a well-known Ramallah lawyer and a member of a notable local family. Shehadeh had spoken publicly in earlier years in favor of making peace with Israel, at a time when it was unfashionable to do so, and as a result had received threats against his life from Palestinians. He was killed violently, by stabbing, yet the police would not investigate the murder, despite the family's appeals. The killer didn't use a gun, which gave the case a low priority. Later, Shehadeh's son, Raja, discovered that his father had been receiving threatening letters from an imprisoned criminal with a grievance against Shehadeh. Raja Shehadeh is convinced that this man murdered his father in revenge when he was released from prison. Yet the man was never questioned by the police. Murder is not a threat to the stability of the occupation.

STILL, Nabhan Khrayshah was right when he wrote in his report that Albert Glock was one of the very few Americans to be murdered in the Occupied Territories. Indeed, it was one of the firmest principles of the *intifada* that foreigners were not to be harmed. For the Palestinians, this was a matter of pure self-interest. The foreigners, most of whom were Americans or Europeans, who visited or worked in the West Bank were generally on the Palestinians' side: they were mostly aid workers, doctors, teachers, and the like, but also they were journalists, who played the important role of reporting Israeli actions against the Arab population to the world outside. Even as tourists foreigners were valuable. Tourists spent money in the Palestinian-owned souvenir shops in the Old City of Jerusalem, or on guides at the Christian holy sites in the West Bank. The tourism industry is one of the oldest in the world: a century and a half ago, the first package tourists came to see the sights of the Holy Land, on trips organized by the London firm of Thomas Cook. Foreign visitors were not instinctively distrusted, instead carefully exploited.

Travelers to the West Bank frequently report being mildly startled to notice a little American flag dangling from the rearview mirror in taxis. In conversation with the taxi driver, who often speaks serviceable English, visitors learn that he spent a couple of years in Brooklyn or Chicago. It is common around Bir Zeit to see an ostentatious new villa under construction, which one learns is being built by a Palestinian who spent twenty years in the dry-cleaning business in America. The family has come back, one is told, to shield the builder's adolescent children from the temptations of American society. The village of Deir Dibwan, southeast of Bir Zeit, consists almost entirely of the flashy houses of returned Palestinian Americans. As a member of one of the most politicized people on earth, the average Palestinian is usually able to distinguish between Americans and American government policy. Palestinians tend to like the first and hate the second.

Knowing this, Albert Glock may have considered himself invulnerable. Obviously, he wasn't. Even after sixteen years of teaching at Birzeit, and becoming a familiar figure in the area, he was still as endangered as any Palestinian resident of the West Bank. The police offered little protection from random violence. In 1984, a commission found that there was no effective police force to protect Palestinians and enforce law and order in the Occupied Territories. Generally, the police would investigate crimes against Palestinians only when a complaint had been made, and often not even then. Knowing that it was unlikely that the police would help—that files would be lost, that investigations would drag on for years without result—Palestinians generally did not bother to make complaints. It was a state of affairs that could be described as institutionalized incompetence.

The *intifada* made a bad situation worse. The few hundred Palestinians who worked as policemen in the Israeli force in the Occupied Territories resigned at the start of the uprising. What law and order there was tended to come in the form of vigilante justice. By the fourth year of the *intifada*, when a Palestinian entered a police station to make a complaint, the Israeli policeman at the desk would tell him, "Go and complain to Yassir Arafat."

In the hours after the shooting, Gabi Baramki had called the American consulate in East Jerusalem to ask someone to come to the scene. He thought a dying American might get American rights, American justice. He was as wrong about that as Glock was about his safety. An American who could not bear to return to what he called "the bubble" of his native land, Albert Glock had died instead like a Palestinian. He was buried in the cemetery of the Lutheran Church in Ramallah with a Palestinian flag draped across his coffin.

———

I HAD LITTLE realistic expectation of uncovering much about how the police investigation was conducted. Lois Glock told me she had given a brief statement at the police station in Ramallah but was not formally questioned. She even had to tell the officer who took her statement what questions to ask. Hamdan Taha, Hamed Salem, Maya el-Farabi, and other members of the Institute of Archeology were questioned once. Hamed Salem told me that he was asked if Glock had any enemies, but that otherwise the questioning was "routine." "My impression was that the inquiry was not serious," he said.

Hamed Salem's remark pointed to one of the problems the police faced in investigating the murder: it was an agency of the Israeli government. Palestinians did not trust the police and would not be expected to cooperate with them.

Studying news reports from the time, I found that three days after the killing, on the day of the funeral, the police did raid a number of homes in the Ramallah area, and they arrested and held without charge about fifty people. The people arrested were all at home because the curfew imposed on the area after the shooting of the settlers in al-Bireh was still in force. (The continuation of the curfew into a seventh week meant that only foreigners and the especially courageous among the Palestinian population were able to attend Glock's funeral.) Those arrested included eight Birzeit students and four staff members, one of whom, Khalil Abu Arafeh, an architecture professor and political cartoonist, told me that the arrests were for "political activities related to the *intifada*." The immediate reason may have been that on that day, January 22, Hanan Mikhail-Ashrawi, the Palestinian spokeswoman to the Washington peace talks, was due to return home, possibly to be confronted by an angry demonstration by people opposed to the talks. A political demonstration of this kind would be a greater threat to order in the West Bank than the murder of an archeology professor, and as a result a higher enforcement priority for the police.

The police maintained that they were giving the case greater consideration than usual. A forensic team had been despatched to the murder scene. The area was cordoned off and searched. A spokesman wrote to Peter Glock some months later: "In this incident, in the light of its gravity and importance, a special investigation team was established, headed by an officer with the rank of superintendent."

A few months after the shooting, Lois and her son Jeff were given access to the diplomatic correspondence about the case of Albert's murder. I had this documentation in my apartment in Bir Zeit. (I was so nervous about its being seized by Israeli or Palestinian authorities that I locked it away every time I went out.) The papers showed that in the months that followed, the American consulate persisted in making diffident inquiries of the Israelis, but with little outcome:

> Congen [consul general] reminded the INP chief superintendent of the intense USG [U.S. government] and family interest in the investigation's progress and pointed out that the police have shared none of the substance of the investigation. The officer provided his assurances that the case is still being actively investigated and that Congen will be provided details as soon as it is possible to do so. He further promised to provide a progress report on Monday, February 24.

A month and a half later, the promised progress report had not appeared, but the consul general remained serene. "Congen remains in regular contact with the Israeli National Police concerning the investigation into the killing of Albert Glock. To date there is no further information or progress toward resolution of the case."

The Glocks pushed hard to keep the investigation going, especially Lois, who stayed on in Beit Hanina for the next two years. There was obvious political sensitivity to the case, and the American consulate in Jerusalem (which unlike American consulates anywhere else in the world operates with equal authority to the embassy in Tel Aviv) had been pressing the Israeli authorities, without much success, for information on the progress of the investigation. They helped Lois to arrange meetings with Israeli officials, perhaps in the hope that this polite lady, with her neat bun of gray hair, could succeed where they had not. In April 1992, when Lois and her son Jeffrey met the officers responsible for the case, they assured the Glocks that everything possible was being done. The officers insisted that the case remained open, that a ballistics test had been conducted. All they could do was wait for the gun to be used again. More information, however, they would not divulge: the investigation was being conducted on the "covert" level. The police said they were depending on information from a local network of informers, and these had offered no useful information.

The Glocks' persistence contrasted with what increasingly appeared to American officials to be a laconic Israeli response. After both U.S. Secretary of State Warren Christopher and Senator Byron Dorgan of North Dakota (where Peter Glock was a constituent) signaled their concern with the low intensity of the Israeli investigation, the American consul in Jerusalem wrote to her superior, the consul general: "I am personally not surprised that Congress and the Glock family are frustrated with the lack of progress. I share their frustration."

The Glocks were dismayed by the Israeli investigators' air of fatalism. Waiting for a particular gun to be used again was a strangely passive way to conduct a murder investigation. The Glocks felt the Israelis were keeping something to themselves. Perhaps because of the obligation of tact to the bereaved, the police seemed hesitant to admit that the Occupied Territories were outside the pale of justice. There, only war and politics existed, and law and order meant keeping the population quiet and submissive. The pursuit of a suspect in a murder that had nothing to do with the immediate status quo of the occupation was a vain hope.

———

THERE WAS a sentence in one of Glock's letters that I had carefully transcribed and often reread. "There are no archeological facts, only hypotheses and relative explanations." The presence of fragments of collar-rim storage jars in an Iron Age site in the Judaean Hills meant to some that the inhabitants of the site were Israelite; to others it indicated a Canaanite settlement. One saw what one wanted to see in the sparse facts available.

He also wrote, "In the case of excavated archeological data, the evidence is almost always incomplete, fragmented, displaced so that the original image appears distorted."

I thought of this as I considered another hypothesis, one that overlapped with the Palestinian belief that Glock was killed by an undercover unit. This second hypothesis was that the killing was the work of extremists among the Israeli settlers in the West Bank. The settlers were in an angry mood at the time of Glock's murder. A month earlier, a mob from the settlement of Pesagot went on a rampage in Ramallah, in protest at the shooting, by Palestinians, of members of a neighboring settlement. For the settlers, killing Glock would weaken Birzeit, demoralize the Palestinians, and show whose land it was. They had been promising vigilante action to fight the *intifada*, and now, perhaps, they were carrying it out. According to this theory, Glock was killed because he was an Arab-loving American, or because of the political threat of his archeology.

But the hypothesis didn't hold water: Glock was invisible to the settlers. It seemed unlikely that they had read his articles in *American Archeologist* or *Birzeit Research Review* and had been offended by his ideas about Palestinian archeology. The only Glock most settlers would have heard of was a brand of pistol. Still, the extremists among them were a menacing and trigger-happy presence in the locality. In an earlier incident, a group of settlers had entered the Birzeit campus and sprayed automatic gunfire at random. And five days before Glock was shot, according to a news report, armed settlers vandalized the home of Birzeit professor Riyad Malki while Israeli soldiers looked on without intervening. But Malki was an outspoken political activist and a highly visible local leader of the PFLP, while Glock studiously avoided any contact with settlers.

Only Palestinians persisted in taking seriously the idea that Glock was murdered by settlers, and it revealed more about them than it did about the murder. To the Palestinians, the settlers were so frightening, irrational, and unpredictable that they might actually do something as unlikely and counterproductive to their own cause as to murder an American citizen.

Something else happened in the town of Bir Zeit on the day Albert Glock was shot. Back at the start of my investigation, when I met Lois Glock at her daughter's home in New Jersey, she told me that a few days after the funeral, Sumaya Nasir, the wife of my landlord Munir Nasir, sent a message to Lois that she had something important to say to her. The Nasirs were friends of the Glocks, and it would have been natural for Sumaya to contact Lois after her husband's death to offer condolences. But it was clear from the urgency of the message that it was not just an expression of sympathy. Lois went to the Nasirs' house in Bir Zeit—a pleasant compact house built on a steep slope of the rocky hillside, surrounded by trellises growing sweet black grapes that the Nasirs made into wine.

Sumaya told Lois that on the day Albert Glock was shot, no more than an hour before the shooting happened, she had seen a notorious and dreaded figure driving through Bir Zeit in his white BMW. The man was a Palestinian collaborator who carried a gun and lived in an Israeli settlement. She felt a tremor of fear when she saw him. "Whenever he was in the town," Sumaya said, "something bad would happen."

His name was Awwad, and he was a native of Bir Zeit. As a boy, he had acquired a reputation in the town as a thief, and later had "got into trouble with drugs and girls." Eventually he married and fathered some children, but had recently been imprisoned on a charge of rape. Sumaya befriended Awwad's wife after the rest of the town ostracized her. Sumaya would bring gifts of food and clothes to her house.

While Awwad was in prison he was recruited by the GSS as a collaborator. In exchange for an early release, he would serve as their agent in Bir Zeit, submitting information about individuals in the town, especially those who were active in the *intifada*. It was a common practice. There were thousands of such collaborators in the Occupied Territories, many of them criminals like Awwad.

Munir Nasir said Awwad had made himself useful to the GSS in prison by taking part in the torture and interrogation of Palestinian prisoners.

Awwad returned to Bir Zeit to live with his family. He was issued a gun for self-defense. His duties in the town amounted to more than collecting information: he served as a hired thug. He would oversee beatings of *intifada* activists and acts of sabotage in the town. Sumaya saw him one night cutting telephone wires. Munir Nasir told me that Awwad was the leader of a group of collaborators that had kidnapped a local activist and had beaten him severely. For this attack, Awwad earned a reprimand from his masters for exceeding his brief. "He is a very harsh man," Munir told me. "He would kill a man like he would kill a chicken."

In retaliation, Awwad's house was attacked. Eventually it became impossible for him and his family to live in the town any longer, so they were moved to an Israeli settlement near Hebron. This was a usual practice when collaborators were exposed. By the time of Glock's death there were about three thousand exposed Palestinian collaborators living inside Israel and in Israeli settlements in the Occupied Territories, living in a kind of limbo, unable to return to their own people, yet unable to assimilate into Israeli society either.

Awwad still had relatives in the town, and he would make occasional visits after he had moved away, arriving in his white BMW. Even after he had left, his presence in the town was still associated with trouble. Munir told me of an armed encounter with activists near the Bir Zeit post office about a year before Glock's death, in which Awwad used a local woman as a human shield. The details were hazy, as ever in this land of rumor and suspicion.

So when Sumaya Nasir saw Awwad in Bir Zeit in his car that day, and later heard that Albert Glock had been shot only an hour later, she suspected the hand of Awwad. He was a local man, with local knowledge. This was my third hypothesis. Awwad could have known that the el-Farabi house offered good cover for a gunman, as it sloped down off the road and permitted a quick escape to Ramallah. He could easily have had in his possession the type of Israeli army weapon that was used in the killing. He could have pulled the trigger himself, or, more likely, been on the scene to supply information to the men who did.

The question was, Whose interests was he serving? Why would he have done it? He would have had no personal motive for killing Dr. Glock, and certainly no political motive, no point to make. If he was involved in the killing in any way, he was either assisting his GSS handlers in an Israeli-sponsored attack, which was unlikely, or, less likely still, helping Palestinian vigilantes. Any hypothesis claiming an Israeli plan to kill Glock was weak, it seemed to me; and Awwad could not have worked with Palestinian activists because of his status as a collaborator. Sumaya had her reasons for dreading the sight of Awwad, but his presence in the town that day was probably no more than a chilling coincidence.

STILL, I continued to examine the question of collaborators in Palestinian society at the time of the murder. I had been brooding over the awful and ironic possibility that Albert Glock may have been judged a collaborator himself. According to a detailed report by Btselem, published in 1994, the definition of the term expanded wildly during the latter part of the *intifada* to encompass not just collaborators like Awwad, but anyone who was judged by the hard-core activists to be helping the Israelis or hindering the *intifada*. Their definition of who was a collaborator became extreme, unforgiving, paranoid. The label, once applied, could be fatal to the person who bore it. I had to consider that this is what happened to Glock. The climate of suspicion and fear in which people were labeled, rightly or wrongly, as collaborators —and then attacked— was a vast and murky subject.

Collaborators like Awwad undermined the fabric of Palestinian society: they dissolved trust and replaced it with suspicion. They were therefore among the first targets of violence in the *intifada*'s early days—a time when people took pride in the fact that the *intifada* was a nonviolent movement. Collaborators were an exception: they had betrayed neighbors and friends. When the uprising broke out, they were spontaneously attacked in the streets, their houses were vandalized, and they were forced to fall back on their Israeli-issued guns for self-defense.

In that first wave, many collaborators resigned from their positions, made public confessions (in Gaza, typically from the loudspeaker in the minaret of a mosque), and repented. The more stubborn among them were given warnings to desist by the *intifada*'s invisible leadership, in the form of graffiti daubed in paint on the walls of their houses. If the collaborator still remained defiant, he was beaten, often viciously. The violence against collaborators was at its most intense in the two overcrowded and impoverished pressure cookers of the *intifada*, Gaza and Nablus. Forty collaborators were killed in the first year.

As the *intifada* progressed, the label of collaborator was attached to people suspected of a wider range of perceived offenses. For example, "intermediaries" were now classed as collaborators. These were Palestinians with good contacts in the Israeli administration (typically because they had once acted as informers) who would intercede on a person's behalf—to help him get a work permit or an exit permit—in exchange for money. It was petty corruption, and it was expensive and humiliating to engage the services of an intermediary (*waasit*, in Arabic), but often it was the only way to get what one needed from the administration. The intermediaries were judged to be collaborators because they undermined the cardinal principle of the *intifada*: that the Palestinians should separate themselves from Israeli institutions and refuse to bend the knee to oppressive Israeli bureaucracy.

Land dealers were almost always considered collaborators. They sold property to Israelis, something regarded as treason. *Mukhtars*, the traditional village headmen, were often collaborators. They represented their village or *hamula* (clan) in dealings with the Israeli authorities, and in some villages were the nearest equivalent to a municipal authority. Some *mukhtars* received a salary from the Israeli administration, for which they were expected to perform official services. They were required, for example, to supply the GSS with information, or to make public announcements about government expropriations of land. As the *intifada* went on, activities of this sort came to be seen as perpetuating the occupation. Some of the *mukhtars* were asked to resign by the UNL. Some refused, and of those who refused, some were issued with Israeli weapons to defend themselves. In May 1991, eight months before the killing of Albert Glock, the *mukhtar* of al-Bireh (near Ramallah) was killed by unknown masked men. He had been assisting the security forces in house-to-house searches for wanted suspects, and had defied the warnings painted on his house to desist.

The Btselem report on undercover activities in the territories said that even Yassir Arafat himself was called a collaborator after he signed the first agreement with Israel in September 1993, in leaflets published by Hamas and by two leftist parties.

By the time of Glock's death, the revolutionary justice of the *intifada* had run out of control: about nine hundred Palestinians would ultimately be killed by Palestinian activists on suspicion of collaboration, and nearly half of these killings were committed in 1992. "Anticollaborator killing" became a cloak for the settling of scores in personal or interclan disputes—murders that had nothing to do with preventing collaboration with the enemy. Rather than a cure, anticollaborator violence was becoming part of the sickness of a traumatized society. The alarm of the *intifada* leadership is apparent in the communiqué that was issued immediately after the killing of Albert Glock. The same communiqué—*bayan* no. 79—that denounced Glock's killing also attempts to rein in the vigilantes:

> No authority is above the authority of the *intifada*. . . . It has been stated before that the Unified Leadership warns against the killing of people suspected of collaboration with the occupation and that these killings tarnish the reputation of the *intifada* and become a very heavy burden on it. It emphasizes that there will be an investigation into the killings and measures will be taken to punish all those who do not abide by the restraint they should show in dealing with collaborators.

Could Albert Glock have been killed as a collaborator? Glock may have been seen as one because the word on the Palestinian street was that he was a foreigner who was standing in the way of a qualified Palestinian. He was therefore undermining Palestinian society. There were plenty of Birzeit students in the Ramallah area who belonged to groups that were active in the punishment of collaborators. The message of the assassination would have been in a display of popular justice against a troublesome outsider.

The collaborator hypothesis had serious weaknesses, however. Glock would have been the first and only foreigner to have been killed by a vigilante group. No one claimed responsibility for the killing. There was no graffiti on the wall of Glock's house or the el-Farabi house denouncing Glock as a collaborator. The public statements by the political parties, the umbrella under which the vigilantes acted, all denounced the killing. There was no point committing a killing in the name of anticollaborator justice if no attempt was made to broadcast the reason for it, and who did it.

Still, there was another way in which Glock's murder could have originated in this climate of retribution. It surely meant something that Glock was killed outside the house of Maya el-Farabi, his favored teaching assistant. What, if anything, did their relationship have to do with his death? I had a kind of clue: among the material in my Glock archive was a videotape, an unedited but professionally made recording of the excavation at Ti'innik. Glock had commissioned the tape as part of a series of teaching videos. It was shot in 1987, about six months before the *intifada* began. The tape gave me a poignant insight into the private world that Glock had created for himself at Birzeit.

The tape showed daily life in the ramshackle village (cows swinging their tails under trees, old men on small trotting donkeys, women baking bread in a traditional oven, boys watering scrawny goats), cutting abruptly to long takes of the excavation. The images were especially vivid because the tape was unedited: life was captured proceeding at its own ambling pace. There was no commentary, so the sounds of voices mumbling banal things mingled with the buzz of insects and the bleating of animals.

One image stuck in my mind: Albert sitting at a table with Maya and some of the students, sorting potsherds. The tabletop is a pool of light, and everything around it is pure blackness, as if they were sitting on a stage. They are sorting pottery fragments according to their age—an easy, sociable task, like shelling peas at a kitchen table.

"Byz ... Byz ... Byz ..." Albert says on the sound track,

thoughtfully examining one fragment after another and putting it into the appropriate box. "Byz" means Byzantine pottery. "Mam . . . Mam . . ." he says, meaning Mamluk. Maya is sitting beside him. It is a scene without context, of pure scholarly activity.

Glock was wearing a black shirt and black jeans. He looked younger than his age at the time, which was sixty-two, and he had the craggy profile of a midwestern farmer. It was the first time I had seen a moving image of him, and watching the tape was like conjuring up his spirit. By now I knew this man well. Six years separated us, and we had never met or spoken, yet we had visited the same places, walked along the same streets, seen the same views. I knew his handwriting and his poor spelling, which came out in writing done late at night. I was familiar with his tendency toward British spelling rather than American (a habit that signified to me his choice of a deracinated, expatriate identity, free from the burden of being American). I knew all his illnesses: he suffered from bursitis (an inflammation of the shoulder), eczema, rheumatoid arthritis, all of which kept him in constant pain. When Lois was away, he didn't look after himself, and then he would get stomach upsets and dehydration. He had had an operation on his foot for a planter's wart. He had an allergy to olive blossoms. I even knew what he had in his stomach when he died.

I also knew what was in his heart. At the time the tape was made he wrote in his diary of an anxiety about his life verging on despair. He had often described in his diary over the years the frustration that he felt about failing to make himself understood. Now this anxiety about his inability to communicate had grown into a sense of isolation.

Glock was mainly worried about not being able to communicate with Maya. He was always thinking about Maya, his colleague, muse, and the object of his doomed longings, as well as his personal symbol of Palestine. Their close professional bond was well known at Birzeit, and resented by some as favoritism.

One of the first rumors after the news of the killing broke was that he had been killed because he and Maya were having an affair. The killing would therefore have been the work of vigilantes acting to punish an offense against morality. This became the second most commonly heard explanation of the murder, after the belief that Glock was killed because of his archeology. The rumor even reached the American consul's office in Jerusalem. In a cable to Washington reporting on the murder and events immediately after it, the consul general wrote, "There has also been speculation that some of the family members of the (female) research assistant felt obliged to defend family honor."

One of the bizarre features of the *intifada*, according to the Btselem report, was the powerful influence of morbid notions joining together fear of female sexuality, sexual temptation, the insuperable strength and ingenuity of the Israelis, betrayal, and the loss of honor. The result was a vague but powerful sexual paranoia that manifested itself in a number of particularly vicious killings, mostly in Gaza. These notions were embodied in the word *isqat*, tripping up or knocking down. *Isqat*, it was believed, was an Israeli tactic to weaken the moral fiber—and hence, the strength of resistance—of Palestinian men by tempting them sexually, for example, by using Palestinian women who were secret Israeli collaborators posing as prostitutes. After the victim had succumbed to temptation, GSS agents would appear and threaten to publicize his transgression unless he agreed to collaborate with them. (The woman would have been tricked into becoming a prostitute-collaborator herself by the same method of extortion, having been secretly photographed by GSS agents in an act of illicit sex.) The idea was popular and pervasive, but Btselem could not identify a single case of *isqat* in the realm of fact. It was a horror story, part of the folklore of the *intifada*.

These fears produced a strange linkage between patriotism and sexuality. The power of such fantasies intensified as the *intifada* ground on and the hardship of everyday life grew steadily harder to bear. The economic deprivation caused by being cut off from one's job in Israel, and the claustrophobic effect of curfews and closures that lasted for weeks at a time inspired a fanatical puritanism in young Palestinians. The *intifada* nurtured Hamas, the Islamic Resistance Movement, which one would naturally associate with this attitude, but the tendency was equally strong among activists of the mainstream parties. Pleasure was abolished. The

earlier insurrectionary exuberance of the *intifada*—when the slogan "Don't worry, be happy" was daubed on the stone walls of the
Old City of Jerusalem—gave way to an austere perseverance. Wedding parties became subdued affairs. Women were exhorted to
dress modestly, to cover their arms and heads. The activists of the
intifada assumed the role of defending the honor of women, a role
traditionally taken by the *hamula*. But now there were harsh penal-
ties for offenses against this code. Modesty in women became a
sign of patriotism. The tabernacle of Palestinian patriotism, it
seemed, had become Palestinian women's bodies.

In this climate of sexual paranoia, the perceived affair of Albert
and Maya would have been treason, collaboration, the weakening
of the moral fabric. It was *ikhtilaat* or *khalwah*—in Islamic law,
terms denoting the illicit mixing of the sexes. Killing Glock on his
lover's doorstep—rather than anywhere else—would signal the
crime for which he had been punished. The Israeli police never
investigated this angle.

The problem with this theory was that if anticollaborator vigilantes suspected a forbidden affair, they would have killed Maya,
not Albert. The victims of honor crimes were always female, and it
seemed unlikely that vehement fundamentalists would change
their pattern and kill the man instead. And none of the people I
spoke to who were familiar with the case genuinely suspected that
the two were having an affair. Their relationship may have been
anguished and neurotic—at least on Albert's part—but I concluded it was nothing more than that.

I WAS STILL intrigued by the hypothesis that Glock's murder was
an anticollaborator killing. I tracked down the author of the Btselem report on such killings in the Occupied Territories, Salah Abd
al-Jawwad, who was a sociology professor at Birzeit. He had told
Lois Glock that the killing might have been an anticollaborator
punishment, but Lois's notes did not detail why he thought this. I
went to his house in al-Bireh to ask him.

Abd al-Jawwad was the son of a former mayor of al-Bireh. He
told me that he had been in prison six times, held under the
administrative detention law that allowed the Israeli authorities to

jail anyone for six months without charge. His report was a brave piece of work that contained an abundance of uncomfortable facts about the violence of the *intifada*. (I have used it to write the above account of the culture of anticollaborator violence.) There was a lot in it that damaged the reputation of the *intifada* and there would have been few Palestinians who would dare to be as honest in print as he was.

I knew of another instance of the courage of Salah Abd al-Jawwad. He had been disgusted by what he saw as the craven reluctance of many of Albert Glock's Birzeit academic colleagues to attend his funeral: they did not want to be seen making a public gesture of sympathy for a man who had been cast in the role of an enemy of the Palestinian cause. Not only did Salah refuse the excuse that a curfew was in place that day, he pushed his way through the crowd of mourners to take a corner of Glock's coffin on his shoulder.

Abd al-Jawwad did not believe that Glock was killed in the wave of anticollaborator violence. Instead, he thought Glock was killed by an Israeli undercover unit, because of the political potency of his archeological work. "We are talking about people who are determined, and who are ready to do anything to obtain what they want," he said, leaning forward to make his point. "They have shown this time and time again." Like the man at al-Haq, he emphasized that the Israelis always carry out killings dressed as Arabs. "Sometimes they kill people who are totally mysterious targets: you don't know who could have done it because you can't tell why someone would have wanted to kill them."

He gave the example of the Palestinian terrorist Abu Nidal, whose group is said to be thoroughly infiltrated by Israeli agents, to the extent that it has become an instrument of Israeli policy. His group has killed more Palestinians than Israelis, Abd al-Jawwad insisted, but it continues to kill Israelis so that it is seen to be a Palestinian faction.

Abd al-Jawwad rejected the honor crime hypothesis. If the *hamula*, the clan, to which the family belonged were offended by Glock's behavior, they might smash his car, not kill him. There were no warnings. And the killing was too professional for a family feud.

Salah Abd al-Jawwad's views were intriguing, but they did not greatly advance my investigation. There was more than a little hollow-eyed paranoia in his outlook, though for a Palestinian, paranoia is usually justified. When I left his house after two hours of exhausting talk, something rather peculiar happened. I was walking back through al-Bireh and noticed a strange-looking man walking a few paces ahead of me on the sidewalk. He was small and dark-complexioned and was wearing a dark blue suit, which is unusual for the West Bank. As I drew near to him I saw him reach down and pick up from the pavement a stone, which he put in his coat pocket. This apparently contrived delay brought him up level with me, and once he was walking abreast of me, he began to talk. He spoke English in an eccentric "what-ho old-chap" Terry-Thomas sort of accent, but was very inquisitive. In the course of a short conversation he managed to extract from me my nationality, my occupation, and my first name. Was this the sort of informer Salah was writing about, checking out a foreigner who was visiting a well-known Palestinian nationalist intellectual? In the multiple worlds of Israel and Palestine, paranoia was contagious.

AFTER THREE MONTHS in the West Bank, I still hadn't seen Hamdan Taha, the man who had struggled with Glock over a job at the Institute of Archeology in the months before Glock's death.

As the weeks turned into months, and as the weather got colder in the Judaean Hills and we began to use the bottled-gas heater in our chilly Bir Zeit apartment, the need to meet with him began to weigh heavily on my mind. I feared that I had made the mistake of oversimplifying him: I had drawn him in my mind with a few exaggerated strokes, creating a kind of caricature, a character in a murder story.

I was the chronicler of Glock's life and death, the narrator of his tragedy, and had become accustomed to seeing everything from Glock's point of view. According to this point of view, Taha was a sort of villain. But as time passed I would come to feel that Taha, too, was a victim of this assassination. Imagine his predicament: after nearly a decade abroad, he returns to the university where his academic career began, expecting a job. His old mentor doesn't want to give him one. Taha does what you do at a university with a highly charged political atmosphere: he makes a noise about it. He has a talent for politics: he knows how to mobilize people. Then something happens that wasn't in the script: a month after the dispute is settled, his boss and mentor is murdered. When he hears the news, on a rainy Sunday afternoon in January, he wails with grief. He could not have anticipated this as he fought for his job. He has tragically underestimated the violence of the *intifada*, and Glock's blood spills across his path.

I knew from what I had read in Glock's papers and from many conversations with his colleagues that he didn't like Taha. But Glock didn't like most people he met. His approach to archeology was irreconcilable with Taha's, and both men had a crusading conviction that their version of the Palestinian archeological mission was the right one. Glock wanted a small, exclusive band of archeological technicians who would work for years, away from the common gaze, to produce world-class scholarship that would be the foundation of a Palestinian archeology. Taha was an evangelist: he wanted to teach the archeology of Palestine to Palestinian undergraduates, to make it part of their liberal education, to raise the awareness of as many students as possible about their archeological heritage.

Taha's talent for politics became apparent in the years after Glock was killed. He served out his contract at Birzeit, lecturing in archeology—not in the Institute of Archeology but in the History Department. Then he was asked to join a preparatory committee of the new Palestinian Authority to form what would become the Palestinian Department of Antiquities. Several archeologists told me he had been nominated for the job by Sari Nusseibah, the president of al-Quds University, a well-known moderate in Palestinian affairs. Taha seemed ideally suited for the job, which required someone with a zeal for Palestinian archeology and hardheaded political ability. Taha had both. His job was to build a Palestinian Department of Antiquities from scratch, and when the final status discussions began—under the Oslo Agreement, the thorny issues were left to the end of the process—to negotiate with Israel over the return of such treasures of cultural property as those in the Rockefeller Museum in East Jerusalem, which had been seized by Israel in 1967 as the spoils of war. His opposite number in these negotiations would be the formidable Itzak "the bulldozer" Magen.

The Hamdan Taha I eventually met bore no resemblance to the vague and ineffectual figure Glock described in his letters and diaries. As head of the Palestinian Department of Antiquities, Taha had established a formidable reputation. He began his work in the extreme heat of Jericho, one of the world's strangest human ecologies. A luxuriant oasis in the fierce heat of the Judaean desert, with abundant plantations of tropical fruit, Jericho is both the lowest (258 meters below sea level) and the oldest continuously inhabited human settlement on earth, where excavation has revealed defensive walls dating to 8000 B.C.E. In the first stage of the Oslo process, Israel ceded this self-contained town and parts of the Gaza Strip to Palestinian control.

The Palestinian Department of Antiquities was established in Jericho in 1994, in a single room, with no files, no equipment, no collection of artifacts, and only a handful of staff. (Itzak Magen was required under the Oslo Agreement to hand over files pertaining to antiquities sites in the areas now under Palestinian control, but he has never done so.) From the moment he assumed his post, Taha showed that he was capable of swift and severe action in defense of Palestinian antiquities. The head of a foreign archeological institute in Jerusalem told me that a local businessman who had plans to build a bank was advised (incorrectly) by architects that there would be a two-week interregnum between the departure of the Israeli administration and the arrival of the PA. They saw in this interregnum an opportunity to begin construction work without the constraint of a permit. Bulldozers were brought in and began to dig a hole on a site in the center of the town. Modern Jericho is built right on top of ancient Roman Jericho, and before long the bulldozers were churning up a large Roman mosaic. As soon as news of this emerged, Taha slapped an order on the site, stopping further work and notifying the businessman that henceforth he would be permanently denied permission to excavate. Taha made it known that anyone who sought to dig without a permit would be punished the same way. The arrival of the Palestinian Department of Antiquities meant that regulations governing excavation would be even tighter than under the Israelis.

The other field in which Taha demonstrated his fierce determination to protect Palestinian antiquities was the antiquities trade. His policy, he told me, was simply to end it. When the West Bank was governed, archeologically speaking, by Itzak Magen, control over the illicit trade in antiquities was lax. It was easy for Palestinians to sell to Israeli and Palestinian dealers the ancient objects they found or deliberately dug up in the ground, in *khirbahs*, in caves, or when plowing a patch of ground for planting. It was the custom of the country, a branch of agriculture: this was how the Dead Sea Scrolls became known to the world. Taha sought to impose the nationalistic view that the antiquities and archeological artifacts in Palestinian soil were the inalienable cultural property of Palestine, and rather than be sold, they should be in a museum or research institute, without exception. An Israeli collector in Jerusalem told me, "Hamdan Taha is completely ruthless. All the antiquities dealers—and I mean Palestinians—were much happier under the Israelis."

I saw Hamdan Taha before I met him. After I had been in the West Bank a few weeks, I attended a lecture that he gave at the Albright Institute. The subject of his talk was an excavation that his department was conducting outside Jenin. I found the diffidence of his manner startling. He hardly looked up from his text, which he read word for word in halting yet precise English, and when he did look up his glance was a timid plea for agreement with his scholarly audience. He spoke so quietly I could hardly hear him.

After three months in Bir Zeit, I picked up the phone and called him. It was easy, after all. He sounded positively anxious to see me, and we arranged an appointment. A few days later I climbed the stone steps to his office, which was in a beautifully restored Ottoman-era house in downtown Ramallah, and sat before him at his desk. I asked him to tell me about his relationship with Glock.

Taha's desk was big. It suited him. He seemed to me the type of person who is fulfilled behind a desk, whose identity melds with the office he holds and comes to embody. His voice was as quiet as I expected, but sitting before him I could detect the steel in him. His hair was tousled and untidy, which probably caused people to make the mistake of thinking him vague or disorganized. But as he spoke I could sense the willpower that these deceptive traits concealed.

Taha talked about the attitude of the Palestinians to archeology and to politics in the 1970s and 1980s, and how these began to change at the time of the *intifada*. It was important to start teaching archeology at Birzeit, he said, to defend "the cultural identity of the Palestinian people." His account was so impersonal that one might have thought he was being evasive, but he was trying to convey the significance of archeology at Birzeit, and to recognize a debt to its founder. "We owe it all fully to Albert Glock," he said.

This was turning into a formal panegyric, so I steered him onto his dispute with Glock in the months before he died. His tone of voice didn't change. He conceded that the teachers' union and the student council had become involved in the dispute, but insisted that the protests were against the university administration, not against Dr. Glock. "No one campaigned directly against Dr. Glock, because it was not up to him to decide if a member of the staff was hired or not," he said. This struck me as hairsplitting: Glock may not have had the final say about appointments, but his recommendations about who should be hired carried considerable weight.

Taha acknowledged that there were strikes organized by the teachers' union, backed by the student council. "But," he continued, "the fact is we had reached an agreement in the office of Dr. Baramki on the conditions under which I would teach. Dr. Glock's death came one month after."

As he sat behind his broad desk, sweat was pouring down Dr. Hamdan Taha's temples. He tried to make me see that he had been caught up in a process he neither controlled nor understood. He felt himself to be in the position of a wounded innocent, shocked by what he saw going on around him. "In 1991, I had just come back from Germany, where I was living a normal human life with my family. I had come back into a situation that was completely new. The *intifada* was at an end—everything was out of control. It was a very frightening time." He paused, as if reliving in memory. "To pass through Ramallah at three o'clock in the afternoon was like walking through a ghost town: in all the streets, all the tall buildings were occupied by soldiers. You couldn't plan ahead for even one day because it was so difficult to move. Even on the road between Bir Zeit and Ramallah there were army checkpoints between the villages. There were soldiers everywhere in the streets, and curfews. They would order people out of their houses to clear the stones from the streets that the *shabab* had thrown, and to paint over their graffiti. . . ."

Taha turned to Glock's murder. The police questioned him once about the case. "They asked about the conflict [at the institute]. I made it clear to them that the issue was settled; it was dealt with by the teachers' union."

I asked him who he thought killed Glock. His answer was unidiomatic, and obscure. "Someone who was hunting in dirty water." He continued, "I'm sure that the killer did not want Dr. Glock personally. It was against the whole Palestinian people, and American-Palestinian relationships. Otherwise, I have no hypothesis." He had used the same rather formal words in a conversation with Jeff Glock, which Jeff had recorded in a notebook, copied, and given to me.

I left Taha's office after two and a half hours, and walked through downtown Ramallah—on the streets where Taha had walked so fearfully when it was the battleground of the *intifada*—feeling drained and exhausted. Taha was indeed a casualty of this assassination. He had had an encounter with horror that was too close. He could not have emerged from the experience unharmed. After meeting him and witnessing his clenched pain, I could never seriously think of him as a suspect.

CHAPTER FOURTEEN

TWICE IN THE DAYS after the shooting of Albert Glock, the *Jerusalem Post* suggested that blame for the killing lay with the Islamic Resistance Movement, Hamas. At first glance this looked like nothing more than instant theorizing. Hamas was opposed to negotiating with Israel, so they assassinated an American in an attempt to throw a wrench into the works and bring the peace process to a halt. I could shrug it off as a serious line of inquiry were it not for glimmers in the half-light that hinted it might be true. For one thing, the Israeli police had told Lois and Jeff Glock that the gun that had been used in the killing of Dr. Glock had previously been used by a Hamas guerrilla in an attack on a Palestinian collaborator (Rasmiyah Quran). I had at least to consider the possibility that someone associated with Hamas had pulled the trigger on that dismal January afternoon.

Gabi Baramki had dismissed the notion out of hand. "A nationalist murder?" he said. "That's impossible." I also remembered that Jamil al-Tarifi, the Afarat loyalist who chaired the PLO's committee of inquiry into the murder, had warned Nabhan Khrayshah not to include Hamas in his investigation. Hamas activists were our people, their thinking ran; therefore, they can't be guilty. And Hamas had issued a statement from its headquarters in Amman denying responsibility.

There weren't many Palestinians in the Occupied Territories who did not have at least a grudging respect for Hamas. The group practically ran Gaza, providing schools and medical clinics and social services to the Strip's impoverished residents. The leader of Hamas, the preacher Sheikh Ahmad Yasin, who was languishing in an Israeli jail, set a severe example of unyielding dedication and

EDWARD FOX

self-discipline that the movement's members zealously followed. In the minds of Israelis, they were fanatics who would volunteer as suicide bombers for the dubious military goal of the random killing of Israeli civilians. But to Palestinians they were honorable people—if cruel in some of their methods—and unlike many members of the Palestinian high command, conspicuously incorruptible. The guerrilla operations Hamas carried out throughout the 1990s—including the gruesome suicide bombings inside Israel itself—were consistent and specific in their objectives: they were always revenge attacks against the Jewish state. To kill an American academic was not how Hamas did things.

But there was something else that compelled me to risk contradicting Gabi Baramki and Jamil al-Tarifi, and the major part of Palestinian opinion. Thanks to Lois Glock, I had a document— five blurry, typed, photocopied pages, translated from the Hebrew into unidiomatic English. The pages contained an enigmatic clue that might, if I could find other facts to support it, show that Albert's murder was indeed a Hamas operation. The document was a charge sheet, a list of indictments filed in Israeli military court against a man suspected being a high-ranking activist in the military wing of Hamas. His name was Muhammad Salah, and out of his strange story emerged a possible answer to the question of who killed Albert Glock.

MUHAMMAD SALAH HAD LIVED with his wife and three children in the Chicago suburb of Bridgeview, where he made a living as a used-car dealer. He was born in 1953 in East Jerusalem, then under Jordanian rule, but had acquired American citizenship. On January 13, 1993, he arrived at Ben Gurion Airport in Israel on a flight from Chicago. According to his own account, he was traveling on behalf of Islamic charities in the Chicago area (where the Muslim community is estimated to number three hundred thousand, one of the largest in America) to distribute donations to Palestinian families in the Occupied Territories—in particular, the families of deportees. A month earlier, the Israeli government had taken the radical step of rounding up 415 of the leading members of Hamas and the smaller Islamist group, Islamic Jihad, and deporting them into the Israeli-controlled "security zone" in southern Lebanon, after a Hamas military cell had kidnapped and murdered an Israeli border policeman.

Salah traveled to Jerusalem in a taxi and took a room in the YMCA in East Jerusalem. Twelve days later, he was arrested as he attempted to enter the Gaza Strip at the Erez checkpoint. The Israeli police searched his room in the Jerusalem YMCA and found $97,000 in cash on the top shelf of the closet. They held him in prison for nine months, awaiting trial. In October 1993, the Israeli government tried him in the military court in Ramallah, where the laws governing courts inside Israel do not apply, and where acquittals are practically unheard-of. The prosecutor charged him with a string of loosely defined offenses, whose common theme was "rendering services to an illegal organization." The judge heard that Salah was the designated leader of the "military branch" of Hamas. Salah denied it and would continue to deny it, even after he had finished serving his sentence and returned to the United States.

The charge sheet, translated from Hebrew into English, was a strange mixture of accusation and fact, and served to present an Israeli army judge with everything he needed to convict. Salah stood accused of belonging to a radical Islamic group whose aim was "to help in the fight against Israeli authority in Judaea and Samaria," and of coordinating its paramilitary activities. The indictment also claimed that in the twelve days between his arrival in Israel and his arrest at the Erez checkpoint, he had not really been distributing money to needy families but had, in fact, been meeting with Hamas activists in the West Bank, listening to reports on their activities, and giving them sums of money amounting to hundreds of thousands of dollars to buy weapons and to finance further paramilitary action.

Since Salah held American citizenship, his arrest was brought to the attention of the American consul. The consul, Kathy Riley, requested a translation of the charge sheet. Riley had taken a close interest in the Glock case, and had met Lois Glock a number of times, helping her to arrange meetings with Israeli police officers to push forward the investigation into the killing. As she read the document, she spotted a paragraph that seemed to refer to Glock's assassination, albeit obscurely and puzzlingly.

> The accused [Muhammad Salah] met with Adel Awadallah, Hamas activist in Ramallah who gave information and names of Hamas activists in the Ramallah District. . . . He also gave information on the assassination of a doctor from Birzeit University in 1991 by members of Hamas, because he was in the habit of cursing Moslems.

Adel Awadallah was a well-known Hamas activist from al-Bireh who later earned an aura of notoriety as Israel's most wanted fugitive. But who was the "doctor from Birzeit University"? Was this a reference to the killing of Albert Glock? The year is wrong, and it doesn't refer to Glock by name, and the reason for the assassination—"because he was in the habit of cursing Moslems"—defies understanding. But there was only one "doctor" at Birzeit University who had been assassinated, and that was Albert Glock.

Salah was sentenced in early December to five years in jail, and he served it in a prison in Nablus and then in Tel Mond prison near Tel Aviv. His case wasn't given a full trial. Instead, he received his five-year sentence as the result of a plea bargain between his defense lawyer and the military prosecutor. Cases against Palestinians in the military courts usually ended this way: defense lawyers knew that acquittal was almost impossible, so they frequently agreed to a plea bargain as a way of getting the shortest possible sentence for their client. But it was strange for the trial of a man alleged to be the "designated head of the military branch of Hamas" to end this way, without the presentation of the evidence against him.

The reference to the doctor from Birzeit University was vague, but I suspected there was more to be found in this murky story, if only I could uncover it.

———

MUHAMMAD SALAH HAD been represented in the military court by Lea Tsemel, a prominent and courageous Israeli human rights lawyer based in East Jerusalem. Lois Glock, who had obtained a copy of the translated charge sheet from Consul Kathy Riley, had been to see her, seeking an explanation of the cryptic reference. Tsemel told her that the charge sheet used against Muhammad Salah was a summary of the transcript of an interrogation he had undergone while in detention before his trial. Lea Tsemel had the original transcripts, which were in Hebrew, and gave Lois a rough translation. I wanted to see these transcripts myself, in the belief that there must be something in them that would tell me more about how Hamas might have been involved in Glock's murder.

Lea Tsemel was hard to reach. When after several attempts I succeeded in getting her on the telephone, she dealt with my request with decisive brevity. "I am very busy," she said in an abrupt, husky, impatient voice. "I don't have time to sit with you to discuss it in my office. But tomorrow I am going to the military court in Jenin. You can come with me, and we can talk about it in the car. And you can come with me to the court. It is something you should see." She told me to meet her at her office at 8:30 the following morning, and we would travel together up to Jenin.

Since this was my only opportunity to secure this busy lawyer's undivided attention, I seized the offer. Early the following morning, I traveled from Bir Zeit to Jerusalem. At 7:30 in the morning, I found myself stuck in a rush hour unlike anywhere else in the world, as the multitudes of West Bank Palestinians who still had jobs or business in Jerusalem flowed into the city that had been declared foreign and forbidden to them. My bus turned off the main road a few kilometers before the checkpoint at the Jerusalem boundary, just as the end of the line of vehicles queuing for inspection began to appear, and bounced along some back roads, bypassing the checkpoint. There was a stream of cars and minibuses in front of us, and a similar stream behind us, traveling almost bumper to bumper, over waste ground and building sites. My fellow passengers, dressed for the office, sat pressed together silently and with stony expressions. They were outwitting the Israelis, but the novelty had obviously worn off by now, and they plainly would have preferred not to be entering the city by stealth. After a bumpy twenty-minute detour, we rejoined the main road and continued the journey to Jerusalem. No one in the bus said a word.

Tsemel's office was across the street from the American Colony Hotel, and down the road from Orient House, the Jerusalem head-quarters of the PLO. A colleague was waiting for her: a Palestinian lawyer who like her worked as a defender in the military courts. A little after 8:30, Tsemel arrived, in a rush. She wore a plain dark suit and was bustling toward us carrying a heavy pile of legal files and the kind of black gown worn by Oxford and Cambridge undergraduates. Evidently, the Israeli military courts maintained a vestige of the medieval conventions of English courtrooms. She was also managing to hold a mobile telephone and a Styrofoam cup of coffee, and bundled herself and all of these things into the front seat of the car. Once we were all inside, Tsemel's Palestinian colleague, Abed Daousheh, grasped her hand in greeting, held it tightly, and kissed it on the palm and on the back, with his head lowered, in an ardent display of love and respect.

Abed Daousheh drove. We traveled north along the narrow highway that winds through the middle of the West Bank toward Jenin, and Tsemel told me about Muhammad Salah.

"After he was arrested, he was interrogated by the GSS," she said. "And he gave a long, detailed confession, which was taped. In his confession, he says that he went around the West Bank meeting Hamas people, and one of these people told him that they had carried out the action against Glock." That was all she knew about Salah's connection to Glock.

Because he had been taped, it was difficult to acquit Salah, she said. "We were faced with a lot of material by the prosecution, a lot of facts, and these facts corroborated other facts. Basically, he was charged with transferring money to Hamas to buy weapons, to reconstruct Hamas. Whenever Hamas were beaten by the Israelis, he would come, distributing money, to help bring them back up to strength. This time, he was caught with a suitcase with about $100,000 in it—he was a hot potato.

"Then the trial started," Tsemel went on, twisting around in the front seat to face me. "We began by complaining about how he was interrogated, that he was tortured into making a confession, and that therefore the evidence was incorrect. We said, you can't charge him on the basis of this confession."

"The GSS was afraid that the trial would be covered in the American press," she said. "Here in Israel, it's totally kosher if you torture a Palestinian. Why not, since he's a terrorist anyway? But if this were published in the United States, it would have enormous effect. So the security services had an interest in not letting the trial go too deep." In the end, the prosecutor agreed to the plea bargain.

The interrogation revealed a trove of information about the activities and organization of the hitherto little-known military branch of Hamas. One of the revelations in it was that Hamas planned to kill Sari Nusseibah, because he had been promoting the Oslo process of peace with Israel. "In the eyes of Hamas," Tsemel said, "Nusseibah was guilty of calling for Palestinians to forsake the concept of an independent Palestinian state. He also represented Palestinians who had become 'foreignized' because he had married an Englishwoman. He was like a European intellectual, and Hamas was suspicious of that."

LEA TSEMEL TOOK on the Palestinian cause in the sixties, as a young leftist, an admirer of Che Guevara. In those days, it was possible to connect the Palestinian liberation struggle with other liberation struggles around the world in a spirit of Marxist internationalism. "It was all the same struggle," she said. All were marching toward the same goal of worldwide proletarian revolution.

But the Palestinians did not want to belong to a global liberation movement, she found. They were nationalists, not internationalists. "If you were a foreigner, especially an Israeli," she said, "they were ultimately suspicious of you. There was always the possibility that you were a spy. They would always want to know who you were working for really. Even this Albert Glock, who wore a *kaffiyeh* and taught at Birzeit."

In time, as Tsemel told it, the Palestinian liberation movement closed completely to outsiders as an internationalist cause with the rise of Hamas, a movement with an ideology intended to be incomprehensible to foreigners. No Western leftist or liberal could subscribe to the xenophobic rhetoric of the Hamas

Charter, for instance, with its reference to the fraudulent *Proto-cols of the Elders of Zion*. Its Islamist creed called for self-sufficiency among Muslims, and a strict code of behavior that was deliberately the opposite of anything its leaders saw as Western. Women had to wear the all-covering veil, and movie theaters and video shops had to close. A code of austerity and an attitude almost of mourning should prevail, they thought, for Palestine would be liberated only when Palestinians returned to a repristinized Islam. This view was gaining ground at Birzeit at the time Albert Glock was killed. Adherents of this severe ideology would regard with suspicion a well-meaning secularist foreigner. The campaign against Glock gave them the cause they needed to kill him.

"That's my guess," Lea Tsemel said, "and it's a brutal guess."

SHE ALSO TOLD me about the mysterious Rasmiyah Quran, the Ramallah woman lawyer who was attacked twice, once allegedly by the same man whose name was now linked with the killing of Albert Glock, Adel Awadallah.

"Rasmiyah Quran," Lea said, "was a lawyer who represented Fatah people. Then they found that she was collaborating with the security services, which was probably true. She had a file of active Fatah members, people who had been accused of recruiting young people into Fatah. She was arrested and charged with aiding an illegal organization. But then she was mysteriously released, and the release was very suspicious: people would not usually be released on such charges. They would normally get long prison sentences. Evidently, she was released in exchange for her agreement to continue supplying information about Fatah members. That made her a collaborator, and that's why they tried to kill her."

ON THE DRIVE BACK to Jerusalem, I arranged with Lea to return to her office the following day to study the transcript of the GSS interrogation of Muhammad Salah, hoping to find in it an elaboration of the cryptic reference to the "killing of the doctor at Birzeit." For the next seven days, I sat in the waiting room of her cramped office suite with my laptop computer and a six-inch-high stack of paper that contained the Salah transcript. Around me, smoking and worrying, sat Lea's clients, waiting to see her or one of her colleagues, in the hope that one of them would plead for their loved ones before the merciless court of the occupation. As I worked my way through the transcripts, a story of extraordinary complexity unfolded.

The papers before me had been submitted to the U.S. Federal District Court in Manhattan. They formed part of the government of Israel's request for the extradition to Israel of another Palestinian resident of the United States named Musa Abu Marzouq. Israel alleged that Abu Marzouq was one of the leaders of the military branch of Hamas. Abu Marzouq acknowledged that he was a member of the ruling council of the political branch of Hamas, but he denied that he was involved in the organization's military affairs. Lea Tsemel had these papers because she was also to represent Abu Marzouq.

The documents represented all the evidence the Israeli government could muster to make the case that Abu Marzouq was a dangerous terrorist kingpin. The prize exhibit in this wealth of material was the interrogation of Muhammad Salah. Salah's arrest gave the Israeli authorities their biggest ever haul of information about how the military branch of Hamas worked, and all the military operations they had carried out until Salah's arrest in 1993.

MUSA ABU MARZOUQ WAS ARRESTED in July 1995 at John F. Kennedy airport in New York. He was returning to his home in Virginia from a trip to the Arabian Gulf, accompanied by his wife and four children. Abu Marzouq held a green card, which allowed him to live and work legally in the United States. When an immigration officer entered Abu Marzouq's information into the computer, a mark against his name flashed up on the screen. Agents from the airport's FBI office appeared and arrested Abu Marzouq on suspicion of violation of immigration rules.

The FBI agents took Abu Marzouq and his family into a room for questioning. The agent who led the arrest later described the interrogation in an affidavit. The agent asked Abu Marzouq if he was carrying an address book. Abu Marzouq said no, he wasn't. Then he and his wife were body-searched, and an address book fell to the floor from the folds of his wife's clothing. The agent said the address book was Abu Marzouq's, and it contained an extensive collection of the names, addresses, and telephone numbers of Hamas activists. (This conclusion must have been reached some time after the arrest, as it was unlikely that the FBI agents could read Arabic and identify the names of Hamas activists on the spot.)

In fact, Abu Marzouq's immigration status was perfectly in order. What he did not know was that at the request of the Israeli security services, his name had been placed on the U.S. Immigration and Naturalization Service's blacklist. Israel believed he was responsible for ordering Hamas guerrilla attacks that resulted in a number of deaths of Israelis and Palestinians. In due course, the Israeli government submitted a request for his extradition to Israel to face trial on charges of terrorism: this was the real object of his detention. In Israel, the charges against him were "murder, attempted murder, manslaughter, harm with aggravating intent, harm and wounding under aggravating circumstances and conspiracy." Abu Marzouq's arrest and incarceration were the result of extraordinary American cooperation with Israel in its war against Hamas, to the extent of misusing the immigration laws to make an arrest that itself was of dubious legality.

Abu Marzouq was held in prison for twenty-two months awaiting his extradition hearing. As his imprisonment dragged on, Abu Marzouq challenged the Israeli government—through the medium of interviews with journalists who came to see him in the Metropolitan Correctional Facility in Manhattan where he was being held—to proceed with his trial without delay. He was daring them to try him, confident that the case would collapse.

Eventually the Israeli prime minister Benyamin Netanyahu unexpectedly announced that the State of Israel was dropping its case for Abu Marzouq's extradition, for "reasons linked to security and the prevention of terrorism." Abu Marzouq and his family then left the United States for Jordan, where King Hussein had granted them asylum "on humanitarian grounds."

THE HEART of the Israeli government's case against Musa Abu Marzouq was the information extracted from Muhammad Salah in the months of interrogation that he underwent in an Israeli jail from February to June 1993. The interrogation sessions were tape-recorded, then meticulously transcribed and translated into Hebrew and then into English, with every word, every obscure phrase, every broken sentence reproduced and typed. The final document contains about two hundred thousand words. Muhammad Salah's revelations were intended to make the case that Musa Abu Marzouq was the prime mover and coordinator of Hamas's paramilitary actions.

While in prison, Salah was subjected to a regime of physical and psychological coercion that can only be described as torture. Salah described this treatment in an affidavit submitted to the U.S. District Court as part of Musa Abu Marzouq's defense. He was held in a tiny, freezing cell with no bed, and deprived of sleep for up to forty-eight hours at a time. Sleep deprivation as a means of breaking a prisoner's resistance was euphemistically called "waiting" in the interrogator's lexicon. He was kept awake by being bound in a sitting position onto a child's chair for long periods, an unnatural posture that quickly becomes extremely painful. At other times he was handcuffed to a chair with a sack over his head, and at night his cell was blasted with loud music. Mostly, the torture was psychological. He was forced to undress and stand naked in the interrogation room, and an interrogator threatened to photograph him in that state with a Polaroid camera if he did not cooperate. He was threatened with violence against himself, against his family outside, and with long imprisonment.

This had the desired effect. An earlier interrogation had yielded little. But after Salah's torture the haul of information was richer.

Salah said that he had been sent by a Hamas leader in the United States to go to Israel in the summer of 1992 "in order to set up the military branch of Hamas in the West Bank and I agreed." He was advised to contact two local activists for this purpose: one was a student at the Islamic University in Hebron, and the other was Adel Awadallah in al–Bireh, the Hamas activist who, according to Muhammad Salah's charge sheet, "gave information on the assassination of a doctor from Birzeit University in 1991 by members of Hamas."

The student from Hebron asked for $50,000 to buy vehicles and weapons. In such revelations I could see how Albert Glock's killing might have been arranged. Salah said he met the student in a mosque in Ramallah and gave him the sum he asked for. Salah then met Adel Awadallah, who had just been released from prison and said he needed time to get organized: three or four months, he estimated. Before he had gone to prison Awadallah had destroyed his lists of recruits: it would take that long to reestablish his contacts.

Salah was asked to make a second trip to Israel and the territories in January 1993 to revive the Hamas military organization after its numbers had been depleted by the Israeli deportations. Again, he made the rounds of Hamas activists in the West Bank and Gaza, giving $100,000 to the head of the Gaza branch and $60,000 to Adel Awadallah in Ramallah. This time Gaza's chief spoke of Uzis, Kalashnikovs, M–16s, and underground shelters, and Adel Awadallah reported the murder of an Israeli intelligence agent.

By this time, Salah's interrogator (identified in the transcript as "Nadav") and his men must have realized that they had a first-class informant in their hands, and they determined to make the most of the opportunity. What they did next was cunning in the extreme. They instructed two Palestinian prisoners to pose as Hamas activists and persuade Salah to give them a full report on his activities to prove his good standing in the organization. It was a technique that the GSS regularly used to extract information from Palestinian prisoners. Over the next few months, Salah wrote a long document in Arabic describing in detail all his activities as a Hamas activist and organizer, whom he met, what they did, and so on. The document consisted of about a hundred pages of handwritten Arabic. This was translated and included with the interrogation transcripts. Once he had written this, the collaborators handed it over to their Israeli employers, who read it and then brought Salah back for further interrogation. When Salah learned what had happened, he knew he was in deep, and the interrogation began again. Salah now had the choice of either talking or enduring a long prison sentence. Henceforth, he was bargaining for his freedom.

The interrogations that followed form the longest and most substantial section of the transcripts. Salah read from his Arabic document, and gave a commentary on it, elaborating and explaining, as Nadav probed him with questions. A picture emerged of the inner workings of Hamas in the early 1990s: for the GSS, it was a rare and valuable glimpse inside a secretive organization that had become, in only two years, a real threat to Israel's containment of the Occupied Territories. In Salah's account, the military branch of Hamas came across as earnest, amateurish, paranoiac, and unworldly in outlook, but staunchly dedicated to the simple project of striking blow after blow against Israel, undaunted by their tiny resources compared to those of an overwhelmingly powerful state.

The movement was only loosely organized, he said: a sense of common purpose held it together, rather than a strictly controlled institutional system. Salah would come to the territories to hear the reports of the Hamas groups in Gaza and the West Bank, and distribute money as needed. Each of these groups acted according to its own judgment; there was no reference to a central command for authorization to carry out an attack. This was partly in order to keep strategic information compartmentalized, so that the arrest and interrogation of one activist would not bring down the whole organization.

The transcripts reveal a dismal cloak-and-dagger world in which Hamas activists communicated by messages left in secret locations: a certain water culvert, a hole in the wall in the fourth compartment along in the men's toilets of a mosque, a Coca-Cola can by the side of the road. This had the disadvantage that lines of communication were hard to maintain and paramilitary actions correspondingly hard to organize. If Albert Glock had been killed in a Hamas operation, the Salah interrogation indicated that the murder would have been the work of a small, isolated cell with little or no central direction and poor lines of communication.

Awadallah told Salah about military actions his group had

performed. One of them was an attack on an Israeli army jeep. Nadav was bemused by the fact that Hamas carried out the attack without claiming responsibility for it, and he pressed Salah for an explanation. Salah answered that Awadallah told him that "it was an operation about which an announcement isn't made."

"The Jews know who perpetrates the actions about which notices are not given," Salah explained. "It is Hamas." This strategy of being implicitly responsible for every guerrilla action maximized the psychological threat of Hamas, giving them an air of omnipresent menace.

In seeking to explain Hamas's strategic thinking to his Israeli interrogator, Salah gave another example of an action by Awadallah's group for which no claim of responsibility was issued. This was "the operation of the doctor." This, at last, was the information that was referred to in Muhammad Salah's charge sheet.

Nadav asked him for more, but Salah answered that Awadallah gave him "no details of [the doctor's] name and how the thing was done." But he only said that it was a doctor who cursed. I don't know details [except that] he is a doctor at Bir Zayit [sic] university."

Nadav pounced on this. "What does it mean? Read it to me another time."

"He [Awadallah] recalled the operation with the doctor."

"Yes, how did he recall it? Remind me and leave the document alone! Explain it in your own words."

"He only told me—"

"Yes?"

"That [there are] operations about which announcements are not made."

Salah apparently knew no more than the little that Awadallah told him, but Nadav continued to press him.

"Why did they kill him?"

"Because he talks crudely."

"Yes?"

"Do you know what the definition of talking crudely is?"

"That means he is bad," Nadav said. "He curses Muslims or such things?" Glock had been transformed by this time into an enemy figure in the Ramallah area, where Awadallah was based, and at the high point of the campaign against him on the Palestinian street he could have been seen by Hamas zealots as someone who was "bad" and "cursed Muslims."

Nadav continued to find it hard to fathom Hamas's thinking, and Salah's lack of curiosity about the killing of the "doctor."

"Doesn't it matter why an operation was performed? Against whom? And why? That means, don't you have to agree?" he asked.

"No! Matters are not that well organized that [I can say] 'Oh Adel, consult with me before you do something.' "

Nadav led Salah through the material in his Arabic document several times, and each time Salah repeated the brief reference to the killing of the doctor in Bir Zeit by Awadallah's group. Salah doesn't name him, because Awadallah didn't give him a name.

Even if this is not a reference to Albert Glock, the GSS certainly believed it was. In his affidavit accompanying the interrogation transcript, Nadav wrote, "Muhammad Salah met with Adel Awadallah . . . who reported to Muhammad Salah on the prior military activities of Hamas in Ramallah and sought Muhammad Salah's advice for future operations. Muhammad Salah and Adel Awadallah discussed the murder of the 'doctor' because he 'spoke crudely' about Islam and the Muslim people."

Nadav attached a footnote at the word "doctor": It read, "Muhammad Salah was referring to the murder of Dr. Albert Glock on January 19, 1992. Dr. Glock had been the Director of the Institute of Archeology at Birzeit University, near Ramallah." The details are correct in every particular. This explicit statement shows that in 1993, when the interrogation of Muhammad Salah took place, the GSS were satisfied that the killing of Albert Glock was the work of Hamas.

Nadav did not linger on the matter of the doctor. "Let's go on," he said. He had heard enough. For the GSS, the Glock case was a distraction from the war against Hamas, which was more important.

Who exactly was this Adel Awadallah? He is a person one can study only from a distance, with no sure knowledge of his inner motivations, his personality, the forces in his character that made him dedicate himself to the Islamic movement. The little that is known about him would fit onto a single card in a Western terrorism expert's card index. He was born in al-Bireh in 1967, the year of the Israeli capture of the West Bank, and grew up under the occupation. He studied engineering at the University of Bethlehem, married a woman from al-Bireh, had two children, and ran a small shop. When the *intifada* began, he became politically active and was in and out of Israeli prisons, under arrest and in administrative detention. The earliest report of him is in connection with the first of several attacks on Rasmiyah Quran, in April 1991. During one of his periods of administrative detention, a fellow prisoner (quoted in the newspaper *Ha'aretz*) described him as "a quiet type, authoritative, with powers of persuasion and diplomacy."

EVERY NIGHT, as I rode back to Bir Zeit in a succession of battered minibuses and shared taxis, I savored the thought that I was really on to something. Of course, the reference to "the doctor" in Salah's testimony didn't prove that Albert Glock was killed by Hamas. But the hypothesis had its strengths. First, as the Israeli request for Abu Marzouq's extradition pointed out, with wicked logic, "the information contained in this report is considered especially reliable," because Muhammad Salah was tricked into giving information he would not have chosen to tell Israeli investigators. Salah refused to put his signature to a Hebrew version of his confession because he doesn't speak or understand Hebrew. He also protested that he spoke only after being tortured, but he has never denied the content of the transcript. If the transcripts are a work of fiction, they are a stunningly effective piece of literary illusionism.

It's true that Hamas issued a public statement after the killing denying involvement in it, and indeed denouncing it. But the transcripts show that if Hamas did carry out the killing, and then chose to deny it, it would not be the first time they had denied responsibility for an action they were embarrassed by.

Salah's testimony also shows that the money he distributed

enabled Hamas to build up inventories of weapons and cars. Prices on the black market were high: a pistol cost 2,000 Jordanian dinars, about $3,000. What Salah reported explains how the killers of Albert Glock might have been able to mount a reasonably professional assassination, with at least two people to execute it, a weapon, and a car to take them to and from the scene.

MUHAMMAD SALAH SERVED his sentence and returned to the United States in 1997, where he found himself ensnared in a Kafkaesque legal predicament that has become a national civil rights issue. Because of his connection to Hamas, Salah was subjected on his return to the United States to the forfeiture of all his personal financial and business assets under a draconian civil forfeiture law originally designed to punish money laundering by major drug dealers. Salah now not only pleads innocence of membership of Hamas, but is also fighting the forfeiture order against him. He has engaged a crusading civil rights lawyer, Matthew Piers, to represent him.

I talked to Piers by telephone from London at his office in Chicago in July 1999. He forcefully made the case that the interrogation transcripts were a total fabrication by GSS agents, designed for the purely political purpose of discrediting Hamas.

"If Salah was such a high-ranking Hamas activist," Piers asked rhetorically, "and had turned informer against his own organization, why did the fact not emerge when Salah was a prisoner? Why didn't his fellow prisoners kill him in retaliation? Why would real Hamas activists seek to compromise their own organization, and one of their own activists, by asking him to write *inside an Israeli prison* a detailed report of activities they might have known about already?"

Piers had a point. In this predicament, it would be logical for Salah to try his hand at creative fiction himself, and weave his own web of deceit, thereby protecting both himself and Hamas.

"And if Salah was so important," Piers went on, "why did the Israelis imprison him for only five years, leaving open the risk that he would be able to resume his work for Hamas once he had served his sentence?"

Piers's logic made me think that Salah's testimony rather than being "especially reliable" because it was obtained deviously may have been completely unreliable for that very reason. And a suspect who is having a confession beaten out of him, as Salah clearly was, will say anything to bring the torture to an end. I had nothing to corroborate my theory of Hamas involvement in Glock's death. I believed it because of its internal consistency, and because it fit convincingly into historical context. But there was no other supporting evidence. Of one thing, though, I could be sure: the transcripts were military intelligence, not judicial evidence, and as such—even if they were true—they must always be seen as a weapon of war, not an instrument of justice.

EXACTLY HOW AWADALLAH WAS involved in the killing of Albert Glock, if he was involved at all, was unknowable. Not even the GSS claimed to know that—but then, they weren't especially interested. He might have supplied the gun and the car and given the green light; he might have only known about the murder, or he might have done it himself. Whatever he did, more than one person carried it out. It seems likely that at least one of the culprits may have been a Birzeit student. A student would have had the local knowledge, and known about Albert Glock and the image he had come to represent on the Palestinian street.

I knew that Hamas was well represented at Birzeit, and there was at least one detailed reference in the Salah transcripts to contacts between the Hamas military branch and the Islamicist student faction at the university. Ever since the university reopened several months after Glock's murder, the Islamic bloc, which supported Hamas, had been a considerable force in student politics. Sheikh Yasin, the Hamas leader, was an undergraduate pinup: his face was festooned around the campus.

A Birzeit professor gave me a verbal sketch of a typical student supporter of Hamas.

"This boy comes from a village, and his family is poor. He might be the first boy in his village or refugee camp to go to university. He has three shirts: the one he's wearing, the one that's in the laundry, and one for holidays. All his life, this boy has studied by rote. His education consists of being dictated to. When he comes to Birzeit, for the first time in his life he encounters women who are not his family: he has never been taught how to deal with this. To him, a woman is either your mother, your sister, your wife, or a whore. And it makes him excruciatingly uncomfortable. When he has to talk to the women in the registrar's office, he sweats with anxiety. He feels timid and invisible. He can't see a female student as a colleague. He doesn't have the social intelligence to go Dutch: if he has a cup of coffee with a girl, he feels compelled to pay for both cups, and then has no money for coffee for himself the next day. And then he hears his first Hamas slogan. Suddenly, he feels like somebody.

"Our job is to make someone out of this rascal," the professor said, in a tone of exasperated frankness, "to give him some social intelligence. That's what makes being in the hell of this place worthwhile. Our modus operandi is to civilize him, make him part of the system."

The Hamas supporters had become a real strain on Birzeit's liberal tradition, but the university struggled to accommodate them. In 1997, the administration was forced to suspend a group of Hamas students who set fire to a bus in an anti-Israel demonstration. When, after the creation of the Palestinian Authority, Yassir Arafat ordered a clampdown on Hamas, fifteen Birzeit students were arrested.

AFTER I HAD READ the Abu Marzouq papers, with their obscure clue about the killing of Albert Glock, I felt obliged to contact Hamas itself, to give someone in the organization the chance to comment on what I had read. I didn't expect I would find much encouragement in an attempt to approach the military branch. But Dr. Abd al-Aziz al-Rantisi, the head of the Hamas political branch in the Occupied Territories, the only part of Hamas that was visible above ground, was available to anyone who would make the journey to see him in his office in Gaza City.

He was easy to reach. He even gave me directions to his office from the Erez checkpoint. On the morning of the day I was to see him, I took a minibus from Ramallah to Gaza, and reached Erez at about eleven o'clock.

The bus came to a stop in a vast parking lot, and the passengers hauled their luggage onto the tarmac. The sky was hot, humid, and muffled white; the sun was a torpid yellow. Gaza sat on a flat, featureless coastal plain that seemed set in a void. Its isolation was reinforced by the measures the Israeli military had taken to seal it off from the rest of the world: its fifty-kilometer length was thickly enclosed in barbed wire. The Gaza Strip contained a million people pressed together in the highest population density on earth. The human wreckage of fifty years of demographic upheaval had been swept into this crowded vessel, and then the lid was clamped on tight.

I took a shared cab into the city. It traveled down a long dusty road, through air heavy with the smells of dust, exhaust, and dung. Since I was going to be in Gaza for the day, I had arranged another appointment with the head of the Palestinian Authority's Department of Antiquities office in Gaza, Mu'in Sadeq. His office was my first stop. (Part of my reason for going there was to have an acceptably noncontroversial answer ready if asked by Israeli officials at the Erez checkpoint for the purpose of my visit: I didn't want to say I was visiting Hamas.)

In Gaza, all eyes were on me, as if it were rare for foreigners to penetrate the dense medium that separated Gaza from the rest of the world. In the West Bank, in Ramallah, one walked ostensibly unnoticed through the streets; here, I was a curiosity.

I was shown into Dr. Sadeq's office and offered tea. I gave Sadeq a book that a friend of his in Jerusalem had asked me to bring him. We talked about archeology. He knew Albert Glock, and we made polite small talk about him. We were not alone: a small group of employees who were in the room drinking tea when I arrived stayed to share in the novelty of my visit. The atmosphere was rather jolly. After a decent period of conversation had elapsed, Sadeq offered to take me on a quick tour of the antiquities sites of Gaza, and everyone in the office joined us. We all bundled into Sadeq's rusty car and drove off down the coast road.

At the end of the tour, I had to raise the delicate question of my next appointment. "I have to go to the Hamas office," I said. I anxiously hoped not only that no one would view this adversely, but that someone in the car would be able to tell me where it was. To my surprise, my cautious announcement provoked great excitement.

"Sheikh Yasin is my cousin!" exclaimed the man sitting beside me. Everyone smiled.

"How is his health these days?" I inquired, greatly relieved by the response.

"Oh, he is very well. He is a very nice man!" There seemed to be general agreement to this.

"I will drive you there," Dr. Sadeq said.

We now began a fresh expedition, and we bounced through the potholed streets of downtown Gaza to the Hamas headquarters. The building was close to the beach, not far from Yassir Arafat's "palace," in what real estate agents would describe as a "prime seafront location."

When we arrived at the Hamas office, my companions from the Department of Antiquities all came into the building with me. The Hamas office was neat and well organized. A cheerful young man with a beard sat at the reception desk, and I told him of my appointment to see Dr. al-Rantisi. While we waited for him, my companions took the opportunity to greet old friends in the Hamas HQ: there was much kissing of cheeks and conviviality. Then al-Rantisi appeared, a serious, bearded man with a nut-brown complexion, and the folk from the Antiquities Department left me to it. I shook hands all around and thanked them, and they went back to work. Hamas was clearly very popular in Gaza.

Abd al-Aziz al-Rantisi was a pediatrician by profession, and he had spent eight years in Israeli jails for his affiliation to Hamas. He had also been one of the 415 Palestinian deportees exiled by Israel to the hills of southern Lebanon in 1992. He radiated discipline, willpower, and suppressed pain. I told him about what I had read, the Abu Marzouq papers, the Muhammad Salah interrogation transcripts, and their reference to the killing of the doctor at Bir Zeit. I didn't expect that he could tell me who killed Albert Glock, and indeed he didn't. He gave me what I expected: a broadcast of the Hamas party line on the issue of anticollaborator killings.

As for Muhammad Salah's interrogation, he knew nothing about it. Being a member of the political wing of Hamas enabled al-Rantisi to profess ignorance of the activities of the military wing.

"But what about the killing of the 'doctor'?" I said. This was a run-up to the obtuse, embarrassing, obvious question: "Did Hamas do it?"

"It is impossible, because Hamas forbids political assassination," he said, predictably. "That is a firm policy."

I pressed on (despite having been clearly shown the impregnable firewall that isolated the military branch from the political branch of his organization). "Could he not have been the target of an anticollaborator killing by Hamas?"

"For Hamas to kill a collaborator," he said, "the collaborator would have to be working day and night for the enemy, giving them information, helping them to destroy the homes of our fighters. Such collaborators we consider the same as Israeli soldiers. They are enemies of our people. When you speak of the killing of the doctor in Bir Zeit, you are speaking of something that is forbidden by our religion."

"What about Adel Awadallah?" I asked. "Muhammad Salah said that he was the leader of the group that killed the doctor."

His answer was simple enough, if unrevealing. "The military wing has the same ideology as the political wing, but the military wing makes its own decisions without referring to the political wing. I really know nothing about the military apparatus and how Adel decides. I know nothing about that," he said.

It was the response I expected. I reached the end of my list of questions and thanked him for the interview. A young man in the office walked me to the taxi stand. We shook hands, and by sunset I was out of Gaza and in another country, in Haifa, waiting for a bus in an Israeli bus station. I was glad to say good-bye to Gaza, although I had been touched by the subdued courtesy of the Hamas people I had met, especially Dr. Abd al-Aziz al-Rantisi. I hadn't really expected him to tell me any more than he did.

Since 1998, Dr. al-Rantisi has spent most of his time in a Palestinian Authority prison, a victim of Arafat's effort to stamp out

Hamas for the sake of the Oslo Agreement. When I read that fact in a newspaper, a year after my sojourn had ended, I recalled how he had shuddered when he mentioned his eight years in an Israeli prison. Now he was enduring more of the same under the Palestinian Authority.

ONCE THE INTELLIGENCE from Muhammad Salah's interrogation had been shared with the Israeli police, the police investigation into Albert Glock's murder effectively ended and the initiative passed to the security services. For the security services, the priority was to use this information in the fight against Hamas, not to help the police solve the murder of an American archeologist. All the police could do was wait for the gun used in the Rasmiyah Quran case to be used again, which meant they could wait forever.

In August 1994, more than a year after Muhammad Salah's interrogation ended, and ten months after his secret trial, the American consulate in East Jerusalem arranged a meeting at Israeli police headquarters between Lois Glock, American consular staff, and a police delegation led by chief superintendent Hezy Leder. Leder's presence demonstrated, as he told Lois Glock, "the high priority the government of Israel is putting on solving her husband's murder." The content of their discussion showed how forlorn was the hope of doing so.

According to the American consulate's report on the meeting, both Mrs. Glock and the American consul asked why, knowing Muhammad Salah's account of Adel Awadallah and the killing of the "doctor," the police had not investigated Hamas's possible involvement in the murder.

Hezy Leder's reply was revealing. "Leder assured Mrs. Glock," the American report related, "that both [Muhammad] Salah and Adel Awad[a]llah, the contact of Salah's who informed Salah about the Bir Zeit murder, had been thoroughly questioned to glean any knowledge they might have about the murder of her husband." Muhammad Salah was just a messenger, with no reason to be suspected in the Glock case. Adel Awadallah was the one person who might know who killed Albert Glock, or might even have done it himself, and the police had him in custody, directly under their microscope. Leder told Lois Glock that Awadallah was serving a two-year jail sentence "in connection with the Rasmiyah Quran case." His offense was seen as political, not criminal: he was charged not with assault but with "membership of an illegal organization."

It is a suspicious coincidence that Awadallah was arrested in early 1993, immediately after Muhammad Salah made his revelations about him and other Hamas activists. The GSS would probably have known Awadallah was a Hamas member before Salah's interrogation; but only after this could they have known the extent of his involvement in military actions and his importance as the leader of a Hamas military cell. Awadallah's prison term began while Salah was still being questioned.

The police were not as effective in their questioning of Awadallah as the GSS had been in their interrogation of Muhammad Salah. Awadallah told them nothing. "The police interrogated him extensively about Dr. Glock's murder," Leder said, but admitted, "to date, no hard evidence or suspects have been obtained from that interrogation."

Despite this lack of success, "the police are operating under the assumption that Dr. Glock's murder was a Hamas operation," Leder said. "He emphasized," the American report continued, "that this was only 'assumption' at this point and they had no evidence to back up this assumption." The investigation entered a state of suspended animation, a situation that has remained unchanged to this day.

Awadallah was released from prison in 1995. Shortly after his release, he was arrested again, and held in administrative detention in Megiddo prison for an additional six months, until January 1996. After his last release from prison, Hamas began an intense campaign of bomb attacks on Israeli targets. Awadallah was thought to be behind them, and his name shot to the top of the list of Israel's and the Palestinian Authority's most wanted men. Four major bomb attacks, killing a total of sixty people, most of them Israelis, were attributed to Adel Awadallah from 1996 onward. Two of them in particular made the front pages of newspapers around the world. In July 1997, fifteen Israelis were killed by a bomb in a covered food market in Jerusalem. Awadallah was named as the "senior Hamas bomb maker."

Why then did the GSS countenance Awadallah's release from prison after only two years, when it was fairly obvious what he would do once he was released? Muhammad Salah, after all, got five years for "membership of an illegal organization," and he hadn't even been involved in violence.

There was one possible explanation for this, to my thinking. For the Israeli government, Adel Awadallah was a key to the inner workings of this deadly organization. If the GSS could keep a close watch on him after his return to the West Bank, and his inevitable resumption of military activity, they could hope, in time, for a far richer haul of intelligence about how Hamas worked. Their aim, after all, was to defeat Hamas and extinguish its military wing. Detaining Adel Awadallah for intensive questioning about the Glock murder case would have been a distraction from this long term strategy. As ever in the administration of the Occupied Territories, the work of the police ran a distant second in the order of priorities.

ADEL AWADALLAH'S LAST PURPORTED BOMB ATTACK took place on September 4, 1997, the day before I arrived in Israel. This time the target was the Ben Yehuda Street pedestrian mall in Jerusalem. Four Israelis were killed, and the Israeli government spokesman named Awadallah as the leader of the Hamas cell that was responsible. By now, he was too important a quarry to be dealt with in a courtroom. The yearlong manhunt Israel launched with the assistance of the Palestinian Authority culminated in the kind of audacious, daring, and well-thought-out military operation that Israel reserves for its top-priority enemies.

On Thursday, September 10, 1998 (a year and six days after the Ben Yehuda Street bombing), at about 4:30 in the afternoon, a truck and four vans carrying dozens of men in civilian clothes drove up to a one-room farmhouse outside the village of Khirbet al-Taibe, near Hebron. Al-Taibe was in Area C, the portion of West Bank land still under direct Israeli military control. The men were members of Yamam, a special unit of the Israeli police.

The house was surrounded by orchards and vineyards. Inside the house were Adel Awadallah and his brother Imad, asleep with their AK-47 assault rifles beside them. The vehicles pulled up to the house and the team burst into the building. The agents fired a few shots and Imad and Adel Awadallah were dead. Ten minutes later, an ambulance accompanied by army jeeps arrived to remove the bodies.

A few months after Adel Awadallah was killed, I received a brief message from the Israeli Foreign Ministry, delivered via the Israeli embassy in London. The message read: "According to the information in the possession of the Israeli security authorities, the murder of Dr. Glock was carried out by a cell under the authority of Adel Awadallah." This was the last official word on the killing of Albert Glock. Awadallah himself is now no longer available for questioning.

And that is how it ended. An investigation that began with a footnote in the *Journal of Palestine Studies* came to a halt with a footnote in the transcript of an Israeli GSS interrogation, where "the doctor" at Bir Zeit was identified as Albert Glock. The Israeli police file on the case remains open. Officially, they are still waiting for that gun to be used again. An FBI investigation is "pending."

A PERSON CAN'T EXPLAIN his own personality to another: that is the work of the beholder. Albert Glock lived for twenty years in the hottest part of the furnace of conflict and seemed to need the heat to stay alive. Eventually the heat grew too much even for him. He was a difficult man, but there was a heroic courage in his devoting himself so ardently to what he believed in and never avoiding the consequences.

Glock had no faith whatever in the Arab-Israeli "peace process," but even he no doubt would have been depressed to see the way it collapsed in the fall of 2000. The Palestinian mood had gone from tentative optimism to extinguished hope to renewed rebellion. The uprising of 2000—named "al-Aqsa *intifada*" because it had been sparked by a provocative visit to the al-Aqsa Mosque by the right-wing politician Ariel Sharon—began with none of the exuberance and idealism of the *intifada* before it.

Instead, it was launched in violence worse than that of the earlier *intifada*. Its defining images were of a Palestinian mob in Ramallah lynching two Israeli soldiers, and of a Palestinian boy being pierced by an Israeli sniper's bullet as he cowered in his father's arms. The Palestinians' prospects looked bleaker than they ever did when Albert Glock was alive.

There have been other changes.

At Birzeit, the Palestinian Institute of Archeology survived the blow that sent it reeling when Albert Glock was shot. Its new director, Khaled Nashef, inherited the massive task of bringing the results of Glock's excavation of Ti'innik to final publication. In 1996, Nashef began the excavation of the ruins at the top of Khirbet Birzeit. The site turned out to be of mixed Frankish (Crusader-era) and Mamuk construction, Nashef reported to the archeological community, and concealed a two-story building with partly preserved vaulted roofs, floors, and rooms. The findings were not surprising, but the dig itself relaunched archeology at Birzeit. Meanwhile, Nashef has sought to purge the ghost of Albert Glock from the Palestinian Institute of Archeology, and has not pursued the Ottoman-era archeology that Glock promoted.

Hamdan Taha is still the director of the Palestinian Authority's Department of Antiquities. Because of the glacial pace of progress in the negotiations between Israel and the Palestinian Authority, he has yet to reach a settlement with Israel on cultural property and antiquities.

Maya el-Farabi is now married and lives in the eastern United States, where she works as an archeologist. According to the Glocks, she was approached by the FBI in connection with their investigation of the Glock case but refused to talk to them. (She also declined to talk to me.) Three months after the murder, she wrote to Lois explaining that she could never go back to Birzeit and expressing her view that the university bore responsibility for Dr. Glock's murder.

A request I made to the CIA under the Freedom of Information Act confirmed that Glock was not a spy.

In 1999, a memorial volume of essays by Albert Glock and others was published, entitled *Archeology, History and Culture in Palestine and the Near East: Essays in Memory of Albert E. Glock*, edited by a former Birzeit colleague, Tomis Kapitan. The book contained three essays by Glock on Palestinian archeology, never published during his lifetime, which together form the most forceful expression Glock ever made of the cause to which he dedicated his life.

In the Glock murder case, as in archeology, no answer will be final, because no final answer is possible. Both sides will continue to believe that the other side was responsible for the killing. Any interpretation will always depend on the outlook of the person making the interpretation. In the absence of a reliable investigation and reliable justice in the land he had chosen, the skeptical approach that Albert Glock taught seemed the only one possible in investigating his death. *"Mortui vivos docent,"* he wrote. The dead teach the living.

God alone is omniscient.

NOTES

CHAPTER ONE

This account is derived from interviews in 1997 with Lois Glock, Haifa Baramki, Munir Nasir, Roger Heacock, Hugh Harcourt, and Jeffrey Glock; on notes of interviews conducted by Lois Glock in 1992 and 1993; on Albert Glock's letters and diaries. I also used Jerome Murphy-O'Connor's *The Holy Land: The Indispensable Archeological Guide for Travellers* (Oxford, New York: Oxford University Press, 1992).

CHAPTER TWO

p. 11, "Albert Glock's father": in papers of Albert Glock. "This Is My Life—Autobiography of Ernest Glock. Washburn, Illinois. December 31, 1968," 29 pages, duplicated typescript.

11, "a St. Louis–based organization": information on Lutheran Church–Missouri Synod is from www.lcms.org and the Rev. Bob Smith of the Walther Library, Concordia Theological Seminary, Fort Wayne, Indiana (personal communication).

12, "It was a claustrophobic, confining upbringing": interviews with Richard Glock, Delmer Glock (Albert's brothers), and Peter Glock (son).

15, "inspired, inerrant and infallible word of God" and "the only true visible church on earth": quotes from James E. Adams, *Preus of Missouri and the Great Lutheran Civil War* (New York: Harper & Row, 1977), p. 18.

15, "anti-German feeling" et seq.: the Rev. Bob Smith of the Walther Library, Concordia Theological Seminary, Fort Wayne, Indiana (personal communication).

19, "skeptical white American tending to minority views": Albert E. Glock, "Cultural Bias in Archeology," *Archeology, History and Culture in Palestine and the Near East: Essays in Memory of Albert E. Glock*, Tomis Kapitan, ed. (Atlanta, Ga.: Scholars Press, ASOR Books, vol. 3, 1999), p. 336.

CHAPTER THREE

Among the numerous works consulted in the writing of this chapter, the following were of particular interest.

Karen Armstrong, "The Holiness of Jerusalem—Asset or Burden?" *Journal of Palestine Studies*, 27, no. 3 (Spring 1998): 5–19.

Amnon Ben-Tor, ed., *The Archeology of Ancient Israel* (New Haven, London: Yale University Press/Open University of Israel, 1992).

Amikam Elad, *Medieval Jerusalem and Islamic Worship: Holy Places, Cere-monies, Pilgrimages* (Leiden: Brill, 1995).

Gershon Greenberg, *The Holy Land in American Religious Thought, 1620–1948: The Symbiosis of American Religious Approaches to America's Sacred Territory* (Lanham, New York, London: University Press of Amer-ica/Avraham Harman Institute of Contemporary Jewry: Hebrew Uni-versity of Jerusalem, 1994).

Thomas E. Levy, ed., *The Archeology of Society in the Holy Land* (London: Leicester University Press, 1995).

Burke O. Long, *Planting and Reaping Albright: Politics, Ideology and Interpreting the Bible* (University Park, Pa.: Pennsylvania State University Press, 1997).

Roger Moorey, *A Century of Biblical Archeology* (Cambridge: Lutterworth Press, 1991).

Neil Silberman, *Digging for God and Country: Exploration, Archeology, and the Secret Struggle for the Holy Land, 1799–1917* (New York: Knopf, 1982).

Thomas L. Thompson, *The Bible in History: How Writers Create a Past* (London: Cape, 1999).

Lester Vogel, *To See a Promised Land: Americans and the Holy Land in the Nineteenth Century* (University Park, Pa.: Pennsylvania State University Press, 1993).

P. W. L. Walker, *Holy City, Holy Places? Christian Attitudes to Jerusalem and the Holy Land in the Fourth Century* (New York: Oxford University Press, 1990).

Robert L. Wilken, *The Land Called Holy: Palestine in Christian History and Thought* (New Haven: Yale University Press, 1992).

p. 21, "visit to Palestine": Countless authors tell the story of Helena's mis-sion to Palestine (Evelyn Waugh turned it into a novel: *Helena*). For a historically critical version, see Jan Willem Drijvers, *Helena Augusta: The Mother of Constantine the Great and the Legend of Her Finding of the True Cross* (Leiden: Brill, 1992).

21, "the legend": Tyrannius Rufinus, *Church History*, vol. X, 7–8. Quoted in Drijvers, op. cit., p. 79.

24, "Pilgrimages": see John Wilkinson, *Jerusalem Pilgrims before the Crusades* (Warminster: Aris & Phillips, 1977).

24, "Egeria": see Egeria, *Egeria's Travels, Newly Translated with Supporting Documents and Notes by John Wilkinson* (Warminster: Aris & Phillips, 1981).

25, "Caliph Abu Ali al-Mansur al-Hakim bi-Amrih Allah": see De Lacy Evans O'Leary, *A Short History of the Fatimid Khalifate* (London: Kegan Paul, 1923), pp. 123–88.

26, "Al-Hakim's demolition" et seq.: see John Wilkinson, *Jerusalem Pilgrims before the Crusades.*

26, "the Temple of Solomon itself": Guy Le Strange, *Palestine under the Moslems: A Description of Syria and the Holy Land from A.D. 650 to 1500, Translated from the Works of the Medieval Arab Geographers* (London: Palestine Exploration Fund, 1890 [Khayats reprint, Beirut, 1965]), p. 130.

27, "the sites the modern tourist sees": see Jerome Murphy-O'Connor, *The Holy Land: The Indispensable Archeological Guide for Travellers*, p. 38.

27, "Edward Robinson": see Edward Robinson, *Biblical Researches in Palestine, Mount Sinai and Arabia Petraea* (London: John Murray, 1841, 3 vols.).

27, "We early adopted two general principles": Robinson, *Biblical Researches*, op. cit., vol. 1, p. 377.

28, *"All ecclesiastical tradition"*: Robinson, *Biblical Researches*, vol. 1, p. 374.

28, "I am led irresistibly to the conclusion": Robinson, *Biblical Researches*, vol. 2, p. 16.

29, "painful and revolting": Robinson, *Biblical Researches*, vol. 1, p. 331.

29, "holiest feelings": Robinson, *Biblical Researches*, vol. 1, p. 46.

30, "New England": Robinson, *Biblical Researches*, vol. 1, p. 46.

30, "archeology, manners and customs": "From the original prospectus," *Palestine Exploration Fund Quarterly Statement*, 1, no. 1 (June 1869): 1.

30, "This country of Palestine": Palestine Exploration Fund, "Report of the Proceedings at a Public Meeting Held in Willis's Rooms, St. James's, on Friday, June 22nd, 1865," *Proceedings and Notes, 1865–1869* (London: Palestine Exploration Fund, n.d.), p. 4.

31, "the Garden Tomb": see Gabriel Barkay, "The Garden Tomb: Was Jesus Buried Here?," *Biblical Archeology Review* (March/April 1986); and Sarah Kochav, "The Search for a Protestant Holy Sepulcher: The Garden Tomb in Nineteenth-Century Jerusalem," *Journal of Ecclesiastical History*, 46, no. 2 (April 1995): 278–301.

32, "Russian Orthodox pilgrims": see Ruth and Thomas Hummell, *Patterns of the Sacred: English Protestant and Russian Orthodox Pilgrims of the Nineteenth Century* (London: Scorpion Cavendish, 1995).

p. 32, "vast human skeleton": see Charles George Gordon, *Reflections in Palestine* (London: Macmillan, 1884).

33, "A more widespread notion": see Barbara Tuchman, *Bible and Sword; England and Palestine from the Bronze Age to Balfour* (New York: New York University Press, 1956).

35, "He dug shafts": see Charles Warren, *Underground Jerusalem* (London, 1876).

36, "Dan Bahat": Dan Bahat, "The Western Wall Tunnels," *Ariel*, no. 84 (1991): 55.

36, "According to Masonic legend": see, for example, Israel J. Herman, "King Solomon's Quarries," *haBoneh haHofshi* (The Israeli Freemason), n.d.

37, "hidden away": Charles Warren, *Underground Jerusalem*, p. 531.

38, "enter Paradise on foot": Charles D. Matthews, tr., "The Book of Arousing Souls" (translation of *Ba'ith al-nufus ila ziyarat al-Quds* by Ibn al-Firkah), in *Palestine—Mohammedan Holy Land* (New Haven: Yale University Press, 1949), p. 29.

38, "Zamzam": Guy Le Strange, *Palestine under the Moslems*, p. 221.

39, "sweet waters": Matthews, op. cit, p. 15.

39, "Ethiopian Christians": E. A. Wallis Budge, tr., *The Queen of Sheba and Her Only Son Menyelek: Being the History of the Departure of God and His Ark of the Covenant from Jerusalem to Ethiopia, and the Establishment of the Religion of the Hebrews & the Solomonic Line of Kings in That Country. A Complete Translation of the Kebra Nagast* (London, Boston: Medici Society, 1922), pp. 22–35; and Roderick Grierson, "Dreaming of Jerusalem," in Roderick Grierson, ed., *African Zion: The Sacred Art of Ethiopia* (London and New Haven: Yale University Press, 1993), p. 11. See also Kirsten Stoffregen-Pedersen, *The History of the Ethiopian Community in the Holy Land from the Time of the Emperor Tewodorus II till 1974* (Jerusalem: Ecumenical Institute for Theological Research, 1983).

40, "Who fasts a day in Jerusalem": Charles D. Matthews, "The Book of Arousing Souls," p. 33.

40, "potent factor": Matthews, op. cit., p. xxii.

40–41, "An Anglican bishop": Warren, *Underground Jerusalem*, p. 83.

41, "Jerusalem is the center of the world": Russian Foreign Ministry report, quoted in Derek Hopwood, *Russian Presence in Syria and Palestine 1843–1914* (Oxford: Clarendon, 1969), p. 46.

41, "Russian belief": see Hummell, op. cit.

42, "Its nominal cause": see David M. Goldfrank, *The Origins of the Crimean War* (New York and London: Longman, 1994).

42, "Prussia": see Sir William Treloar, *With the Kaiser in the East: Notes of the Imperial Tour in Palestine and Syria* (London, 1898); and Silberman, *Digging for God and Country*.

43, "all of the major powers": Neil Silberman, "Power, Politics and the Past: The Social Construction of Antiquity in the Holy Land," in Thomas E. Levy, ed., *The Archeology of Society in the Holy Land* (London: Leicester University Press, 1995), p. 14.

44, "The PEF defined Palestine": see Silberman, *Digging for God and Country*.

CHAPTER FOUR

Principal works consulted:

G. Bowman, "Nationalising the Sacred: Shrines and Shifting Identities in the Israeli-Occupied Territories," *Man*, 28 (1993): 431–60.

Magen Broshi, "Religion, Ideology, and Politics and Their Impact on Palestinian Archeology," *Israel Museum Journal*, 6 (1987): 17–32.

William Dever, *Recent Archeological Discoveries and Biblical Research* (Seattle: University of Washington Press, 1990).

Ruth Kark, ed., *The Land That Became Israel: Studies in Historical Geography* (New Haven, London: Yale University Press, 1989).

Philip J. King, *American Archeology in the Middle East: A History of the American Schools of Oriental Research* (Philadelphia: ASOR, 1983).

Neil Silberman, "Promised Lands and Chosen Peoples: The Politics and Poetics of Archeological Narrative," *Nationalism, Politics and the Practice of Archeology* (Cambridge: Cambridge University Press, 1995).

Neil Silberman, "Desolation and Restoration: The Impact of a Biblical Concept on Near Eastern Archeology," *Biblical Archeologist*, 54 (June 1991): 76–86.

Neil Silberman, "The Politics of the Past: Archeology and Nationalism in the Eastern Mediterranean," *Mediterranean Quarterly*, 1 (1991): 99–110.

Neil A. Silberman and David Small, "The Archeology of Israel—Constructing the Past, Interpreting the Present," *Journal for the Study of the Old Testament*, Supplement Series 237 (Sheffield: Sheffield Academic Press, 1997).

p. 45, "Archeology without the Bible": quoted in Amy Dockser Marcus, *The View from Nebo: How Archeology Is Rewriting the Bible and Reshaping the Middle East* (New York, London: Little, Brown, 2000), p. 98.

50, "Benyamin Netanyahu": see Yoav Kaveh, "Messiah now!" *Ha'aretz*, 9 November 1997.

p. 50, "Pesagot settlement": Bryant Wood, "Khirbet Nisya, 1994," *Israel Exploration Journal*, 44, nos. 1–2 (1994): 142–45.

52, "Here in the east": quoted in Neil Silberman, *A Prophet from Amongst You: The Life of Yigael Yadin: Soldier, Scholar, and Mythmaker of Modern Israel* (Reading, Mass.: Addison-Wesley, 1993), p. 157.

53, "a psycho-political role": Amos Elon, "Politics and Archeology," *New York Review of Books*, 22 September 1994, pp. 14–18.

53, "archeological activity in Jerusalem":Yigael Yadin, "Foreword," *Jerusalem Revealed: Archeology in the Holy City, 1968–1974*, Yigael Yadin, ed., [English translation from the Hebrew and abridgement by R. Grafman] (Jerusalem: Israel Exploration Society, 1976).

53, "Maghreb Quarter": see Joanna Oyediran, *Plunder, Destruction and Despoliation: An Analysis of Israel's Violations of the International Law of Cultural Property in the Occupied West Bank and Gaza Strip* (Ramallah: al-Haq, 1997).

55, "Operation Scroll": See "Notes and News," *Israel Exploration Journal* 45, no. 4 (1995): 292.

56, "Whitelam argues": Keith W. Whitelam, *The Invention of Ancient Israel: The Silencing of Palestinian History* (London, New York: Routledge, 1996).

CHAPTER FIVE

Glock diaries and letters. Interviews with Lois Glock and Nancy Lapp.

CHAPTER SIX

Glock diaries and letters. Interviews with Lois Glock, Albert Glock Jr., Jeffrey Glock, Peter Glock, Alice Glock, Neil Silberman, Mark Ziese, Sy Gitin, Hugh Harcourt, Alison McQuitty, Albert Aghazarian, Walid Sharif, Hamed Salem, Phillip Mattar, Shimon Gibson, and Khaled Nashef.

p. 76, "I should preface this discussion": Albert E. Glock, "Cultural Bias in Archeology," *Archeology, History and Culture: Essays in Memory of Albert E. Glock*, Tomis Kapitan, ed. (Atlanta, Ga.: Scholars Press, ASOR Books, vol. 3, 1999), p. 324.

CHAPTER SEVEN

Glock letters and diaries. Interviews with Salim Tamari, Walid Sharif, "Ibtisam el-Farabi," Hamed Salem, Lois Glock, Hamdan Taha, Adel Yahya, Penny Johnson, Gabi Baramki, and Neil Silberman.

93, "I'm a hard man": quoted in profile of Magen: David Shalit and Merav Nesher, "War of Excavations" (Hebrew), *Ha'aretz* (magazine supplement), 2 February 1996.

94, "The soldiers broke down the door": Joanna Oyediran, *Plunder, Destruction and Despoliation*.

106, "powerful nationalist myth": see Silberman, *A Prophet from Amongst You*.

CHAPTER EIGHT

My main sources for the history of the *intifada* are Ze'ev Schiff and Ehud Ya'ari, *Intifada: The Palestinian Uprising—Israel's Third Front*, ed and tr., Ina Friedman (New York: Simon and Schuster, 1990); Saïd K. Aburish, *Cry Palestine: Inside the West Bank* (Boulder: Westview and London: Bloomsbury, 1991); and Norman G. Finkelstein, *The Rise and Fall of Palestine: A Personal Account of the Intifada Years* (London, Minneapolis: University of Minnesota Press, 1996). Interviews with Gabi Baramki, Albert Aghazarian, Salah Abd al-Jawwad, Lea Tsemel, Lois Glock, Sari Nusseibah, Roger Heacock, and Raja Shehadah.

Peteet, Julie, "Male Gender and Rituals of Resistance in the Palestinian Intifada: A Cultural Politics of Violence," *American Ethnologist*, 21, no. 1 (1994): 31–49.

p. 117, "al-Quds radio": Kirsten Nakjavani Bookmiller and Robert J. Bookmiller, "Palestinian Radio and the *Intifada*," *Journal of Palestine Studies*, no. 76, p. 96.

CHAPTER NINE

Albert Glock's letters and diaries. Transcripts of news stories from the FBIS (Foreign Broadcast Information Service). Interviews with Alice Glock, Lois Glock, Raja Shehadeh, Penny Johnson, Su'ad al-Amri, "Ibtisam el-Farabi," Roger Heacock, Phillip Mattar, Adel Yahya, Walid Sharif, Hamed Salem, Hamdan Taha, Gabi Baramki, and Albert Aghazarian.

CHAPTER TEN

Albert Glock's letters and diaries. Letters and notes of Lois Glock. Interviews with Lois Glock, "Ibtisam el-Farabi," Gabi Baramki, Munir Nasir, Mark Taylor, Albert Aghazarian, Roger Heacock, Walid Sharif, and Hamdan Taha.

p. 135, "As in all good science": Albert E. Glock, "Archeology as Cultural Survival: The Future of the Palestinian Past," *Archeology, History and Culture in Palestine and the Near East: Essays in Memory of Albert E. Glock,* Tomis Kapitan, ed. (Atlanta, Ga.: Scholars Press, ASOR Books, vol. 3, 1999), p. 321.

137, "Archeology as Cultural Survival": This article was originally published in *Journal of Palestine Studies,* 23, no. 3 (1994): 70–84.

CHAPTER ELEVEN

Albert Glock's letters and diaries. Interviews with Musa al-Alloush, Faida Abu Ghazaleh, and Phillip Mattar.

p. 151, "The process of excavation": Albert Glock, "Prolegomena to Archeological Theory," *Birzeit Research Review,* no. 4 (Winter/Spring 1987): 6–7.

152, "massive earthquake": see Bailey Willis, in the *Bulletin of the Seismological Society of America,* 28 (1928): 73–103.

155, "The Jewish warrior": See Bazalel Bar-Kochva, *Judas Maccabaeus: The Jewish Struggle against the Seleucids* (Cambridge: Cambridge University Press, 1989), p. 378.

CHAPTER TWELVE

Lois Glock's notes, documents, and correspondence. Interviews with Mark Taylor, Gabi Baramki, Albert Aghazarian, Haifa Baramki, Nabhan Khrayshah, Nadia Abu el-Haj, Lois Glock, Peter Glock, Brig. Hezy Leder, Lea Tsemel, and Hussein Deifallah.

p. 169, "The undercover units": see Middle East Watch, a division of Human Rights Watch, *A License to Kill: Israeli Undercover Operations against "Wanted" and Masked Palestinians* (London, New York, etc.: Human Rights Watch, 1993), and B'tselem, *Activity of the Undercover Units in the Occupied Territories* (Jerusalem: B'tselem, 1992).

169, "We had five bottles": *A License to Kill,* p. 175.

CHAPTER THIRTEEN

Albert Glock's archive; Lois Glock's notes, documents, and correspondence. Interviews with Khalid Batrawi, Linda Menuhin (Israeli National Police), Phillip Mattar, Salah Abd al-Jawwad, Yuval Ginbar, Hamed

Salem, Khalil Abu Arafeh, Hamdan Taha, Salim Tamari, and Arnold Spaer.

John D. Brewer et al., *The Police, Public Order and the State: Policing in Great Britain, Northern Ireland, the Irish Republic, the USA, Israel, South Africa and China* (London: Macmillan and New York: St. Martin's Press, second edition, 1996).

S. Reiser, "The Israel Police: Politics and Priorities," *Police Studies* 6 (1983).

Chapter Fourteen

The principal textual source for this chapter is the mass of documents submitted to U.S. Federal District Court, Manhattan, by the State of Israel in support of their case for the extradition of Hamas leader Musa Abu Marzouq from the United States to Israel.

Interviews with Matthew Piers, Lois Glock, Lea Tsemel, Kathy Riley, Avigdor Feldman, Beverley Milton-Edwards, Mu'in Sadeq, Abd al-Aziz al-Rantisi.

B'tselem, *Collaborators in the Occupied Territories: Human Rights Abuses and Violations* (Jerusalem: B'tselem, 1994).

Beverley Milton-Edwards, *Islamic Politics in Palestine* (London: I. B. Tauris, 1996).

Raja Shehadeh, "The Myth of Law and Order," *Jerusalem Post*, 23 March 1988.

Graham Usher, "What Kind of Nation? The Rise of Hamas in the Occupied Territories," *Race and Class*, 37, no. 2 (October/December 1995); 65–79.

Graham Usher, "Hamas's Shifting Fortunes," *Middle East International*, 24 September 1993.

ACKNOWLEDGMENTS

I have many people to thank, for many people helped me write this book. Most of all, I would like to thank the family of Albert Glock: his sons, Albert Jr., Peter, and Jeffrey, his daughter, Alice, his brothers, Delmer and Richard, and especially his widow, Lois Glock, who over the past four years has always been available at the other end of the telephone to answer my increasingly minute queries about her life with Albert Glock in the West Bank and the aftermath of his murder. At the outset of my work she had the courage to give me unrestricted access to her late husband's personal and professional papers and her own extensive correspondence with Israeli and U.S. government officials, and never sought to influence the outcome of my study of them. She made the decision to entrust this material to me, and I hope that with this book before her she feels that her trust has not been misplaced, and that its publication will achieve the two objectives she had in making the book possible: a sense of emotional closure, and a renewal of public interest in the unsolved crime at the heart of this story.

I am grateful to my partner, Emma Whitlock, for her love and support during the years it took to write this book, especially for joining me in the West Bank when our son Theodore was still a baby. This book is for her.

Stephen Hubbell, my initial editor at Metropolitan Books, was the true begetter of this book, encouraging me to write it and then overseeing its slow extrusion into its present form.

I would also like to thank Sara Bershtel and Riva Hocherman at Metropolitan Books, Michael Fishwick, Arabella Pike, and Kate Morris at HarperCollins, my agent, Gillon Aitken, and, for their involvement with an early prototype of this book, Stuart Proffitt and Elisabeth Furse.

Phillip Mattar, at the Institute for Palestine Studies, Washington, D.C., and a friend of Albert Glock, helped me launch my research, gave me indispensable advice on Palestinian studies, and maintained a supportive interest throughout.

My archeology guru was Rupert Chapman of the Palestine Exploration Fund. I would like to thank him for guiding me around the labyrinthine archives of the PEF, and for giving me numerous ad hoc seminars on the archeology of the Holy Land during many fondly remembered visits to the PEF's headquarters, a haven of Victorian scholarly arcana hidden away behind a piano showroom in the West End of London.

Thanks are also due to Neil Silberman, whose writing on the archeology of the region is the best introduction to the subject for a nonarcheologist, making it understandable without hiding its complexity, and to Susan Brind Morrow, for a pivotal introduction.

In Jerusalem and the West Bank, I would like to express my especial gratitude to Dr. Albert Aghazarian, Dr. Munir Nasir, Richard Harper at the British School of Archeology in Jerusalem, and Sy Gitin and Edna Sachar at the Albright Institute.

In the early stages of working on this book I was aided enormously by an award from the Society of Authors. I acknowledge this with thanks.

A NOTE ON THE
NAMES OF PEOPLE AND PLACES

I have changed the names of some of the people involved in this story in an attempt to defend their privacy. I have not changed the names of political figures and of people serving in governments.

As for place-names, I use Palestine in this book at first as a historical term denoting the area of the Levant or southern Syria that includes what is now the State of Israel and the Occupied Territories, which extended from the Jordan River to the Mediterranean, and from Lebanon in the north to the Negev Desert in the south. This is the sense intended when dealing with the history and archeology of the country. Later, particularly where I follow Albert Glock's life and work among the Palestinians, the name Palestine is often used as it would be understood in the Palestinian Arab context in which Albert Glock had immersed himself; that is, in a political sense, meaning the Palestinian nation, its culture, and history.

Bir Zeit—written as two words—is the name of the town in which Birzeit (written in English as one word) University is situated.

INDEX

EDWARD FOX lives in London, where he writes for *The Independent*, *The Sunday Telegraph*, and *The Times*. *Sacred Geography* is his first book to be published in the United States.